RECAP

APPLY

REVIEW

SUCCEED

REVISION GUIDE

Religious Studies A (9 – 1)

Christianity & Sikhism

Ann Clucas
Marianne Fleming
Peter Smith

Great Clarendon Street, Oxford, OX2 6DP, United Kingdom

Oxford University Press is a department of the University of Oxford. It furthers the University's objective of excellence in research, scholarship, and education by publishing worldwide. Oxford is a registered trade mark of Oxford University Press in the UK and in certain other countries

First published in 2021

British Library Cataloguing in Publication Data
Data available

978-138-201502-8

Digital edition: 978-138-201501-1

10 9 8 7 6 5

Paper used in the production of this book is a natural, recyclable product made from wood grown in sustainable forests. The manufacturing process conforms to the environmental regulations of the country of origin.

Printed and bound by CPI Group (UK) Ltd, Croydon, CR0 4YY

Please note that the Practice Questions in this book allow students a genuine attempt at practising exam skills, but they are not intended to replicate examination papers.

Acknowledgements

The publisher and authors would like to thank the following for permission to use photographs and other copyright material:

Cover photos: Image Source/Getty Images; Tim Smith/Panos Pictures.

Artworks: Jason Ramasami, Q2A Media.

Photos: p18: Renata Sedmakova/Shutterstock; **p19**: GrahamMoore999/iStockphoto; **p54**: Saikat Paul/Shutterstock; **p56**: World Religions Photo Library / Alamy Stock Photo; **p59**: Dead3ye Designs/Shutterstock; **p64**: kevin wheal kent/Alamy Stock Photo; **p66**: Guru Nanak Nishkam Sewak Jatha (GNNSJ); **p67**: John Cole/Alamy Stock Photo; **p70**: Betto Rodrigues/Shutterstock; **p71**: Gapper/India/Alamy Stock Photo; **p72**: Dmitry Rukhlenko/Shutterstock; **p82**: Areeya_ann/Shutterstock; **p94**: Mshch/iStockphoto; **p96**: janrysavy/iStockphoto; **p109**: cinoby/iStockphoto; **p128**: Querbeet/iStockphoto; **p130**: Peter Macdiarmid/Shutterstock; **p135**: adventtr/iStock; **p141**: Jeff J Mitchell/Getty Images.

Carrotflower font © Font Diner – www.fontdiner.com

We are grateful to the authors and publishers for use of extracts from their titles and in particular for the following:

Scripture quotations taken from the **Holy Bible, New International Version Anglicised** Copyright © 1979, 1984, 2011 Biblica. Used by permission of Hodder & Stoughton Ltd, an Hachette UK company. All rights reserved. 'NIV' is a registered trademark of Biblica UK trademark number 1448790.

Excerpts from **The Church of England**: *Nicene Creed*, the *Lord's Prayer* and the *baptism rite*, https://www.churchofengland.org/media/41165/cibaptismandconf.pdf (The Archbishops' Council, 2016). Reproduced with permission from The Archbishops' Council. © The Archbishops' Council. Reproduced with permission rights@hmynsam.co.uk

AQA: *Paper 1: Additional specimen mark scheme*, (AQA 2017). Reproduced with permission from AQA.

AQA: *Paper 1A: Specimen question paper*, (AQA 2017). Reproduced with permission from AQA.

AQA: *Paper 1A: Additional specimen question paper*, (AQA 2017). Reproduced with permission from AQA.

The Church of England: *The Lambeth Conference: Resolutions Archive from 1930*, (The Lambeth Conference, 2005). Reproduced with permission from The Lambeth Conference.

The Church of England: *Marriage, Family and Sexuality Issues: Family*, https://www.churchofengland.org/our-views/marriage,-family-and-sexuality-issues/family.aspx (Archbishops' Council, 2017) Text from the Church of England website is © The Archbishops' Council. Published by Church House Publishing. Used by permission. rights@hymnsam.co.uk

J Fowler: *Hinduism, Beliefs and Practices*, Volume 1, (Sussex Academic Press, 2014). Reproduced with permission from Sussex Academic Press.

Guru Granth Sahib: *Siri Guru Granth Sahib*, One Volume, 3rd Edition, translated by Singh Sahib Sant Singh Khalsa, MD, (Hand Made Books). Reproduced with permission from Dr Sant Singh Khalsa, MD.

S. Hucklesby: *'Mutual cooperation, not mutual destruction' say Churches*, The Methodist Church in Britain website, 23rd May 2015. http://www.methodist.org.uk/about-us/news/latest-news/all-news/mutual-cooperation-not-mutual-destruction-say-churches/ (The Methodist Church in Britain, 2015). © Trustees for Methodist Church Purposes Reproduced with permission from the Methodist Church in Britain. www.methodist.org.uk

Pope Francis: *Address to a Meeting at the Ponitifcal Academy of Sciences*, October 2014. (The Vatican, 2014) © Libreria Editrice Vaticana. Reproduced with permission from The Vatican.

C. Shackle and A. Mandair: *Teachings of the Sikh Gurus: Selections from the Sikh Scriptures*, (Routledge, 2005). Reproduced with permission from Taylor & Francis Group.

N.-G. K. Singh: *The Name of my Beloved: Verses of the Sikh Gurus*, (Sacred Literature Trust, 1996). Reproduced with permission from Pr N.-G. K. Singh.

United Nations: *The Universal Declaration of Human Rights*, http://www.un.org/en/universal-declaration-human-rights/ (United Nations, 1948). Reproduced with permission from United Nations.

Although we have made every effort to trace and contact all copyright holders before publication this has not been possible in all cases. If notified, the publisher will rectify any errors or omissions at the earliest opportunity.

Guru Gobind Singh: *Sri Dasam Granth Sahib*, translated by SriDasam.Org http://www.sridasam.org/dasam (SriDasam.Org, 2005). Copyright holder not established at time of going to print.

The Shiromani Gurdwara Parbandhak Committee: *Sikh Rehat Maryada*, English translation, http://sgpc.net/sikh-rehat-maryada-in-english/ (SGPC, 2016). Copyright holder not established at time of going to print.

Salvation Army: *Positional Statement: Euthanasia and Assisted Suicide*, http://www.salvationarmy.org/ihq/ipseuthanasia (Salvation Army, 2013). Copyright status not established at time of going to print.

The publisher would like to thank Rachel Jackson-Royal for reviewing this book.

Contents

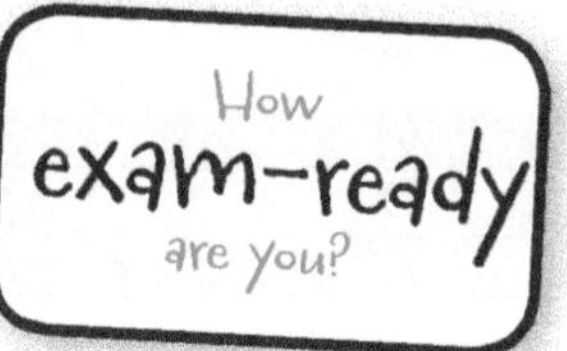

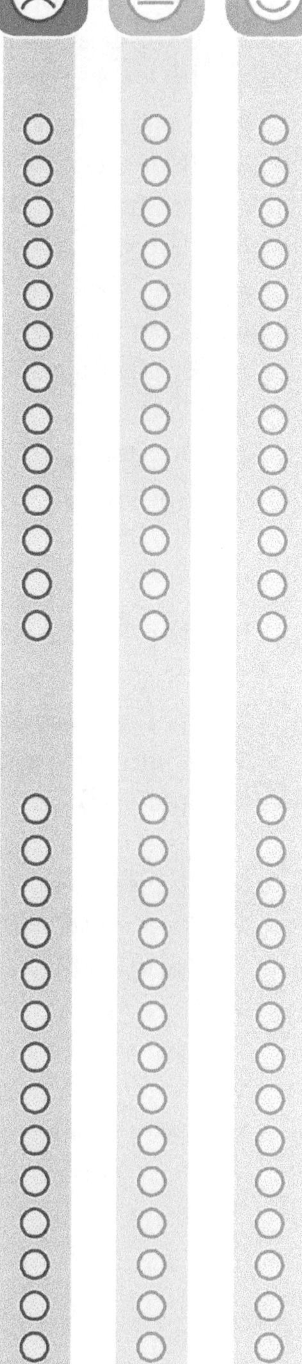

PART ONE: THE STUDY OF RELIGIONS *(continued)*

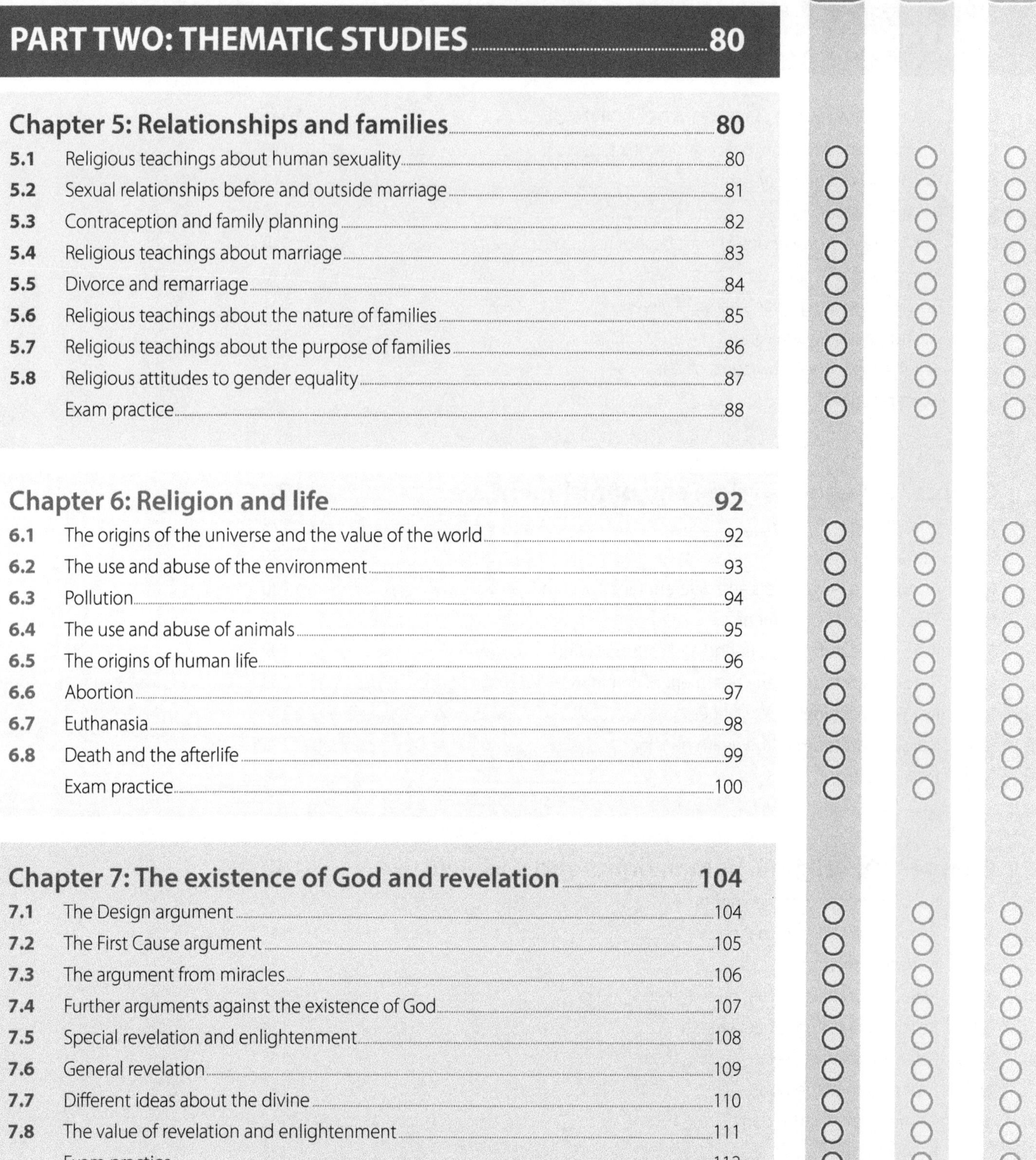

PART TWO: THEMATIC STUDIES 80

PART TWO: THEMATIC STUDIES *(continued)*

Introduction

What will the exam be like?

For your GCSE Religious Studies exam, you will sit two papers.

- **Paper 1 will cover the study of religions.** You will need to answer questions on the beliefs and teachings, and practices, of **two** world religions. There will be separate question and answer booklets for each religion. Chapters 1 and 2 of this revision guide will help you to answer questions on Christianity for Paper 1. Chapters 3 and 4 will help you to answer questions on Sikhism for Paper 1.
- **Paper 2 will cover thematic studies.** There are six themes on the paper. You will need to **choose four themes**, and answer all the questions for each chosen theme. You will need to know about religious beliefs and viewpoints on themes and issues. Except in those questions where the main religious tradition of Great Britain is asked for (see page 9), you can use beliefs from any religion in your answer. For example, you might want to focus on Christianity, including viewpoints from different traditions within Christianity, such as Catholic or Protestant views. Or you might want to include beliefs across six religions, including Christian, Buddhist, Hindu, Muslim, Jewish or Sikh viewpoints. Chapters 5 to 10 of this revision guide cover the six themes, focusing on Christian and Sikh perspectives.

If you are studying **St Mark's Gospel**, then the six themes will appear in Section A of Paper 2. You will need to choose **two themes**. You will then also need to answer the **two questions on St Mark's Gospel** from Section B.

TIP

Each paper is 1 hour and 45 minutes long, and you'll need to answer four full questions. Aim to spend 25 minutes on each question.

What kind of questions will be on the exam?

Each question on the exam will be split into five parts, worth 1, 2, 4, 5 and 12 marks.

The 1 mark question

The 1 mark question tests knowledge and understanding.

It is always a **multiple-choice question** with four answers to choose from. It will usually include the command words: '**Which one of the following...**'

Which **one** of the following is the idea that God is three-in-one?

Put a tick (✔) in the box next to the correct answer.

A Atonement ☐

B Incarnation ☐

C Salvation ☐

D Trinity ☐

[1 mark]

How is it marked?

1 mark is awarded for a correct answer.

The 2 mark question

The 2 mark question tests knowledge and understanding.

It always begins with the command words '**Give two...**' or '**Name two...**'

> Give **two** ways in which religious believers help victims of war.
>
> **[2 marks]**

How is it marked?

1 mark is awarded for 1 correct point.

2 marks are awarded for 2 correct points.

TIP

The examiner is expecting two simple points, not detailed explanations. You would get 2 marks if you answered "1) praying for victims; 2) providing food and shelter". You don't need to waste time by writing in full sentences and giving long explanations.

The 4 mark question

The 4 mark question tests knowledge and understanding.

It always begins with the command words '**Explain two...**'

It might test your knowledge of how a religion influences individuals, communities and societies. Or it might ask for similarities or differences within or between religions.

TIP

Here, 'contrasting' means different. The question is asking you to explain two different ways in which Holy Communion is celebrated.

> Explain **two** contrasting ways in which Holy Communion is celebrated in Christianity.
>
> **[4 marks]**

How is it marked?

For the first way, influence or similar/contrasting belief:

- 1 mark is awarded for a simple explanation
- 2 marks are awarded for a detailed explanation.

For the second way, influence or similar/contrasting belief:

- 1 mark is awarded for a simple explanation
- 2 marks are awarded for a detailed explanation.

So for the full 4 marks, the examiner is looking for two ways/influences/beliefs and for you to give detailed explanations of both. The examiner is expecting you to write in full sentences.

What is a detailed explanation?

An easy way to remember what you need to do for the four mark question is:

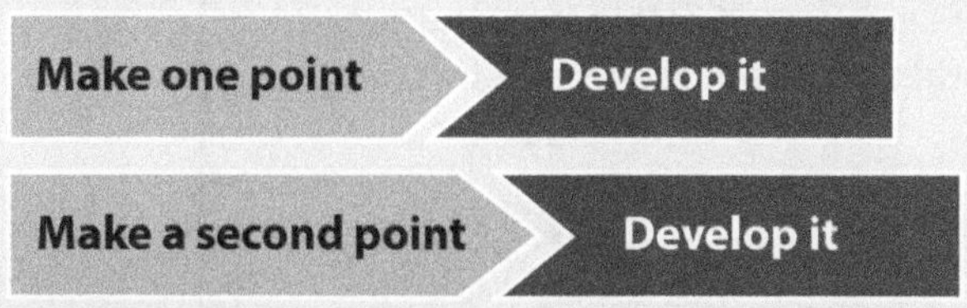

But how do you develop a point? You might do this by:

- giving more information
- giving an example
- referring to a religious teaching or quotation.

> **TIP**
> One point you might make to answer this question is to say "Catholics celebrate Holy Communion by receiving offerings of bread and wine." This would get you 1 mark. For a second mark you could develop the point by giving further information: "During the service they believe the bread and wine become the body and blood of Jesus Christ." There is more you could probably say, but as you'd get 2 marks for this, it would be better to turn your attention to thinking about a second contrasting way in which Holy Communion is celebrated, and then developing that second point.

The 'Great Britain' question

Sometimes, in the Themes paper, there may be additional wording to the 4 mark question, asking you to '**Refer to the main religious tradition of Great Britain and one or more other religious traditions.**'

> Explain **two** similar religious beliefs about abortion.
>
> In your answer you should refer to the main religious tradition of Great Britain and one or more other religious traditions.
>
> **[4 marks]**

The main religious tradition of Great Britain is Christianity, so in your answer **you must refer to Christianity**. You can refer to **two different denominations within Christianity**, or you can compare **a Christian belief with that from another religion**, such as Buddhism, Hinduism, Islam, Judaism or Sikhism.

> **TIP**
> You can't, for example, refer to two different groups within Sikhism, or compare Sikhism and Islam. There must be a reference to Christianity or you won't get full marks for this question however detailed your answer is.

For theme C: the existence of God and revelation, the wording will say: 'In your answer you should refer to the main religious tradition of Great Britain **and non-religious beliefs.**' You must refer to Christianity and a non-religious belief.

This type of question will only be asked about certain topics. We point them out in this revision guide using this feature:

> You might be asked to compare beliefs on contraception between Christianity (the main religious tradition in Great Britain) and another religious tradition.

The 5 mark question

The 5 mark question tests knowledge and understanding.

Like the 4 mark question, it always begins with the command words '**Explain two...**' In addition it will also ask you to '**Refer to sacred writings or another source of religious/Christian belief and teaching in your answer.**'

> Explain **two** reasons why Christians pray.
>
> Refer to sacred writings or another source of Christian belief and teaching in your answer.
>
> **[5 marks]**

How is it marked?

For the first reason/teaching/belief:

- 1 mark is awarded for a simple explanation
- 2 marks are awarded for a detailed explanation.

For the second reason/teaching/belief:

- 1 mark is awarded for a simple explanation
- 2 marks are awarded for a detailed explanation.

Plus 1 mark for a relevant reference to sacred writings or another source of religious belief.

So for the full 5 marks, the examiner is looking for two reasons/teachings/beliefs and for you to give detailed explanations of both, just like the 4 mark question. **For the fifth mark, you need to make reference to a writing or teaching that is considered holy or authoritative by a religion.** The examiner is expecting you to write in full sentences. You might aim to write five sentences.

What counts as 'sacred writings or another source of religious belief and teaching'?

Sacred writings and religious beliefs or teachings might include:

- a quotation from a holy book, for example the Bible or the Guru Granth Sahib
- a statement of religious belief such as the Apostles' Creed or the Mool Mantra
- a prayer such as the Lord's Prayer or the Ardas prayer
- a statement made by a religious leader, for example the Pope or one of the Gurus
- a quotation from a religious text such as the Catechism of the Catholic Church.

If you can quote exact phrases this will impress the examiner, but if you can't then it's fine to paraphrase. You don't need to include the exact verse that a quotation is from, but it would be helpful to name the holy book, for example, to specify that it is a teaching from the Bible.

The 12 mark question

The 12 mark question tests analytical and evaluative skills. It will always begin with a statement, and then ask you to **evaluate the statement**. There will be bullet points guiding you through what the examiner expects you to provide in your answer.

From Paper 1:

'The Bible tells Christians all they need to know about God's creation.'

Evaluate this statement. In your answer you should:

- refer to Christian teaching
- give reasoned arguments to support this statement
- give reasoned arguments to support a different point of view
- reach a justified conclusion.

[12 marks]
[+3 SPaG marks]

TIP

The examiners are not just giving marks for what you know, but for your ability to weigh up different sides of an argument, making judgements on how convincing or weak you think they are. The examiner will also be looking for your ability to connect your arguments logically.

From Paper 2:

'War is never right.'

Evaluate this statement. In your answer you:

- should give reasoned arguments in support of this statement
- should give reasoned arguments to support a different point of view
- should refer to religious arguments
- may refer to non-religious arguments
- should reach a justified conclusion.

[12 marks]
[+3 SPaG marks]

TIP

For Paper 2, on thematic issues, you can use different views from one or more religions, and you can also use non-religious views.

How is it marked?

Level	What the examiner is looking for	Marks
4	A well-argued response with two different points of view, both developed to show a logical chain of reasoning that leads to judgements supported by relevant knowledge and understanding. ***References to religion applied to the issue.***	10–12 marks
3	Two different points of view, both developed through a logical chain of reasoning that draws on relevant knowledge and understanding. ***Clear reference to religion.***	7–9 marks

TIP

This question is worth the same amount of marks as the 1, 2, 4 and 5 mark questions combined. Try to aim for at least a full page of writing, and spend 12 minutes or more on this question.

2	One point of view developed through a logical chain of reasoning that draws on relevant knowledge and understanding. OR Two different points of view with supporting reasons. ***Students cannot move above Level 2 if they don't include a reference to religion, or only give one viewpoint.***	4–6 marks
1	One point of view with supporting reasons. OR Two different points of view, simply expressed.	1–3 marks

Tips for answering the 12 mark question

- **Remember to focus your answer on the statement you've been given** – for example, 'War is never right.'
- **Include different viewpoints, one supporting the statement, one arguing against it** – for example, one viewpoint to support the idea that war is *never* right, and an alternative viewpoint to suggest that war is sometimes necessary.
- **Develop both arguments showing a logical chain of reasoning** – for example, draw widely on your knowledge and understanding of the subject of war, and try to make **connections** between ideas. Write a detailed answer and use evidence to support your arguments.
- **Be sure to include religious arguments** – a top level answer will explain how religious teaching is relevant to the argument.
- **Include evaluation** – you can make judgements on the strength of arguments throughout, and you should finish with a justified conclusion. If you want to, you can give your own opinion.
- **Write persuasively** – **use a minimum of three paragraphs** (one giving arguments for the statement, one for a different point of view and a final conclusion). The examiner will expect to see extended writing and full sentences.

Spelling, punctuation and grammar

Additional marks for **SPaG – spelling, punctuation and grammar** – will be awarded on the 12 mark question.

A maximum of 3 marks will be awarded if:

- your spelling and punctuation are consistently accurate
- you use grammar properly to control the meaning of what you are trying to say
- you use specialist and religious terminology appropriately. For example, the examiner will be impressed if you use appropriately the term 'resurrection' rather than just 'rising from the dead'.

In Paper 1, SPaG will be awarded on the Beliefs question for each religion.

In Paper 2, SPaG will be assessed on each 12 mark question, and the examiner will pick your best mark to add to the total.

Always try to use your best written English in the long 12 mark questions. It could be a chance to pick up extra marks for SPaG.

How to revise using this book

This revision guide takes a three step approach to help with your revision.

RECAP 	This is an overview of the key information. It is not a substitute for the full student book, or your class notes. It should prompt you to recall more in-depth information. Diagrams and images are included to help make the information more memorable.
APPLY 	Once you've recapped the key information, you can practise applying it to help embed the information. There are two questions after each Recap section. The first question will help you rehearse some key skills that you need for the questions on the exam that test your knowledge (the 1, 2, 4 and 5 mark questions). The second question will help you rehearse some key skills that you will need for the 12 mark question, which tests your evaluative skills. There are suggested answers to the Apply activities at the back of the book.
REVIEW 	At the end of each chapter you will then have a chance to review what you've revised. The exam practice pages contain exam-style questions for each question type. For the 4, 5 and 12 mark questions, there are writing frames that you can use to structure your answer, and to remind yourself of what it is that the examiner is looking for. When you've answered the questions you can use the mark schemes at the back of the book to see how you've done. You might identify some areas that you need to revise in more detail. And you can turn back to the pages here for guidance on how to answer the exam questions.

The revision guide is designed so that alongside revising *what* you need to know, you can practise *how* to apply this knowledge in your exam. There are regular opportunities to try out exam practice questions, and mark schemes so you can see how you are doing. Keep recapping, applying and reviewing, particularly going over those areas that you feel unsure about, and hopefully you will build in skills and confidence for the final exam.

Good luck!

1 Christianity: Beliefs and teachings

1.1 The nature of God

RECAP

Essential information:

- [ ] Christianity is the main religion in Great Britain.
- [ ] Christianity has three main traditions: Catholic, Protestant and Orthodox.
- [ ] Christianity is **monotheistic**, meaning that Christians believe in one Supreme Being, **God**.

Different branches of Christianity

CHRISTIANITY

- **Catholic** – based in Rome and led by the Pope.
- **Orthodox** – split from Catholic Christianity in 1054 CE and practised in Eastern Europe.
- **Protestant** – split from Catholic Christianity in the 16th century and branched out into different **denominations** (distinct groups), e.g. Baptist, Pentecostal, Methodist, United Reformed Churches. Protestants agree that the Bible is the only authority for Christians.

TIP

If you are asked about similarities and differences in a religion, try to remember that even though Christianity has different denominations, they all share the same belief in God.

What do Christians believe about God?

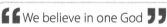

- There is only one God:

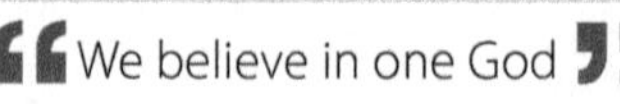

> "We believe in one God"
>
> *The Nicene Creed*

- God is the creator and sustainer of all that exists.
- God works throughout history and inspires people to do God's will.
- People can have a relationship with God through prayer.
- God is spirit (John 4:24) – neither male nor female – but has qualities of both.
- God is **holy** (set apart for a special purpose and worthy of worship).
- Jesus is God's son – the true representation of God on earth (Hebrews 1:3).

TIP

See page 15 for more Christian beliefs about God.

APPLY

A Christians believe that there is only one God. Refer to scripture or another Christian source of authority to support this idea.

B 'Christianity is a major influence on people's lives.'

Write a paragraph to **support this statement**.

1.2 God as omnipotent, loving and just

RECAP

Essential information:

Christians believe:

- ☐ God is **omnipotent**, almighty, having unlimited power.
- ☐ God is **benevolent**, all-loving and all-good.
- ☐ God is **just**, the perfect judge of human behaviour who will bring about what is right and fair or who will make up for a wrong that has been committed.

Some qualities of God

Omnipotent	Benevolent	Just
• God is the Supreme Being who is all-powerful. • God has unlimited authority.	• God uses his power to do good. • God shows his love by creating humans and caring for them. • God showed his love by sending God's Son, Jesus, to earth.	• God is a just judge of humankind. • God will never support injustice, ill-treatment, prejudice or oppression.

The problems of evil and suffering

The problems of evil and suffering challenge belief in these qualities of God:

- If God is benevolent, **why does God allow people to suffer**, and to hurt others?
- If God is omnipotent, **why does God not prevent evil and suffering**, such as the suffering caused by natural disasters?
- If God is just, **why does God allow injustice** to take place?

Christians believe a just God treats people fairly, so they trust God even when things seem to be going wrong.

TIP

See page 109 for more arguments in response to these challenges to belief in God.

APPLY

A Give **two** ways in which Christians believe God shows his benevolence.

B Write the response a Christian would make to someone who said that a loving God would not allow suffering. Think of **two** arguments and develop them.

TIP

In the 12 mark exam answer, using the key terms 'omnipotent', 'benevolent' and 'just' where appropriate, and spelling them correctly, may gain you more marks for SPaG.

RECAP

Essential information:

- [ ] Christians believe there are three persons in the one God: Father, Son and Holy Spirit. This belief is called the **Trinity**.
- [ ] Each person of the Trinity is fully God.
- [ ] The persons of the Trinity are not the same.

TIP

The Apostles Creed and/or the Nicene Creed, Christian statements of belief, are useful to know when discussing the Trinity. They begin 'I/We believe in one God' and include references to 'the Father Almighty', 'the Son' and 'the Holy Spirit'.

The Trinity

- God is understood by Christians as a relationship of love between Father, Son and Holy Spirit.
- In describing God as Trinity, 'person' does not mean a physical being, although Jesus did have a physical presence in history.

God the Father, the creator of all life, acts as a good father towards his children. He is all powerful (omnipotent), all loving (omnibenevolent), all knowing (omniscient) and present everywhere (omnipresent).

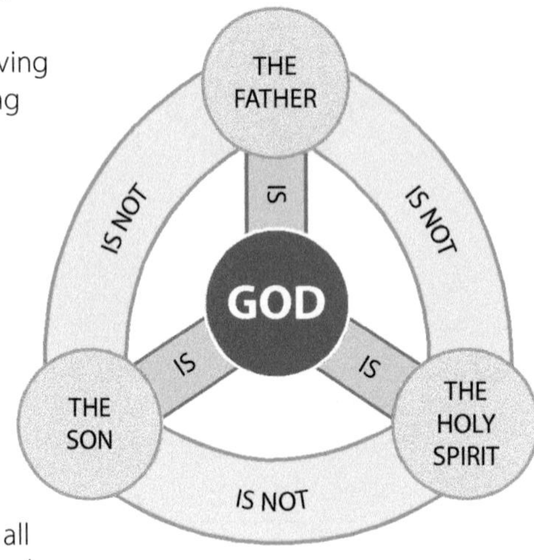

God the Holy Spirit is the unseen power of God at work in the world, who influences, guides and sustains life on earth.

God the Son became incarnate through Jesus, who was both fully human while on earth and fully God at all times. Jesus is called the **Son of God** to show his special relationship to God the Father.

APPLY

A Here are **two** Christian beliefs about the Trinity. Develop each point with further explanation or a relevant quotation:

1. *"The Trinity is the Christian belief that there are three persons in the one God."* ____________________

2. *"One of the persons of the Trinity is God the Father."* ____________________

B Here are some arguments that could be used to evaluate the statement, 'The Trinity is a helpful way of describing God.' Sort them into arguments in support of the statement, and arguments in support of different views. **Write your own justified conclusion.**

1. The Trinity is a helpful idea because it describes God as a loving relationship of persons.	5. If God is One, then how can God have three persons?
2. The love of God the Son is shown in Jesus' mission and sacrifice.	6. The Holy Spirit is the outpouring of love between Father and Son that encourages Christians to love their neighbour.
3. The Trinity seems contradictory.	7. Jesus was a Jew and believed in the oneness of God.
4. The love of God the Father is shown in his sending his Son to earth to save humankind.	8. The Trinity is not helpful to people of other faiths as they may think that Christians believe in three different Gods.

1.4 Different Christian beliefs about Creation

RECAP

Essential information:

- [ ] Christians believe in **creation** by God, the act by which God brought the universe into being.
- [ ] God, the Father, chose to design and create the earth and all life on it.
- [ ] The Holy Spirit was active in the creation (Genesis 1:1–3).
- [ ] The **Word**, God the Son or Jesus, was active in the creation (John 1:1–3).
- [ ] The Trinity, therefore, existed from the beginning and was involved in the creation.

Creation: *Genesis 1:1–3*

> **In the beginning, God created the heavens and the earth**. Now the earth was formless and empty, darkness was over the surface of the deep, and the Spirit of God was hovering over the waters. And God said, "Let there be light," and there was light.
>
> *Genesis 1: 1–3* [NIV]

- Many Christians believe that the story of the creation in Genesis, while not scientifically accurate, contains religious truth.
- Some Christians believe that God made the world in literally six days.
- God created everything out of choice and created everything 'good'.
- Christians believe that God continues to create new life today.
- Although God the Father is referred to as the creator, the Holy Spirit was active in the creation, according to Genesis.

Creation: *John 1:1-3*

> In the beginning was the Word, and **the Word was with God, and the Word was God**. He was with God in the beginning. Through him all things were made; without him nothing was made that has been made.
>
> *John 1: 1–3* [NIV]

- In John's gospel, everything was created through the Word, who was both with God and was God.
- The Word refers to the Son of God who entered history as Jesus.
- Christians believe that the Son of God, the Word of God, was involved in the creation.

TIP
See pages 92 and 104–105 for more detail on different Christian beliefs about creation.

APPLY

A Explain **two** ways in which belief in creation by God influences Christians today.

B Here is an argument in support of the statement, 'The Bible is the best source of information about the creation.'

Evaluate the argument. Explain your reasoning.

"The Bible contains the truth about the creation of the world by God. God is omnipotent, so God can just say 'Let there be light' and it happens. The Bible is God's word, so it is true. Other theories about the creation, like evolution and the Big Bang theory, have not been proved."

TIP

Show the examiner that you are aware of contrasting views within Christianity about the way Genesis 1 is interpreted, that is, between those who take the story literally and those who do not.

1.5 The incarnation and Jesus, the Son of God

RECAP

Essential information:

- ☐ Christians believe that Jesus was God in human form, a belief known as the **incarnation** (becoming flesh, taking a human form).
- ☐ Christians believe that Jesus was the Son of God, one of the persons of the Trinity.

The incarnation

> "This is how the birth of Jesus the Messiah came about: His mother Mary was pledged to be married to Joseph, but before they came together, **she was found to be pregnant through the Holy Spirit.**"
>
> *Matthew 1:18* [NIV]

- On separate occasions an angel appeared to Mary and Joseph explaining that it was not an ordinary conception and it was not to be an ordinary child.
- The gospels of Matthew and Luke explain that Mary conceived Jesus without having sex.
- The virgin conception is evidence for the Christian belief that Jesus was the Son of God, part of the Trinity.
- Through the incarnation, God showed himself as a human being (Jesus) for around 30 years.

> "**The Word became flesh** and made his dwelling among us."
>
> *John 1:14* [NIV]

Son of God, Messiah, Christ

- Jesus was fully God and fully human, which helps explain his miracles and **resurrection** (rising from the dead).
- His words, deeds and promises have great authority because they are the word of God.
- Most Jews expected a Messiah who would come to save Israel and establish an age of peace, but Jews do not believe that Jesus was that person.
- Christians believe that Jesus is the Messiah, but a spiritual rather than a political one.
- Gospel writers refer to Jesus as the Christ ('anointed one' or Messiah), but Jesus warned his disciples not to use the term, possibly because his opponents would have him arrested for **blasphemy** (claiming to be God).

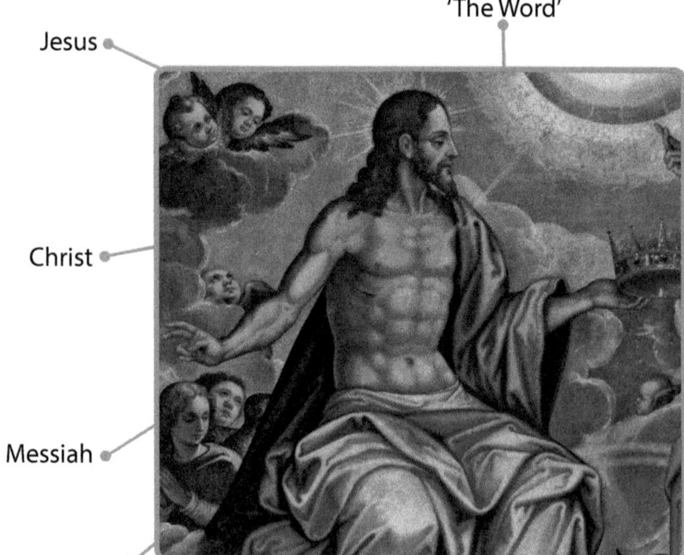

APPLY

A Explain **two** Christian beliefs about Jesus' incarnation. **Refer to sacred writings in your answer**.

B **Develop this argument** to support the statement, 'The stories of the incarnation show that Jesus was the Son of God' by explaining in more detail, adding an example, or referring to a relevant religious teaching or quotation.

"The stories of the incarnation in the gospels of Matthew and Luke show that his mother, Mary, was a virgin. Joseph was not the natural father of Jesus. Jesus' conception was through the Holy Spirit, so really God was his father. That is why he is called the Son of God."

TIP

In a 5 mark question, you need to give a detailed explanation of each belief and then support your answer by quoting from scripture or sacred writings for full marks. The sacred writings may refer to just one of the beliefs or to both of them.

1.6 The crucifixion

RECAP

Essential information:

- ☐ Jesus was sentenced to death by Pontius Pilate, a death by **crucifixion** (fixed to a cross).
- ☐ Jesus forgave those who crucified him and promised one of the men crucified with him that he would join God in paradise.
- ☐ Jesus' body was buried in a cave-like tomb.

INRI

Jesus' crucifixion – what happened?

- Although Jesus was fully God, he was also fully human so suffered pain and horror.
- Jesus' last words before dying were:

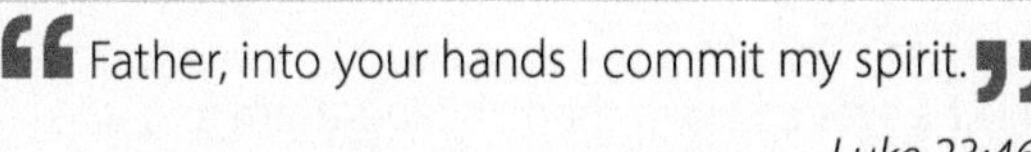

> "Father, into your hands I commit my spirit."
>
> *Luke 23:46* [NIV]

- A Roman centurion acknowledged Jesus was innocent, and said he was the Son of God (Mark 15:39).
- The Roman guards made sure Jesus was dead.
- Joseph of Arimathea was permitted to bury Jesus in a cave-like tomb, rolling a large stone to block the entrance.
- Jesus' burial was rushed because the Sabbath was about to begin.

Jesus' crucifixion – why is it important?

- Jesus' sacrifice on the cross gives hope to Christians that **their sins will be forgiven if they sincerely repent**.
- Christians believe that **God understands human suffering** because Jesus, who is God, experienced it.
- **Christians accept that suffering is part of life**, just as it was a part of Jesus' life.

TIP
See page 25 for more detail on why the crucifixion was important.

APPLY

Here are two ways in which Jesus' crucifixion influences Christians today:

1) Their sins are forgiven.
2) They have hope when they are suffering.

Develop both points by **explaining in more detail or by adding an example**.

TIP

Keep rereading the statement to make sure you are answering the question asked.

Read the following response to the statement, 'The crucifixion is the most important belief for Christians.' Underline the **two** best arguments. Explain how this answer could be improved.

"Jesus was arrested in the Garden of Gethsemane and brought to trial, first before the Jewish Council and then before the Roman Governor, Pontius Pilate. In the gospels it says that Pontius Pilate did not think Jesus was guilty of anything, so he didn't want to have him killed. Instead he had him flogged. The Jewish leaders called for Jesus' death, so Pilate gave in to their wishes and sentenced Jesus to death. After about six hours of agony on the cross, Jesus died. A Roman centurion said that because Jesus was innocent, he must surely be the Son of God. When Jesus died, he took the sins of everyone on himself. This is called the atonement. If Jesus had not died, he would not have risen from the dead."

1.7 The resurrection and ascension

RECAP

Essential information:

- ☐ The gospels say that after Jesus died and was buried, he rose from the dead. This event is known as the **resurrection**.
- ☐ The **ascension** of Jesus took place 40 days after his resurrection, when he returned to God the Father in **heaven**.
- ☐ There would be no Christian faith without the resurrection.

The resurrection of Jesus – what happened?

- Early on Sunday morning, some of Jesus' female followers, including Mary Magdalene, visited the tomb to anoint Jesus' body.
- Jesus' body was not there.
- Either a man or two men, who may have been angels, told the women to spread the news that Jesus had risen from the dead.
- Over the next few days, Jesus appeared to several people including Mary Magdalene and his disciples. He told them he had risen from the dead, as he predicted he would before the crucifixion.

"And if Christ has not been raised, our preaching is useless and so is your faith. But Christ has indeed been raised from the dead [...] For as in Adam all die, so in Christ all will be made alive."

1 Corinthians 15:14, 20, 22 [NIV]

The ascension of Jesus – what happened?

- After meeting with his disciples and asking them to carry on his work, Jesus left them for the last time, returning to the Father in heaven. This event is called the ascension.

"While he was blessing them, he left them and was taken up into heaven."

Luke 24:51 [NIV]

The significance of these events for Christians today

The significance of the **resurrection**:

- Shows the power of good over evil and life over death.
- Means Christians' sins will be forgiven if they follow God's laws.
- Means Christians will be resurrected if they accept Jesus, so there is no need to fear death.

The significance of the **ascension**:

- Shows Jesus is with God in heaven.
- Paves the way for God to send the Holy Spirit to provide comfort and guidance.

TIP

This quote shows that Christianity would not exist without the resurrection. It also shows that the resurrection is important because it is significant evidence for Christians of the divine nature of Jesus.

APPLY

A Give **two** reasons why the disciples believed Jesus was alive after his resurrection. (AQA Specimen question paper, 2017)

B 'The resurrection is the most important belief for Christians.'

Develop this response to the statement, by adding a relevant religious teaching or quotation.

"Without the resurrection, there would be no Christian faith. Jesus' death would have been the end of all the hopes the disciples placed on him. He would have been just like all the other innocent victims put to death for their beliefs."

1.8 Resurrection and life after death

RECAP

Essential information:

- [ ] Jesus' resurrection assures Christians that they too will rise and live on after death.
- [ ] Christians have differing views about what happens when a person who has died is resurrected.
- [ ] Belief in resurrection affects the way Christians live their lives today.

Different Christian views about resurrection

Some Christians believe a person's soul is resurrected **soon after death**.	Other Christians believe the dead will be resurrected at **some time in the future**, when Jesus will return to judge everyone who has ever lived.
Catholic and Orthodox Christians believe in bodily resurrection. This means resurrection is **both spiritual and physical**: the physical body lost at death is restored and transformed into a new, spiritual body.	Some other Christians believe resurrection will **just be spiritual**, not physical as well.

> "So will it be with the resurrection of the dead. The body that is sown is perishable, it is raised imperishable; it is sown in dishonour, it is raised in glory; it is sown in weakness, it is raised in power; it is sown a natural body, it is raised a spiritual body. If there is a natural body, there is also a spiritual body."
>
> *1 Corinthians 15:42–44* [NIV]

TIP

This quote explains some of the differences between a living body and a resurrected body. For Catholics and Orthodox Christians, it suggests there is a physical element to resurrection, as it talks about the resurrected body being a 'body', even if it is a spiritual one.

Impact of the belief in resurrection

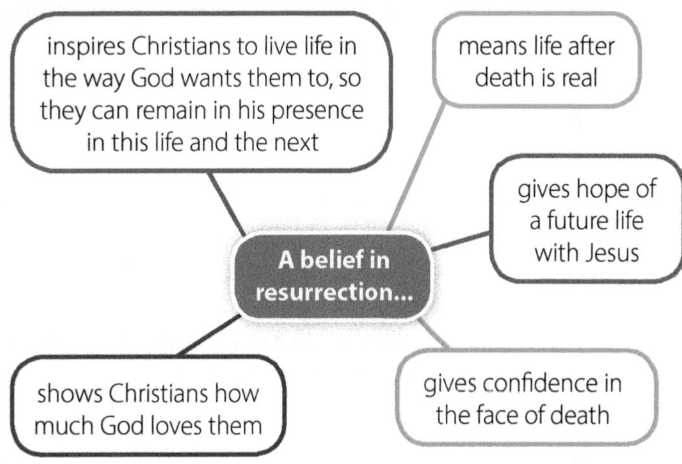

A belief in resurrection...
inspires Christians to live life in the way God wants them to, so they can remain in his presence in this life and the next
means life after death is real
gives hope of a future life with Jesus
gives confidence in the face of death
shows Christians how much God loves them

APPLY

A Explain **two** ways in which a belief in resurrection influences Christians today.

B The table below presents arguments for and against the belief in bodily resurrection. **Write a paragraph** to explain whether you agree or disagree with bodily resurrection, having evaluated both sides of the argument.

TIP

If you need to give different points of view in your answer to an evaluation question, you could include contrasting non-religious perspectives as well as religious perspectives.

For	Against
Jesus rose from the dead and appeared to his disciples.	Science has shown the body decays after death, so there cannot be a physical resurrection.
The gospels insist he was not a ghost, as he ate with them and showed his wounds to them.	Some people are cremated so their bodies no longer exist.
Yet he could appear and disappear suddenly, so it seems that his body was transformed.	Stories of the resurrection appearances may have been exaggerated.
Paul says 'the body that is sown is perishable, it is raised imperishable', suggesting the natural body is raised as a spiritual body, but a body nevertheless.	The disciples may have felt Jesus' presence spiritually rather than seeing him physically.
Catholic and Orthodox Christians believe people's bodies are transformed into a glorified state in which suffering will not exist.	Christians believe in the soul and it is the soul that rises again, not the body.

1.9 The afterlife and judgement

RECAP

Essential information:

- [ ] Christians believe in an **afterlife** (life after death) that depends on faith in God.
- [ ] The afterlife begins at death or at the **Day of Judgement**, when Jesus will come to judge the living and the dead.
- [ ] Judgement will be based on how people have behaved during their lifetimes, as well as their faith in following Jesus. This has an effect on how Christians choose to live their lives today.

The afterlife

Christian beliefs about life after death vary, but many believe that:

- They will be **resurrected** and receive **eternal life** after they die.
- This is a gift from God, and **dependent on faith** in God.
- They will be **judged by God** at some point after they die, and either rewarded by being sent to heaven or punished by being sent to hell.
- This judgement will happen either **very soon after death** or **on the Day of Judgement**. This is a time in the future when the world will end and Christ will come again to judge the living and the dead.

Some of these beliefs about the afterlife are found in the **Apostles' Creed**, which is an important statement of Christian faith.

> "He ascended into heaven, and is seated at the right hand of the Father, and he will come to judge the living and the dead: I believe in [...] the resurrection of the body; and the life everlasting."
>
> *The Apostles' Creed*

Judgement

- Christians believe that after they die, God will judge them on their **behaviour and actions** during their lifetime, as well as their **faith in Jesus** as God's Son.
- In the Bible, Jesus' **parable of the Sheep and the Goats** describes how God will judge people.
- This parable teaches Christians that **in serving others**, **they are serving Jesus**, so this is the way they should live their lives.

> "For I was hungry and you gave me something to eat, I was thirsty and you gave me something to drink, I was a stranger and you invited me in, I needed clothes and you clothed me, I was ill and you looked after me, I was in prison and you came to visit me."
>
> *Matthew 25:35–36* [NIV]

- Before he died, Jesus told his disciples he would prepare a place for them in heaven with God. He also made it clear that **having faith in him and following his teachings** was essential for being able to enter heaven when he said:

> "I am the way and the truth and the life. No one comes to the Father except through me."
>
> *John 14:6* [NIV]

APPLY

A Explain **two** Christian teachings about judgement. **Refer to sacred writings or another source of Christian belief and teaching in your answer.** (AQA Specimen question paper, 2017)

B **Evaluate the statement**, 'The afterlife is a good way to get people to behave themselves and help others.' Refer to two developed Christian arguments, and two developed non-religious arguments. **Write a justified conclusion.**

TIP

When writing a justified conclusion, do not just repeat everything you have already said. Instead, weigh up the arguments and come to a personal view about their persuasiveness.

RECAP

Essential information:

- [ ] Many Christians believe God's judgement will result in eternal reward or eternal punishment.
- [ ] **Heaven** is the state or place of eternal happiness and peace in the presence of God.
- [ ] **Hell** is the place of eternal suffering or the state of being without God.

What happens after God's judgement?

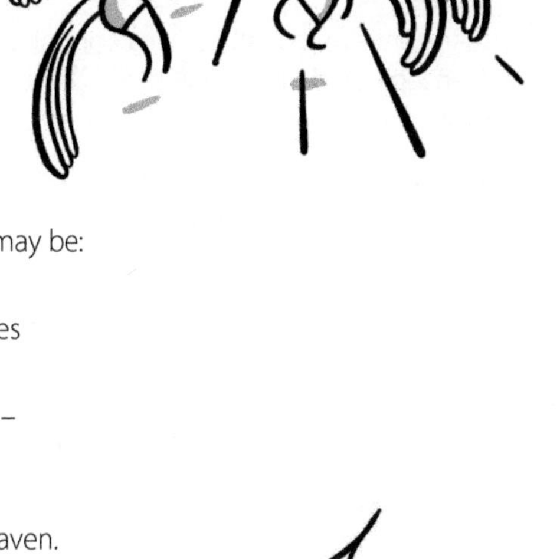

- After God's judgement, Christians believe they will either **experience eternal happiness in the presence of God** (heaven), or **be unable to experience God's presence** (hell).
- Catholics believe some people might enter an intermediate state, called purgatory, before they enter heaven.
- Knowledge of these states is limited and linked to imagery from the past.

Heaven and purgatory

- **Heaven** is thought to be either a **physical place** or **spiritual state** of peace, joy, freedom from pain and a chance to be with loved ones.
- Traditional images of heaven often show God on a throne with Jesus next to him and angels all around him, or a garden paradise.
- Christians differ in their views about **who is allowed into heaven**, where there may be:
  - only Christians (believers in Jesus)
  - Christians and other religious people who have pleased God by living good lives
  - baptised Christians, regardless of how they lived their lives.
- However, many Christians believe heaven is a reward for **both faith and actions** – not just one of these – as the parable of the Sheep and the Goats seems to show (see page 22).
- **Purgatory** is an intermediate state where souls are cleansed in order to enter heaven. This is a Catholic belief.

Hell

- **Hell** is seen as the opposite of heaven – a state of existence without God.
- It is often pictured as a **place of eternal torment** in a fiery pit ruled by Satan (a name for the Devil), who is the power and source of evil.
- However, many people question whether a loving God would condemn people to eternal torment and pain in hell.
- Christians who believe God would not do this see hell as an **eternal state of mind** of **being cut off from the possibility of God**.
- Hell would then be what awaits someone who did not acknowledge God or follow his teachings during their life.

APPLY

A Give **two** reasons why some people do not believe in hell.

B **Make a list of arguments** for and against the idea that heaven and hell were invented to encourage people to behave themselves.

TIP

If this question said 'some Christians', you should offer Christian objections to the idea of hell. 'Some people' means you can give non-religious reasons if you wish.

1.11 Sin and salvation

RECAP

Essential information:

- [ ] **Sin** is any thought or action that separates humans from God.
- [ ] **Original sin** is the in-built tendency to do wrong and disobey God, which Catholics believe all people are born with.
- [ ] The ways Christians can be saved from sin to gain salvation include following God's **law**, receiving God's **grace**, and being guided by the **Holy Spirit**.

The origins and meanings of sin

A sin is any **thought or action that separates humans from God**. Sinful thoughts (such as anger) can lead to sinful actions (such as murder).

- Some sins, like murder or assault, are illegal.
- Other sins, like adultery, are not illegal but are against the laws of God.

Christians believe that all humans commit sins. Some Christians (particularly Catholics) also believe humans are born with an in-built tendency to sin, called **original sin**.

- The idea of original sin comes from Adam and Eve's disobedience of God, when they ate the fruit of the tree of knowledge of good and evil which was forbidden by God. This was the first (original) sin.
- The result of their sin was separation from God, and the introduction of death into the world.

Christians believe **God gave people free will**, but they should use their freedom to make choices God would approve of, otherwise they will separate themselves from God. God provides people with the guidance to make good choices in his law, for example the Ten Commandments (Exodus 20:1–19), the Beatitudes (Matthew 5:1–12) and other Christian teachings.

Salvation

- **Salvation** means to be saved from sin and its consequences, and to be granted eternal life with God.
- Salvation **repairs the damage caused by sin**, which has separated people from God.

There are two main Christian ideas about how salvation can come about:

- Through **doing good works** – the Old Testament makes it clear that salvation comes through faith in God and obeying God's law.

> "In the same way, faith by itself, if it is not accompanied by action, is dead."
>
> *James 2:17* [NIV]

- Through **grace** – salvation is given freely by God through faith in Jesus. It is not deserved or earned, but is a free gift of God's love.

> "For it is by grace you have been saved"
>
> *Ephesians 2:8* [NIV]

- Christians believe it is the **Holy Spirit** who gives grace to Christians and continues to guide them in their daily lives, to help them achieve salvation.

APPLY

A Explain **two** Christian teachings about the means of salvation. **Refer to sacred writings or another source of Christian belief and teaching in your answer.** (AQA Specimen question paper, 2017)

B 'As nobody is perfect, it is impossible not to sin.' **Evaluate this argument** and explain your reasoning.

"It is perfectly possible to live a good life without sin. Jesus lived his life without sin. Many saints have lived good lives without acting badly to other people. It is true that nobody is totally perfect, but that's different. Sin separates you from God and goes against God's law, and there are many people who stay close to God and keep his commandments, so I disagree with the statement."

1.12 The role of Christ in salvation

RECAP

Essential information:

- [ ] Christians believe that salvation is offered through the life and teaching of Jesus.
- [ ] Jesus' resurrection shows that God accepted Jesus' sacrifice as **atonement**. This means that through the sacrifice of his death, Jesus restored the relationship between God and humanity that was broken when Adam and Eve sinned.

TIP

To remember the meaning of 'atonement', think of it as 'at-one-ment', because Jesus' death and resurrection make people at one with God.

The role of Jesus in salvation

Christians believe Jesus' life, death and resurrection had a crucial role to play in God's plan for salvation because:

- Jesus' crucifixion **made up for the original sin** of Adam and Eve.
- The death of Jesus, as an innocent man, was necessary to **restore the relationship between God and believers**, to bring them salvation.
- Jesus' resurrection shows the goodness of Jesus defeated the evil of sin. It was proof that God had accepted Jesus' sacrifice on behalf of humankind.
- Jesus' resurrection means humans can now receive forgiveness for their sins.
- Jesus' death and resurrection made it possible for all who follow his teachings to **gain eternal life**.

> For the wages of sin is death, but the gift of God is eternal life in Christ Jesus our Lord.
>
> *Romans 6:23* [NIV]

TIP

This quote shows the Christian belief that death came into the world as a punishment for sin, but salvation is offered through the life and teaching of Jesus.

Atonement

- Atonement **removes the effects of sin** and allows people to restore their relationship with God.
- Many Christians believe that through the sacrifice of his death, Jesus took the sins of all humanity on himself and paid the debt for them all. He **atoned for the sins of humanity**.
- This sacrifice makes it possible for all who follow Jesus' teachings to **receive eternal life** with God.

> [...] if anybody does sin, we have an advocate with the Father – Jesus Christ, the Righteous One. He is the atoning sacrifice for our sins, and not only for ours but also for the sins of the whole world.
>
> *1 John 2:1–2* [NIV]

APPLY

A Give **two** reasons why the death and resurrection of Jesus is important to Christians.

B Here are some sentences that could be used to evaluate the statement, 'Salvation is God's greatest gift to humans.'

Sort them into arguments in support of the statement, and arguments in support of different views. Try to put them in a logical order. What do you think is missing from these statements to make a top level answer? Explain how the answer could be improved.

1. Atheists do not consider salvation important because they do not think there is a God who saves people.	5. Without salvation, humankind would have to pay the price of human sin.
2. God shows his great love for people by sending his Son to save us.	6. People may doubt the truth of Jesus' resurrection so they don't see the need for a belief in salvation.
3. Even some religious people may think there are greater gifts to humans, such as nature or life itself.	7. Some people may question whether God is loving if God demands the death of his Son in payment for human sin.
4. Everyone needs forgiveness from God.	8. Humans should be grateful every day of their lives for Jesus' sacrifice on their behalf.

Test the 1 mark question

1 Which **one** of the following is the idea that God became human in Jesus?

A Atonement B Incarnation C Resurrection D Creation **[1 mark]**

2 Which **one** of the following is the idea that God is loving?

A Omniscient B Omnipotent C Benevolent D Immanent **[1 mark]**

Test the 2 mark question

3 Give **two** ways that Christians believe salvation can come about. **[2 marks]**

1) ______

2) ______

4 Give **two** Christian beliefs about life after death. **[2 marks]**

1) ______

2) ______

Test the 4 mark question

5 Explain **two** ways in which a belief in Jesus' crucifixion influences Christians today. **[4 marks]**

• **Explain one way.**	*One way in which a belief in Jesus' crucifixion influences Christians today is that they believe that the crucifixion was a sacrifice Jesus chose to make for them*
• Develop your explanation with more detail/an example/ reference to a religious teaching or quotation.	*in order to give them the opportunity to be granted forgiveness by God, so they can live in confidence that their sins have been forgiven.*
• **Explain a second way.**	*A second way in which a belief in Jesus' crucifixion influences Christians today is that it helps Christians who are suffering because they know Jesus suffered as well.*
• Develop your explanation with more detail/an example/ reference to a religious teaching or quotation.	*For example, Christians who are suffering persecution for their faith will be comforted to know that Jesus understands what they are going through because he too was innocent and suffered for his beliefs.*

6 Explain **two** ways in which the belief in creation by God influences Christians today. **[4 marks]**

• **Explain one way.**	
• Develop your explanation with more detail/an example/ reference to a religious teaching or quotation.	
• **Explain a second way.**	
• Develop your explanation with more detail/an example/ reference to a religious teaching or quotation.	

TIP

The student has explained the influence a belief in Jesus' crucifixion has on a Christian's attitude (their confidence in being forgiven and their comfort in dealing with their own suffering). You could also discuss the influence of this belief on a Christian's life (e.g. it might encourage them to spread the message of Jesus or to make the sign of the cross when they pray to remind themselves of Jesus' sacrifice).

7 Explain **two** ways in which the belief that God is loving influences Christians today. **[4 marks]**

Test the 5 mark question

8 Explain **two** Christian beliefs about salvation.

Refer to sacred writings or another source of Christian belief and teaching in your answer. **[5 marks]**

• **Explain one belief.**	*One Christian belief about salvation is that salvation can be gained through good works.*
• Develop your explanation with more detail/an example.	*These good works may be following teachings such as the Ten Commandments, the Golden Rule and 'love your neighbour'. Worshipping and praying regularly also help Christians to earn salvation.*
• **Explain a second belief.**	*A second Christian belief about salvation is that it is gained through grace.*
• Develop your explanation with more detail/an example.	*God gives salvation to people who have faith in Jesus. It is a gift for the faithful.*
• Add a reference to sacred writings or another source of Christian belief and teaching. If you prefer, you can add this reference to your first belief instead.	*Paul wrote in his letters that it is through grace, which is a gift from God, that people are saved, not simply through their good works.*

TIP

The references to scripture here count as development of your first point.

9 Explain **two** Christian teachings about God.

Refer to sacred writings or another source of Christian belief and teaching in your answer. **[5 marks]**

• **Explain one teaching.**	
• Develop your explanation with more detail/an example.	
• **Explain a second teaching.**	
• Develop your explanation with more detail/an example.	
• Add a reference to sacred writings or another source of Christian belief and teaching. If you prefer, you can add this reference to your first teaching instead.	

TIP

You only need to make one reference to scripture in your answer. It can support either your first or your second point.

10 Explain **two** Christian teachings about atonement.

Refer to sacred writings or another source of Christian belief and teaching in your answer. **[5 marks]**

Test the 12 mark question

11 'The stories of the incarnation prove that Jesus was the Son of God.'

Evaluate this statement. In your answer you should:

- refer to Christian teaching
- give reasoned arguments to support this statement
- give reasoned arguments to support a different point of view
- reach a justified conclusion.

[12 marks]
[+3 SPaG ma

REASONED ARGUMENTS IN SUPPORT OF THE STATEMENT ● **Explain why some people would agree with the statement.** ● Develop your explanation with more detail and examples. ● Refer to religious teaching. Use a quote or paraphrase or refer to a religious authority. ● **Evaluate the arguments.** Is this a good argument or not? Explain why you think this.	*Christians believe in the incarnation. This means that God took human form in Jesus. The stories of Jesus' birth show he was not conceived in the normal way. The fact he was conceived through the actions of God and born of a virgin proves that he was special and if God was involved it is likely that Jesus was his son. However, even though he was a physical person, he was also God at the same time. John's gospel calls Jesus 'the Son of God' and says he was the Word made flesh, living among us. This supports the idea that Jesus was both God and human.*
REASONED ARGUMENTS SUPPORTING A DIFFERENT VIEW ● **Explain why some people would support a different view.** ● Develop your explanation with more detail and examples. ● Refer to religious teaching. Use a quote or paraphrase or refer to a religious authority. ● **Evaluate the arguments.** Is this a good argument or not? Explain why you think this.	*Many people do not agree that Jesus was conceived through the actions of God and believe that Mary, his mother, was not a virgin. If the stories of the incarnation are not correct, they cannot be used as evidence that Jesus was the Son of God although his actions showed he was very special.*
CONCLUSION ● **Give a justified conclusion.** ● Include your own opinion together with your own reasoning. ● **Include evaluation.** Explain why you think one viewpoint is stronger than the other or why they are equally strong. ● Do not just repeat arguments you have already used without explaining how they apply to your reasoned opinion/conclusion.	*It may be true that the title 'Son of God' does not mean that there is such a close relationship between Jesus and God. It is possible that he was chosen by God, maybe when he was baptised, to do good works on earth and tell people about Christianity without there being a family relationship between himself and God. If this is true, there is no such thing as incarnation as far as Jesus is concerned.*

TIP

The question is about stories (plural) so it would improve the answer to mention details of Jesus' conception in the gospels of Matthew and Luke.

TIP

This argument could be developed further for more marks. For example, after the sentence that ends 'not a virgin' you might add 'Mary was engaged to Joseph, making it possible that Joseph was Jesus' father.'

TIP

The conclusion shows logical chains of reasoning. It evaluates different interpretations of the title 'Son of God' in relation to the stories of the incarnation. The examiner will want to see that you can link ideas together when developing your argument, and not just repeat what you have said already.

12 'There is no such place as hell.'

Evaluate this statement. In your answer you should:

- refer to Christian teaching
- give reasoned arguments to support this statement
- give reasoned arguments to support a different point of view
- reach a justified conclusion.

TIP
Spelling, punctuation and grammar is assessed on each 12 mark question, so make sure you are careful to use your best written English.

[12 marks]
[+3 SPaG marks]

REASONED ARGUMENTS IN SUPPORT OF THE STATEMENT ● **Explain why some people would agree with the statement.** ● Develop your explanation with more detail and examples. ● Refer to religious teaching. Use a quote or paraphrase or refer to a religious authority. ● **Evaluate the arguments.** Is this a good argument or not? Explain why you think this.	
REASONED ARGUMENTS SUPPORTING A DIFFERENT VIEW ● **Explain why some people would support a different view.** ● Develop your explanation with more detail and examples. ● Refer to religious teaching. Use a quote or paraphrase or refer to a religious authority. ● **Evaluate the arguments.** Is this a good argument or not? Explain why you think this.	
CONCLUSION ● **Give a justified conclusion.** ● Include your own opinion together with your own reasoning. ● **Include evaluation.** Explain why you think one viewpoint is stronger than the other or why they are equally strong. ● Do not just repeat arguments you have already used without explaining how they apply to your reasoned opinion/conclusion.	

TIP
It's essential to include evaluation because this is the key skill that you are being tested on in the 12 mark question. You can evaluate after each viewpoint, and/or at the end as part of your justified conclusion.

13 'The best way to gain salvation is to obey God's law.'

Evaluate this statement. In your answer you should:

- refer to Christian teaching
- give reasoned arguments to support this statement
- give reasoned arguments to support a different point of view
- reach a justified conclusion.

[12 marks]
[+3 SPaG marks]

Check your answers using the mark scheme on page 157. How did you do?
To feel more secure in the content you need to remember, re-read pages 14–25.
To remind yourself of what the examiner is looking for, go to pages 7–13.

2 Christianity: Practices

2.1 Worship

RECAP

Essential information:

- ☐ **Worship** is the act of religious praise, honour or devotion. It is a way for Christians to show their deep love and honour to God.
- ☐ Worship can take different forms, including liturgical, non-liturgical and informal worship.
- ☐ **Private worship** is when believers praise or honour God in their own home.

Why do Christians worship?

- To praise and thank God
- To ask for forgiveness
- To seek God's help for themselves or others
- To deepen their relationship with God and strengthen their faith

Different forms of worship

Type of worship	What form does it take?	Examples	Why is it important for Christians?
liturgical worship is a church service that follows a set structure or ritual	• takes place in a church • priest leads the congregation and may perform symbolic actions • formal prayers with set responses • Bible passages are read out, there may be a sermon • music and hymns	the Eucharist for Catholic, Orthodox and Anglican Churches	• worldwide set order for service that is familiar to everyone • ritual passed down through generations gives a sense of tradition • Bible readings follow the Christian calendar and teach Christian history and faith
non-liturgical worship is a service that does not follow a set text or ritual	• takes place in a church • often focused on Bible readings followed by a sermon • may also have prayers and hymns but there is no set order, the number and type can change from week to week	services in non-Conformist churches, e.g. Methodist, Baptist, United Reformed	• services can be planned and ordered to suit a certain theme • non-Conformist churches place an emphasis on the word of God in the Bible
informal worship is a type of non-liturgical worship that is 'spontaneous' or 'charismatic' in nature	• community or house churches meet in private homes and share food • Quaker worship is mainly silent, people speak when moved by God to offer their thoughts or read from the Bible • 'charismatic' worship may involve dancing, clapping, calling out and speaking in tongues	community or house churches, Quaker worship, charismatic ('led by the spirit') worship of the Pentecostal Church	• the style of worship in house churches is similar to the worship of early Christians • people can share readings and prayers and can take an active part in church by calling out or speaking without formal training • service may have an emotional impact with a feeling of personal revelation from God

APPLY

A Going on pilgrimage, celebrating festivals and religious art are also forms of worship. Give **two** more ways that Christians worship.

B 'Worship is most powerful when believers follow a set ritual.'

List arguments to support this statement and arguments to support a different point of view.

TIP

The arguments should apply to Christianity. Try to use religious language (see key terms in red).

2.2 Prayer

RECAP

Essential information:

- [ ] **Prayer** is communicating with God, either silently or through words of praise, thanksgiving or confession, or requests for God's help or guidance.
- [ ] Christians may use **set prayers** that have been written down and said more than once by more than one person. An example is **the Lord's Prayer**, which is the prayer Jesus taught to his disciples.
- [ ] Christians may also use **informal prayers** (made up by an individual using his or her own words) to communicate with God. Some Christians find they can express their needs to God more easily by using their own words.

The importance of prayer

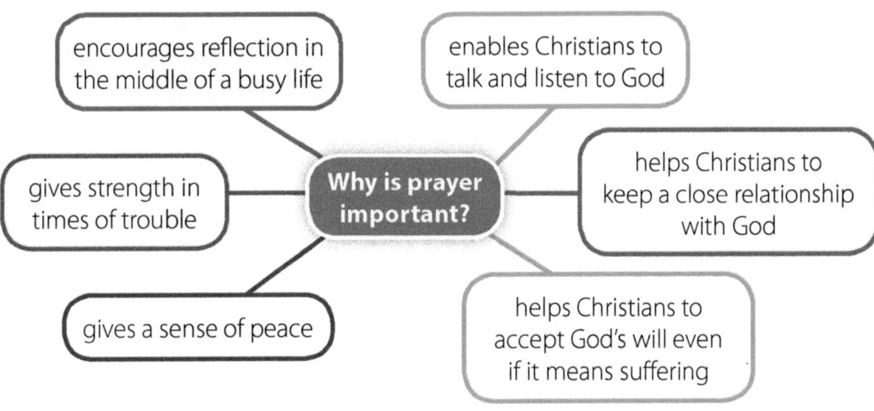

Why is prayer important?
encourages reflection in the middle of a busy life
enables Christians to talk and listen to God
gives strength in times of trouble
helps Christians to keep a close relationship with God
gives a sense of peace
helps Christians to accept God's will even if it means suffering

The Lord's Prayer

> "Our Father in heaven, hallowed be your name,
> your Kingdom come, your will be done,
> on earth as in heaven.
> Give us today our daily bread.
> Forgive us our sins
> as we forgive those who sin against us.
> Lead us not into temptation, but deliver us from evil.
> For the kingdom, the power, and the glory are yours
> now and for ever. Amen."
>
> *The Lord's Prayer*

- When Jesus' disciples asked him to teach them how to pray, he answered with the Lord's Prayer.
- Christians see it as a **model of good prayer**, as it combines praise to God with asking for one's needs.
- It reminds Christians to **forgive others in order to be forgiven**, since prayer is only effective if people's relationships with others are right.
- It reminds Christians that **God is the Father of the whole Christian community**, and it can create a sense of unity when everyone in the congregation says it together.
- The Lord's Prayer is often used in worship and is nearly always said at Holy Communion, baptisms, marriages and funerals. It is also used in schools and in commemoration services in Britain.

APPLY

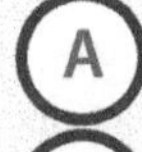

A Give **two** reasons why the Lord's Prayer is important to Christians.

B 'Private worship has more meaning for a Christian than public worship.' (AQA Specimen question paper, 2017)

Develop this argument to support the statement by explaining in more detail, adding an example, or referring to a relevant religious teaching or quotation.

"An individual Christian can choose how they want to worship in private, whereas in public worship they have to follow what everyone else is saying and doing. Therefore private worship has more meaning because they can put their heart and soul into it."

TIP

Always analyse the statement carefully. For example, here 'has more meaning' might depend on an individual's reasons for prayer.

2.3 The sacraments: Baptism

RECAP

Essential information:

- [ ] **Sacraments** are holy rituals through which believers receive a special gift of grace (free gift of God's love). Some Christian denominations recognise seven sacraments while others acknowledge fewer.
- [ ] **Baptism** is the ritual through which a person becomes a member of the Church. It involves the use of water to symbolise the washing away of sin.
- [ ] **Infant baptism** is for babies and young children. **Believers' baptism** is for people who are old enough to understand the significance of the ritual.

The sacraments

- **Catholic and Orthodox** Christians recognise **seven** sacraments: baptism, confirmation, Holy Communion, marriage, Holy Orders, reconciliation and the anointing of the sick.
- Many **Protestant** churches recognise **two** sacraments – baptism and Holy Communion – because they believe Jesus taught people to undertake these.
- Some churches that practise believers' baptism consider it to be important but not a 'sacrament'.
- Some churches, like the Quakers or Salvation Army, do not see any ritual or ceremony as being a 'sacrament'.

Baptism

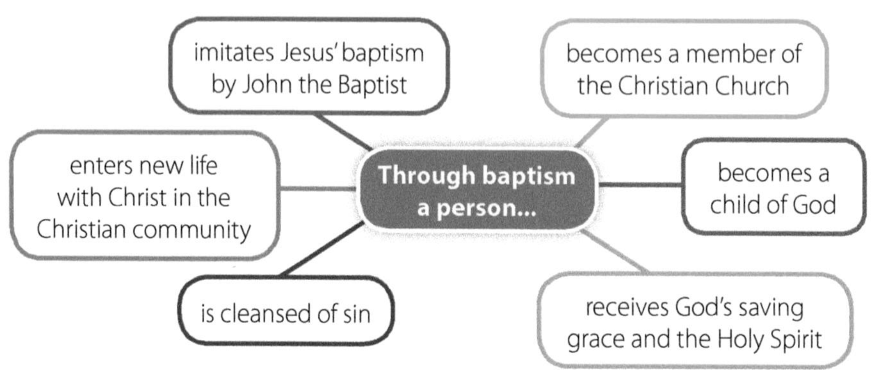

Infant baptism and believers' baptism

	Practised by	Reasons why	What happens
Infant baptism 	Catholic, Orthodox, Anglican, Methodist, and United Reformed Christians	• Removes original sin (Catholic and Orthodox belief). • Allows the child to be welcomed into the Church as soon as possible. • The parents can thank God for their new baby and celebrate with family and friends.	• The priest or minister pours blessed water over the baby's head and says, 'I baptise you in the name of the Father, and of the Son, and of the Holy Spirit.' • Godparents and parents promise to bring up the child as a Christian. • The child is welcomed into the Christian community.
Believers' baptism 	Baptists, Pentecostalists (and other denominations, such as Anglicans who join the church as adults)	• People should be old enough to consciously make a mature decision about their faith. • The decision to live a life dedicated to Jesus is what saves a person, rather than the baptism itself.	• The person is fully immersed in a pool which symbolises cleansing from sin and rising to new life in Christ. • When asked whether they are willing to change their lives, the person gives a brief testimony of their faith in Jesus. • The person is baptised 'in the name of the Father, and of the Son, and of the Holy Spirit.'

APPLY

A Explain **two** contrasting ways in which Christians practise baptism and develop each point.

B 'Parents should not have their children baptised if they have no intention of bringing them up as Christians.'

Evaluate this statement.

2.4 The sacraments: Holy Communion

RECAP

Essential information:

- ☐ **Holy Communion** (also known as the Eucharist, Mass, the Lord's Supper or the Divine Liturgy) is the sacrament that uses bread and wine to celebrate the sacrifice of Jesus on the cross and his resurrection.
- ☐ It recalls the Last Supper of Jesus, using his words and actions.
- ☐ Christians interpret the meaning of Holy Communion in different ways, but all agree that it brings them closer to each other and to God.

The meaning of Holy Communion

Holy Communion is a service which celebrates and gives thanks for the sacrifice of Jesus' death and resurrection (see pages 19–20). It has different meanings for different Christians:

- **Catholics, Orthodox Christians** and **some Anglicans** believe the bread and wine become **the body and blood of Christ**. This means Jesus is fully present in the bread and wine. This is a divine mystery that helps believers share in the saving sacrifice of Jesus' death and resurrection.
- **Protestant Christians** celebrate Holy Communion as a **reminder of the Last Supper**. They do not believe the bread and wine become the body and blood of Christ. Instead, the bread and wine remain **symbols of Jesus' sacrifice**, which helps believers to reflect on its meaning today.

> "For whenever you eat this bread and drink this cup, you proclaim the Lord's death until he comes."
>
> *1 Corinthians 11:26* [NIV]

The impact of Holy Communion

For many Christians, Holy Communion is at the centre of their lives and worship. It affects individuals, local communities and the wider society in a number of ways:

Individuals	Communities	Wider society
• Christians **receive God's grace** by joining in the sacrifice of Jesus. • This helps to strengthen their faith. • They become closer to God.	• Holy Communion **brings the community of believers together** in unity by sharing the bread and wine. • This can provide support and encouragement for those going through a difficult time.	• Holy Communion **acts as a call to love others in practical ways**. • It encourages Christians to work for equality and justice for all. • Many churches collect money during the service to help support those in need, such as the poor or homeless.

APPLY

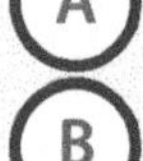

A Explain **two** ways in which Holy Communion has an impact on the lives of believers.

B Use the table below with arguments about the statement, 'It is more important to help the poor than to celebrate Holy Communion.'

Write a paragraph to explain whether you agree or disagree with the statement, having evaluated both sides of the argument.

TIP

Decide on two ways and explain each. Do not simply list a number of ways without developing any of your points.

In support of the statement	Other views
The poor need urgent help, particularly if they are living in less economically developed countries, so of course it is more important to help them than to receive Holy Communion. Christians are taught to love their neighbour so that must come before their own needs. Remembering Jesus' death and resurrection through Holy Communion is nice, but not very useful to anyone. It's just focusing on the past when people should be thinking about the present.	It doesn't need to be such a stark choice. After all, when Christians break bread together at Holy Communion they remember that people in the world are starving and they try to help them. Many churches collect money for the poor during the service of Holy Communion, so celebrating this sacrament encourages people to care for others, not just themselves. 'Eucharist' means 'thanksgiving', so it makes Christians grateful for God's love and this makes them want to share it.

2.5 Celebrating Holy Communion

RECAP

Essential information:

- [ ] In most churches the Holy Communion service has two parts: the ministry of the Word (which focuses on the Bible), and the ministry of Holy Communion (the offering, consecrating and sharing of bread and wine).
- [ ] Christians have different practices when it comes to celebrating Holy Communion.

Differences between Holy Communion services

- In the **Orthodox Church**, Holy Communion is called the Divine Liturgy, and is believed to recreate heaven on earth. Much of the service is held at the altar behind the iconostasis, which is a screen that represents the divide between heaven and earth. The priest passes through the iconostasis using the Royal Doors.
- Holy Communion in the **Catholic and Anglican Churches** is very similar. The main difference is that Catholics believe the bread and wine turn into the body and blood of Christ, whereas many Anglicans believe Jesus is only present in a spiritual way when the bread and wine are being eaten.

Further examples of how Holy Communion services differ from each other include the following:

Orthodox Divine Liturgy	Catholic Mass and Anglican Holy Communion	Holy Communion in the United Reformed Church
Liturgy of the Word: • There are hymns, prayers and a Bible reading. • The priest comes through the Royal Doors to chant the Gospel. • There may be a sermon. **Liturgy of the Faithful:** • The priest receives wine and bread baked by church members. • Prayers are offered for the church, the local community and the world. • Behind the iconostasis, the priest says the words of Jesus at the Last Supper. • Most of the bread is consecrated as the body and blood of Christ. • The priest distributes holy bread and wine on a spoon. • Prayers of thanksgiving are said. • Unconsecrated pieces of bread are given to people to take home, as a sign of belonging to the Christian community.	**Liturgy of the Word:** • There are three Bible readings, a psalm and a homily. • The Creed is said. • Prayers are said for the Church, the local community, the world, and the sick and the dead. **Liturgy of the Eucharist:** • In the Anglican Holy Communion, people give a sign of peace to each other. • Offerings of bread and wine are brought to the altar. • The priest repeats the words of Jesus at the Last Supper over the bread and the wine. • People say the Lord's Prayer. • In the Catholic Mass, the sign of peace is given at this point. • People receive the bread and wine. • The priest blesses people and sends them out to live the gospel.	• The service begins with a hymn and prayer of praise and thanksgiving. • Bible readings and a sermon are given. • Prayers for the world and the needs of particular people are said. • The minister repeats the words and actions of Jesus at the Last Supper. • There is an 'open table' so anyone who wishes may receive Holy Communion. • Sometimes the bread is cut beforehand, other times it is broken and passed around by the congregation. • Wine is sometimes non-alcoholic and is usually distributed in small cups. • The service ends with a prayer of thanksgiving, a blessing, and an encouragement to go out and serve God.

APPLY

(A) Explain **two** contrasting ways in which Holy Communion is celebrated in Christianity. (AQA Specimen question paper, 2017)

(B) **Write a paragraph** in response to the statement, 'Holy Communion services should focus more on the Liturgy of the Word than on the Holy Communion itself.' **Develop your reasons** and include a reference to scripture or religious teaching in your answer.

Holy Communion services have many similarities. Be sure to choose aspects that show a real contrast.

RECAP

Essential information:

- [ ] A **pilgrimage** is a journey made by a believer to a holy site for religious reasons. As well as making a physical journey to a sacred place, the pilgrim also makes a spiritual journey towards God.
- [ ] A pilgrimage gives many opportunities for prayer and worship, and is itself an act of worship and devotion.
- [ ] Two popular pilgrimage sites for Christians are Lourdes (a town in France) and Iona (a Scottish island).

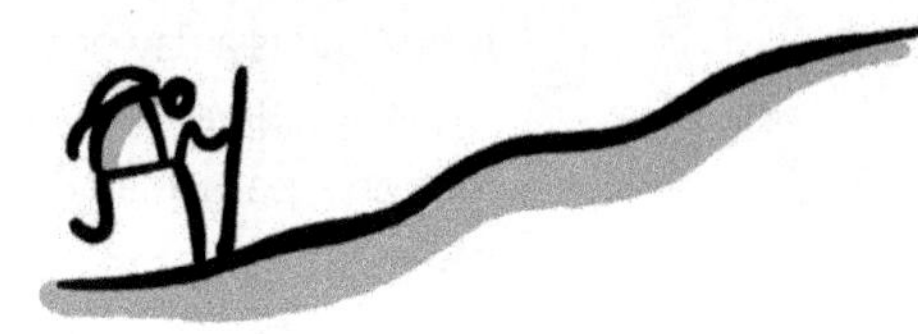

The role and importance of pilgrimage

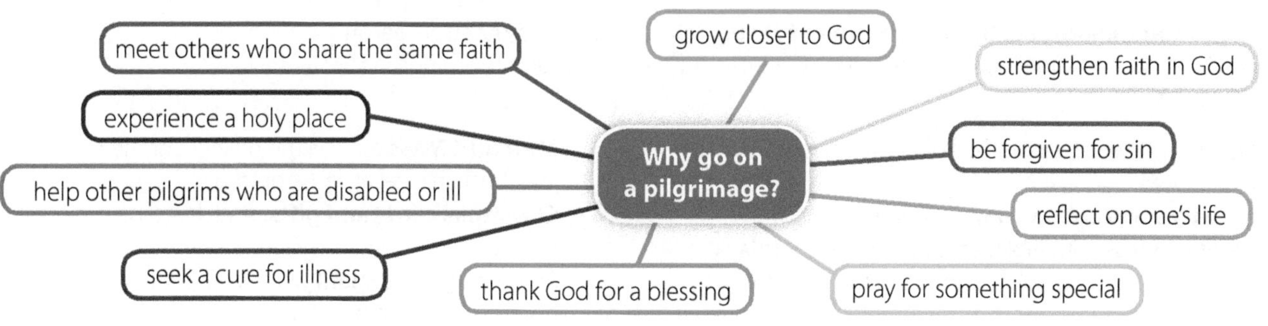
Why go on a pilgrimage?
meet others who share the same faith
grow closer to God
strengthen faith in God
experience a holy place
be forgiven for sin
help other pilgrims who are disabled or ill
reflect on one's life
seek a cure for illness
thank God for a blessing
pray for something special

A pilgrimage can impact on a Christian's life in a number of ways. It can:

- give them a better understanding of their faith
- renew their enthusiasm for living a Christian life
- help them to see problems in a new light
- help them to feel cleansed from sin
- help them to feel more connected to the Christian community
- give them a good feeling about helping other pilgrims who are disabled or ill.

Places of Christian pilgrimage

Place	Significance	Activities
Lourdes (a town in France)	• Where Mary, Jesus' mother, is said to have appeared in a number of visions to a girl called Bernadette. • Mary told Bernadette to dig in the ground, and when she did a spring of water appeared. • The water is believed to have healing properties, and a number of healing miracles are claimed to have taken place here.	• Pilgrims go to Lourdes to bathe in the waters of the spring, or to help other pilgrims who are ill or disabled to bathe in the waters. • Pilgrims also pray for healing or forgiveness. • They may recite the rosary together.
Iona (an island off the coast of Scotland)	• Where St Columba established a monastic community in the 6th century AD. • The community now has an ecumenical centre where pilgrims can stay.	• Because it is quiet, peaceful and a place of natural beauty, pilgrims can spend time praying, reading the Bible, and reflecting or meditating. • Pilgrims can also attend services in the abbey church, take part in workshops, and visit the island's holy or historic sites.

APPLY

Explain **two** contrasting examples of Christian pilgrimage. (AQA Specimen question paper, 2017)

'There is no difference between a pilgrimage and a holiday.'

Develop this argument against the statement by explaining in more detail, adding an example or referring to Christian teaching.

"Although a pilgrimage can seem a lot like a holiday, especially if you travel abroad, there is a big difference. A pilgrimage is a spiritual journey that people undertake for religious reasons rather than just to sightsee."

TIP

You need to explain why the examples are contrasting, rather than just describing the two places, so be sure to explain the different reasons why pilgrims go there.

RECAP

Essential information:

- [ ] A **festival** is a day or period of celebration for religious reasons.
- [ ] Festivals help Christians to remember and celebrate the major events in their religion – particularly the life, death and resurrection of Jesus.
- [ ] **Christmas** commemorates the incarnation and the birth of Jesus. Celebrations begin on 25 December and last 12 days, ending with Epiphany (which recalls the visit of the wise men).
- [ ] **Easter** celebrates the resurrection of Jesus from the dead. Celebrations begin before Easter Sunday and finish with the feast of Pentecost.

Christmas

Christmas **commemorates the incarnation of Jesus**, which is the belief that God became human in Jesus (see page 18). The celebrations reflect Christian beliefs and teachings in the following ways:

- **lights** represent Jesus as the light coming into the world of darkness
- **nativity scenes** show baby Jesus born into poverty
- **carol services** with Bible readings remind Christians about God's promise of a saviour and the events of Jesus' birth
- **Midnight Mass** reflects the holiness of the night and the joy Christians feel at Jesus' birth
- **Christmas cards and gifts** recall the wise men's gifts to Jesus
- Christians **give to charity** in this time of peace and goodwill because God gave humanity the gift of Jesus, his Son.

Easter

Easter is the most important Christian festival, which **celebrates Jesus' rising from the dead** (see page 20).

Holy Week (the week before Easter Sunday) remembers the events leading up to Jesus' crucifixion, including his arrest and trial.

- On **Saturday night**, some churches hold a special service to celebrate Christ's resurrection.
- Orthodox Christians walk with candles in procession, then enter the dark church as if going into Jesus' empty tomb.
- The priest announces 'Christ is risen!' to which people answer 'He is risen indeed.'
- Catholics and Anglicans have a vigil that begins in darkness, before the Paschal candle is lit to symbolise the risen Christ. The service ends with Holy Communion.

On **Good Friday** (the day Jesus was crucified), there are special services and processions led by a person carrying a cross.

- On **Easter Sunday**, churches are filled with flowers and special hymns are sung to rejoice at Jesus' resurrection.
- Services are held at sunrise, and shared breakfasts include eggs to symbolise new life.

> "Christ is risen from the dead, trampling down death by death, and upon those in the tombs bestowing life."
>
> *Traditional Orthodox hymn at the Easter Divine Liturgy*

APPLY

 Give **two** ways in which Christians celebrate the festival of Easter.

 'Christmas is no longer a religious festival.' **Evaluate this statement.**

RECAP

Essential information:

- [ ] **The Church** is the holy people of God, also called the Body of Christ, among whom Christ is present and active.
- [ ] **A church** is a building in which Christians worship.
- [ ] Individual churches and the Church as a whole help the local community in a variety of ways, including the provision of **food banks**. These give food for free to people who cannot afford to buy it.

What does the Church do?

Individual churches and the Church as a whole help the local community in many ways.

Individual churches:

- educate people about Christianity (e.g. Bible study groups)
- are meeting places for prayer and worship
- provide activities for younger people (e.g. youth clubs)
- are places where Christians can socialise and obtain spiritual guidance.

The Church:

- supports local projects such as food banks
- provides social services such as schooling and medical care
- helps those in need
- campaigns for justice.

> "And God placed all things under his [Jesus'] feet and appointed him to be head over everything for the church, which is his body."
>
> *Ephesians 1:22–23* [NIV]

TIP

You could use this quote in your exam to show that Christians think of the Church as the followers of Jesus, who together are the body of Christ on earth.

Examples of the Church helping the local community

The Trussell Trust and The Oasis Project are two organisations that help the local community by providing food banks and other services. The work of these charities is based on Christian principles (such as the parable of the Sheep and the Goats).

The Trussell Trust

- A charity running over 400 food banks in the UK.
- These provide emergency food, help and support to people in crisis in the UK.
- Non-perishable food is donated by churches, supermarkets, schools, businesses and individuals.
- Doctors, health visitors and social workers identify people in crisis and issue them with a food voucher.
- Their aim is to bring religious and non-religious people together to help end poverty and hunger.

The Oasis Project

- A community hub run by Plymouth Methodist Mission Circuit.
- Provides an internet café, creative courses, a job club, training opportunities, a meeting place and a food bank.
- Spiritual and practical help is given to those in need because of ill health, learning disabilities, domestic violence, substance abuse, low income and housing problems.

TIP

You will not be asked about these particular organisations in your exam, but if you learn what they do, you will be able to give detailed examples of how the Church helps in the local community.

APPLY

A Give **two** meanings of the word 'church'.

B Here is a response to the statement, 'There will always be a need to feed hungry people in Britain.' Can you **improve this answer** by including religious beliefs?

"At first this statement appears untrue. No one should be hungry in Britain as there is a welfare state. People who can't work to feed themselves or their families can apply for benefits."

"However, I agree with the statement because people can suddenly be faced with bills they can't pay, or lose their jobs, or become ill so they can't work. It may take many weeks to apply for benefits and be accepted, so what do they do in the meantime? If they don't have much savings they will be really hard up and need the help of food banks."

RECAP

Essential information:

- [ ] Christians should help others in the local community because Jesus taught that people should show **agape** love (a Biblical word meaning selfless, sacrificial, unconditional love).
- [ ] Christians believe it is important to put their faith into action. They do this through many organisations and projects that help vulnerable people in the community.
- [ ] **Street Pastors** are people who are trained to patrol the streets in urban areas. They help vulnerable people by providing a reassuring presence on the street.

The importance of helping in the local community

- Jesus taught that **Christians should help others by showing agape love** towards them. For example, in the parable of the Sheep and the Goats, Jesus teaches Christians they should give practical help to people in need (see page 22).
- Two examples of Christian organisations that provide practical help to local communities are Street Pastors and Parish Nursing Ministries UK.

> "Faith by itself, if it is not accompanied by action, is dead."
>
> *James 2:17* [NIV]

TIP

You could use this quote in your exam to show that Christians believe it is very important to take practical action to help others.

Street Pastors and Parish Nursing Ministries UK

Street Pastors

- An initiative started in London in 2003, by the Christian charity the Ascension Trust.
- Adult volunteers are trained to patrol the streets in urban areas.
- The main aim originally was to challenge gang culture and knife crime in London.
- The focus then widened to responding to drunkenness, anti-social behaviour and fear of crime.
- Street Pastors work closely with police and local councils.
- They listen to people's problems, advise on where they might get help, and discourage anti-social behaviour.
- A similar group called School Pastors was set up in 2011 to discourage illegal drug use, bullying and anti-social behaviour in schools.

Parish Nursing Ministries UK

- This Christian charity supports whole-person healthcare through the local church.
- They provide churches with registered parish nurses, who promote well-being in body, mind and spirit among the local community.
- The nurses help to provide early diagnosis of health problems.
- They train and coordinate volunteers to help combat loneliness or provide support during times of crisis.
- They give additional help to the NHS.
- They encourage people to exercise and have a good diet.
- They focus on the whole person, including listening to people and praying with them if asked. They also direct people to specific services if needed.

TIP

When using Christian charities as examples in your answers, focus on their work and why they do it, rather than details about when they were founded and by whom.

APPLY

A Explain **two** ways in which Street Pastors carry out their Christian duty.

Refer to Christian teaching in your answer. (AQA Specimen question paper, 2017)

B 'All Christians should do something practical to help their community, including praying for their neighbours.'

Develop two religious arguments in support of this statement, and **two** non-religious arguments against it.

2.10 The place of mission and evangelism

RECAP

Essential information:

- ☐ A **mission** is a vocation or calling to spread the faith. The Church has a mission to tell non-believers that Jesus Christ, the Son of God, came into the world as its saviour.
- ☐ Christians spread the faith through **evangelism** (showing faith in Jesus by example or by telling others).
- ☐ They do this to fulfil Jesus' instructions to the disciples to spread his teachings (the **Great Commission**).

The Great Commission

"Therefore go and make disciples of all nations, baptising them in the name of the Father and of the Son and of the Holy Spirit, and teaching them to obey everything I have commanded you."

Matthew 28:19–20 [NIV]

TIP

You can use this quote in your exam to show what the Great Commission involves. Jesus instructs his disciples to baptise people and to spread his teachings.

- Jesus gave a Great Commission to his disciples to **spread the gospel** and **make disciples of all nations through baptism**.
- The **Holy Spirit** at Pentecost gave the disciples the gifts and courage needed to carry out the Great Commission.
- All Christians have a duty to spread the gospel and tell others of their faith, but some become **missionaries** or **evangelists** (people who promote Christianity, for example by going to foreign countries to preach or do charitable work).
- The aims of missionary work and evangelism are to **persuade people to accept Jesus as their Saviour**, and to extend the Church to all nations.

Alpha

- Alpha is an **example of evangelism in Britain**.
- It was started in London by an Anglican priest, with the aim of helping church members understand the basics of the Christian faith.
- The course is now used as an **introduction for those interested in learning about Christianity**, by different Christian denominations in Britain and abroad.
- The organisers describe it as 'an opportunity to explore the meaning of life' through talks and discussions.
- Courses are held in homes, workplaces, universities and prisons as well as in churches.

APPLY

A Give **two** ways in which the Church tries to fulfil its mission.

B **Unscramble the arguments** in the table below referring to the statement, 'Every Christian should be an evangelist.' Decide which arguments could be used to support the statement and which could be used against it.

Write a paragraph to explain whether you agree or disagree with the statement, having evaluated both sides of the argument.

1. If Christians don't help to spread the faith, it might die out.	4. Not every Christian should be an evangelist because some people are just too shy.
2. Some Christians live in countries where they are persecuted, so if they spoke in public about their faith they would be risking death or imprisonment.	5. All Christians have received the Great Commission from Jesus to preach to all nations.
3. Evangelism can happen in small ways, for example Christians can spread their faith to people they meet in everyday life or just give a good example of loving their neighbours.	6. Christians who go around evangelising can annoy people, so it does not help their cause.

2.11 Church growth

RECAP

Essential information:

- ☐ Up to a third of the world's population claim to be Christian (including people who rarely attend church), and around 80,000 people become Christians each day.
- ☐ The Church expects new Christians to help spread the faith as part of their commitment to Jesus.
- ☐ Christ for all Nations is an example of a Christian organisation that promotes evangelism.

The growth of the Church

- The Church is growing rapidly in South America, Africa and Asia, but not in the USA, Europe and the Middle East (where Christians have been persecuted).
- Worldwide around 80,000 people become Christians each day, and over 500 new churches are formed.
- The Church's mission is to make disciples, not just new believers. This means **new Christians are also expected to help spread the faith**.
- Evangelism should therefore be followed up by training new **converts** (people who decide to change their religious faith) in the way of following Jesus.
- Every Christian has a role in **encouraging fellow believers**. They might do this in the following ways.

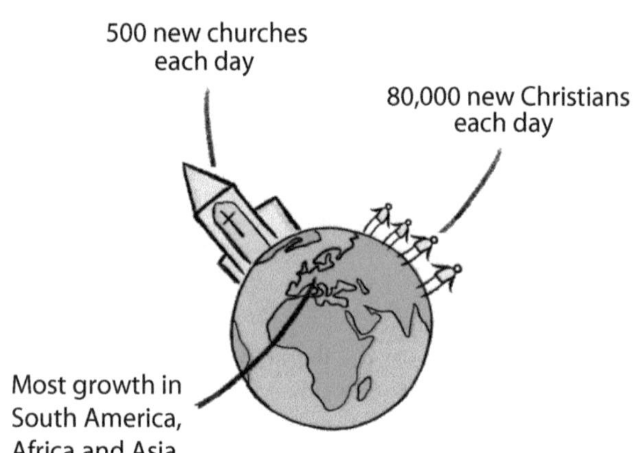

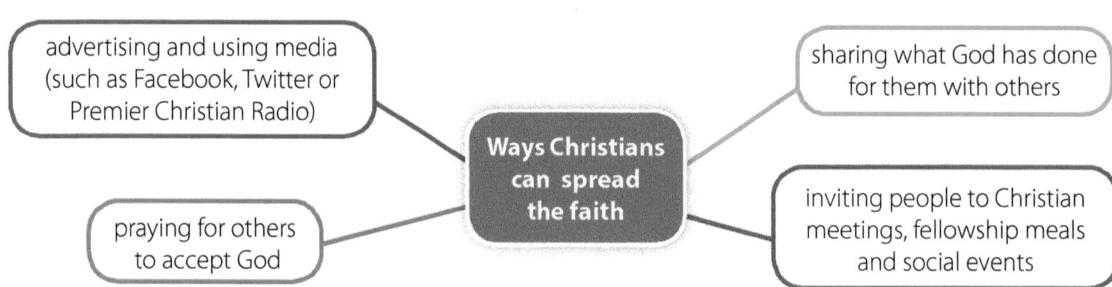

Ways Christians can spread the faith
advertising and using media (such as Facebook, Twitter or Premier Christian Radio)
praying for others to accept God
sharing what God has done for them with others
inviting people to Christian meetings, fellowship meals and social events

Christ for all Nations

- Christ for all Nations is an example of a **Christian organisation promoting evangelism**. They do this by holding evangelistic meetings throughout the world, but particularly in Africa.
- They are led by the evangelists Richard Bonnke and Daniel Kolenda.
- Some of their large open-air rallies held in Africa have drawn crowds of up to 1.6 million people.
- It is claimed that many miracles of healing take place at the meetings.
- Christ for all Nations claims that 74 million people have filled in decision cards to follow Christ at their meetings.

TIP

You will not be asked a specific question about Christ for all Nations in your exam, but being able to give examples of the work of Christian organisations or charities may be very helpful.

APPLY

Give **two** ways in which the Church gets its message to people.

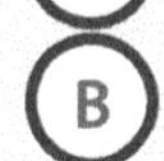

Evaluate this argument in response to the statement, 'Christians should just rely on evangelists for Church growth.' Explain your reasoning and suggest how you would improve the argument.

"Christians should not just rely on evangelists for Church growth because there are not that many specially trained evangelists to promote Christianity. People are more likely to be drawn to Christianity by the inspiration of someone they know, like a neighbour who is kind and considerate and demonstrates the love that Jesus taught."

RECAP

Essential information:

- ☐ The worldwide Church has a mission to restore people's relationship with God and with one another.
- ☐ The Church therefore plays an important role in **reconciliation** (restoring harmony after relationships have broken down), through initiatives to develop peace and understanding.

Working for reconciliation

- Christians believe humans were **reconciled to God** through Jesus' death and resurrection. This means Jesus' death and resurrection helped to **restore the relationship between God and humanity**, which had been broken by sin (see page 24).
- For Catholics, the **sacrament of Reconciliation** also helps to restore people's relationship with God.
- Matthew 5:23–24 teaches that Christians should be **reconciled to each other**.
- Reconciliation is therefore an **important part of the Church's work**. This might involve anything from trying to restore relationships between individual people, to working for peace between different religious groups or nations at conflict.

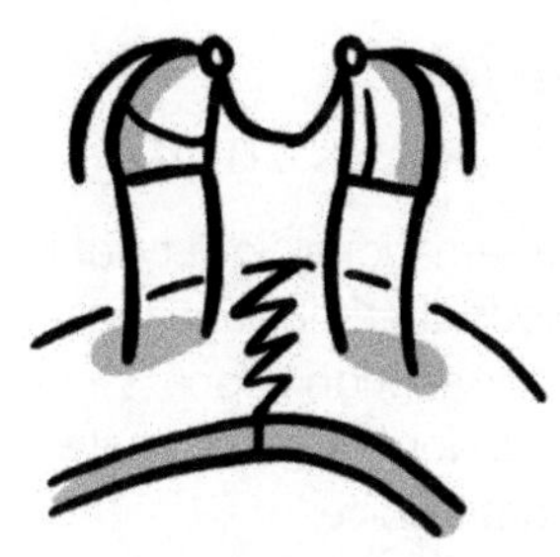

> "For if, while we were God's enemies, we were reconciled to him through the death of his Son, how much more, having been reconciled, shall we be saved through his life!"
>
> *Romans 5:10* [NIV]

TIP

You could use this quote in your exam to show that humanity's relationship with God was restored (or reconciled) through the death of Jesus.

Examples of organisations working for reconciliation

- The **Irish Churches Peace Project** brings Catholics and Protestants together in Northern Ireland.
- The project aims to develop peace and understanding between these two denominations.

- The **World Council of Churches** works for reconciliation between different Christian denominations and members of other faiths.
- For example, the Pilgrimage of Justice and Peace initiative supports inter-religious dialogue and cooperation.

- After the bombing of Coventry Cathedral in World War II, local Christians showed forgiveness to those responsible, and the cathedral became a world centre for peace and reconciliation.
- The cathedral is home to the **Community of the Cross of Nails**, which works with partners in other countries to bring about peace and harmony.

- The **Corrymeela Community** brings together people from different backgrounds, including people of different faiths or political leanings.
- They meet at a residential centre in Northern Ireland to build trust and explore ways of moving away from violence so they can work together constructively.

APPLY

A Give **two** examples of how the Church has helped to work towards reconciliation.

B 'Reconciliation to God is more important than reconciliation to other people.'

Develop this argument to support the statement by explaining in more detail, adding an example, or referring to a relevant religious teaching or quotation.

"Reconciliation to God is more important because God is the Supreme Being. God will judge us when we die and if we are not sorry for our sins we will not receive eternal life with God in heaven."

2.13 Christian persecution

RECAP

Essential information:

- ☐ Christians have faced **persecution** (hostility and ill-treatment) from the beginning of the Church, and Christians are still persecuted worldwide today.
- ☐ For some Christians, persecution can have positive effects: it can strengthen their faith, allow them to share in Jesus' sufferings, and even inspire others to become Christian.
- ☐ The Church helps those who are persecuted through prayer, practical help and financial support, and by raising awareness of persecution and campaigning against it.

What is persecution?

- The International Society for Human Rights estimates 80% of all acts of religious discrimination today are aimed at Christians.
- This persecution happens around the world, but particularly in countries such as North Korea, Somalia, Iraq and Syria.
- It might involve:
  - being forced to pay extra tax
  - job discrimination
  - being forbidden to build churches
  - attacks on Christian homes, churches and families, including murder.

These examples of the kinds of persecution Christians face will be helpful if you need to give an explanation of persecution in your exam.

Some Christian responses to persecution

Response	Supporting quote from scripture
• For some Christians, persecution can have a **positive effect**, as it strengthens their faith and conviction. • It also allows them to share in the suffering of Jesus.	"I want to know Christ – yes, to know the power of his resurrection and participation in his sufferings" *Philippians 3:10* [NIV] This quote shows that one way Christians can get to know Jesus is by sharing in his suffering.
• The Church believes it is important to **act against persecution**, by supporting persecuted Christians wherever possible and campaigning on their behalf.	"If one part suffers, every part suffers with it" *1 Corinthians 12:26* [NIV] This quote refers to the Church. It shows that helping individual Christians also helps the whole Church.
• Christians are **encouraged to show love and forgiveness** towards their persecutors.	"Do not be overcome by evil, but overcome evil with good" *Romans 12:21* [NIV] This quote shows that Christians should respond to evil with love.

Some ways the Church has helped persecuted Christians

- Christians have smuggled Bibles into the USSR (Russia) to strengthen and give comfort to persecuted Christians.
- The Barnabas Fund sends money to support people persecuted for their faith.
- Christian Solidarity Worldwide campaigns for religious freedom for all.

APPLY

Give **two** ways in which Christians support those in countries where it is forbidden to follow Jesus.

Develop one religious argument and one non-religious argument in response to the statement, 'It is not possible to "rejoice and be glad" if you are suffering persecution.'

'Develop' means you need to add some detail to your argument, for example by explaining it more fully and giving examples.

2.14 The Church's response to world poverty

RECAP

Essential information:

- ☐ Christian charities follow the example and teaching of Jesus in working to relieve poverty.
- ☐ Christians believe they should show Jesus to the world through helping the disadvantaged.
- ☐ Three Christian charities that help the poor are Christian Aid, Tearfund and CAFOD.

Helping those in poverty

Christians try to help those living in poverty because Jesus taught that this was important. For example:

- Jesus once told a rich man to sell everything and give to the poor (Mark 10:21).
- The parable of the Rich Man and Lazarus (Luke 16:19–31) tells of a rich man who ends up in hell for ignoring a beggar.
- The parable of the Good Samaritan (Luke 10:30–37) teaches the importance of helping all people.
- Jesus helped outcasts such as lepers, tax collector and sinners.

> "If anyone has material possessions and sees a brother or sister in need but has no pity on them, how can the love of God be in that person? Dear children, let us not love with words or speech but with actions and in truth."
>
> *1 John 3:17–18* [NIV]

TIP

You only need to know about one of these organisations for your exam.

Three Christian charities that help those in poverty are Christian Aid, Tearfund and CAFOD (Catholic Agency for Overseas Development).

Charity	Examples of their work
Christian Aid	• Supports projects to encourage sustainable development. • Provides emergency relief, such as food, water, shelter and sanitation. • Campaigns to end poverty alongside organisations such as the Fairtrade Foundation, Trade Justice and Stop Climate Chaos.
Tearfund	• Works with over 90,000 churches worldwide to help lift people out of poverty. • Supplies emergency aid after natural disasters and conflict. • Provides long-term aid to help communities become more self-reliant, such as education or new farming equipment. • Supported by donations, fundraising events and prayer from churches in the UK.
CAFOD	• Works with local organisations to train, supply and support communities to work their own way out of poverty. • Gives short-term aid such as food, water and shelter during conflicts and disasters. • Lobbies UK government and global organisations for decisions that respect the poorest. • Encourages Catholic schools and parishes to pray, give money and campaign for justice.

APPLY

Here are two ways in which a worldwide Christian relief organisation carries out its mission overseas. **Develop one of the points** by adding more detail and by referring to a relevant religious teaching or quotation.

"One way that Christian Aid carries out its mission overseas is to provide emergency relief when there is a disaster."

"Another way they help is by setting up longer-term programmes that encourage sustainable development."

Write a paragraph either supporting or against the statement, 'Religious charities should just concentrate on emergency aid.' Include a Christian teaching in your answer.

TIP

Emergency aid gives help such as food, water and temporary shelter to people immediately after a disaster. In contrast, long-term aid tries to help people to become more self-sufficient over a longer period of time.

2 Exam practice

Test the 1 mark question

1 Which **one** of the following is a type of worship that follows a set pattern?

A Informal worship
B Private worship
C Non-liturgical worship
D Liturgical worship **[1 mark]**

2 Which **one** of the following is the festival that celebrates the incarnation of Jesus?

A Easter
B Good Friday
C Christmas
D Lent **[1 mark]**

Test the 2 mark question

3 Give **two** ways in which the Church responds to world poverty. **[2 marks]**

1) ______________________________

2) ______________________________

4 Give **two** reasons why prayer is important to Christians. **[2 marks]**

1) ______________________________

2) ______________________________

Test the 4 mark question

5 Explain **two** contrasting ways in which Christians worship. **[4 marks]**

• **Explain one way.**	*Some Christians worship with other people in church on Sunday by going to a service called Holy Communion.*
• Develop your explanation with more detail/an example/ reference to a religious teaching or quotation.	*During the liturgy, they receive bread and wine that they believe is the body and blood of Jesus.*
• **Explain a second contrasting way.**	*Other Christians prefer informal worship, sometimes meeting in someone's home.*
• Develop your explanation with more detail/an example/ reference to a religious teaching or quotation.	*These Christians share their faith by reading and discussing a passage from scripture and praying together in their own words.*

TIP

In this answer formal worship is contrasted with informal worship, but you could also contrast public worship with private worship or liturgical worship with charismatic worship.

6 Explain **two** contrasting ways in which Christians practise baptism. **[4 marks]**

• **Explain one way.**	
• Develop your explanation with more detail/an example/ reference to a religious teaching or quotation.	
• **Explain a second contrasting way.**	
• Develop your explanation with more detail/an example/ reference to a religious teaching or quotation.	

TIP

The question asks for different 'ways' in which Christians practise baptism, not different beliefs about baptism. The clearest contrast is between believers' baptism and infant baptism, but you should focus your answer on the way each of these is carried out, not what people believe about them.

7 Explain **two** contrasting interpretations of the meaning of Holy Communion. **[4 marks]**

Test the 5 mark question

8 Explain **two** ways that Christian charities help the poor in less economically developed countries.
Refer to sacred writings or another source of Christian belief and teaching in your answer. **[5 marks]**

• **Explain one way.**	*One way that Christian charities help the poor in less economically developed countries is by providing emergency aid when there has been a natural disaster, like an earthquake or famine.*
• Develop your explanation with more detail/an example.	*For example, Tearfund, a Christian charity, was set up originally to provide emergency aid in response to the famine in Biafra, Nigeria, where it sent emergency food and clothing to refugees fleeing the famine-struck country.*
• **Explain a second way.**	*A second way that Christian charities help is by providing long-term aid that helps countries become self-sufficient or less dependent on aid.*
• Develop your explanation with more detail/an example.	*CAFOD, for example, works on development projects to give people access to education, healthcare, and clean water.*
• Add a reference to sacred writings or another source of Christian belief and teaching. If you prefer, you can add this reference to your first belief instead.	*These charities are inspired by Christian teachings such as the parable of the Rich Man and Lazarus, where Jesus taught that rich people who ignore the needs of the poor will be punished by God.*

TIP
Here the student has used a parable from the Bible. Another 'source of Christian belief and teaching' could be official statements or documents by leaders of the Church.

9 Explain **two** reasons why Christians practise evangelism.
Refer to sacred writings or another source of Christian belief and teaching in your answer. **[5 marks]**

• **Explain one reason.**	
• Develop your explanation with more detail/an example.	
• **Explain a second reason.**	
• Develop your explanation with more detail/an example.	
• Add a reference to sacred writings or another source of Christian belief and teaching. If you prefer, you can add this reference to your first teaching instead.	

TIP
It is helpful to start by explaining the meaning of 'evangelism' before explaining why Christians practise it.

10 Explain **two** ways that Christians may work for reconciliation.
Refer to sacred writings or another source of Christian belief and teaching in your answer. **[5 marks]**

Test the 12 mark question

11 'The most important duty of the Church is to help people in need.'

Evaluate this statement. In your answer you should:

- refer to Christian teaching
- give reasoned arguments to support this statement
- give reasoned arguments to support a different point of view
- reach a justified conclusion.

[12 marks]

REASONED ARGUMENTS IN SUPPORT OF THE STATEMENT ● **Explain why some people would agree with the statement.** ● Develop your explanation with more detail and examples. ● Refer to religious teaching. Use a quote or paraphrase or refer to a religious authority. ● **Evaluate the arguments.** Is this a good argument or not? Explain why you think this.	*'The Church' in this statement clearly stands for the Christian believers and not the actual building. So what does the Bible say about the duty of Christians? Jesus taught his followers that helping those in need is extremely important and he showed he believed that by the way he acted. If he saw a person suffering from an illness he healed them. He touched lepers in order that they might be cured, even though it was something other people would not do because it was against the law and they feared catching leprosy. He gave sight to the blind, healed the crippled and even cast out evil spirits that were tormenting a naked madman. Jesus did this because he had compassion and pity on those he saw were in need.* *Jesus also showed in his teaching that Christians should help people in need. In the parable of the Good Samaritan it is the traveller who showed pity on the wounded man and helped him that is the hero of the story. Furthermore Jesus warns that those who do not help will face the anger of God on judgement day in the parable of the Sheep and the Goats. The sheep represented the people who helped and were given the reward of eternal life, but the goats did not and were thrown out of God's presence. So you could argue that it is the most important duty of the Church to help people who are in need.*
REASONED ARGUMENTS SUPPORTING A DIFFERENT VIEW ● **Explain why some people would support a different view.** ● Develop your explanation with more detail and examples. ● Refer to religious teaching. Use a quote or paraphrase or refer to a religious authority. ● **Evaluate the arguments.** Is this a good argument or not? Explain why you think this.	*On the other hand, Jesus summed up the duty for Christians and the Church in two commandments. He said that the first, most important commandment is to love God. The second is to love our neighbour as ourselves. If that is the case, then the most important duty of the Church (Christians) is to love and worship God, and this is more important than helping those in need.*
CONCLUSION ● **Give a justified conclusion.** ● Include your own opinion together with your own reasoning. ● **Include evaluation**. Explain why you think one viewpoint is stronger than the other or why they are equally strong. ● Do not just repeat arguments you have already used without explaining how they apply to your reasoned opinion/conclusion.	*In conclusion I would say that the statement is wrong and I would argue that the most important duty is to love God. The only way the Church can show love of God is by loving human beings who need help. So that is also important, but not the most important duty. It merely follows on from the most important duty.*

TIP

The student has developed this argument by referring to the Bible. Although there are no direct quotations, the answer shows excellent knowledge of Jesus' actions and teaching and uses these to support the statement.

TIP

This argument could be developed further for more marks. For example, it could go into more detail about other important duties of the Church (such as preaching the gospel or administering the sacraments), and explain why these are equally or more important than helping people in need.

12 'The best way for Christians to grow closer to God is to go on a pilgrimage.'

Evaluate this statement. In your answer you should:

- refer to Christian teaching
- give reasoned arguments to support this statement
- give reasoned arguments to support a different point of view
- reach a justified conclusion.

[12 marks]

TIP

Look for the key words in questions. Here it is 'best'. The answer should focus on whether or not a pilgrimage is the best way for Christians to grow closer to God or whether there are other ways that might be better.

REASONED ARGUMENTS IN SUPPORT OF THE STATEMENT • **Explain why some people would agree with the statement.** • Develop your explanation with more detail and examples. • Refer to religious teaching. Use a quote or paraphrase or refer to a religious authority. • **Evaluate the arguments.** Is this a good argument or not? Explain why you think this.	
REASONED ARGUMENTS SUPPORTING A DIFFERENT VIEW • **Explain why some people would support a different view.** • Develop your explanation with more detail and examples. • Refer to religious teaching. Use a quote or paraphrase or refer to a religious authority. • **Evaluate the arguments.** Is this a good argument or not? Explain why you think this.	
CONCLUSION • **Give a justified conclusion.** • Include your own opinion together with your own reasoning. • **Include evaluation**. Explain why you think one viewpoint is stronger than the other or why they are equally strong. • Do not just repeat arguments you have already used without explaining how they apply to your reasoned opinion/conclusion.	

13 'A Christian's most important duty is to tell others about their faith.'

Evaluate this statement. In your answer you should:

- refer to Christian teaching
- give reasoned arguments to support this statement
- give reasoned arguments to support a different point of view
- reach a justified conclusion.

[12 marks]

TIP

'To tell others about their faith' is the meaning of evangelism, which is part of a Christian's mission. Try to use these terms in your answer to show the depth of your understanding about this topic.

Check your answers using the mark scheme on pages 157–158.
How did you do? To feel more secure in the content you need to remember, re-read pages 30–43.
To remind yourself of what the examiner is looking for, go to pages 7–13.

3 Sikhism: Beliefs and teachings

3.1 The nature of God

RECAP

Essential information:

- [ ] Sikhism began over 500 years ago in India.
- [ ] Sikhs believe God is beyond human description and has no limits.
- [ ] The **Mool Mantra** (main chant) summarises Sikh beliefs.

How Sikhism began

- Sikhism originated in the Punjab – an area in India where both Muslims and Hindus lived.
- 'Sikh' means learner or disciple.
- The first Sikh **Guru** (spiritual teacher) was Guru Nanak, who was followed by another nine Gurus that developed the religion.
- Sikhs believe their holy book, the **Guru Granth Sahib**, is a living Guru and contains the word of God.

The nature of God

Sikhs believe God is beyond human description. Although 'he' and 'him' are used when talking about God, he has no gender. Human words cannot adequately describe God's greatness.

However, God communicates with humans and can be experienced by them. He is immanent and so is in everything, but also transcendent (above and beyond creation).

TIP

The phrases in the Mool Mantra will give you useful quotes to use when explaining Sikh beliefs.

The Mool Mantra

The Mool Mantra opens the Guru Granth Sahib and summarises Sikh beliefs about God. It is said daily in prayers and recited in worship. The first words of the Mool Mantra are used as a symbol of the Sikh religion.

Mool Mantra	Meaning
One Universal Creator God.	Sikhs are **monotheists**: they believe there is only one God, who is the creator and sustainer of the universe.
The Name is Truth.	God can be reached by humans if they reflect on the truth.
Creative Being Personified.	God is present in the creation he has made. He is also present in people's souls. This makes it possible to have a personal relationship with God.
No Fear. No Hatred.	There is no fear or hatred in God because he is One and not subject to any other being.
Image Of The Undying.	God is eternal and beyond time. He has always existed.
Beyond Birth.	God is not born and cannot die. He is immortal.
Self-Existent.	Nothing brought God into being.
By Guru's Grace.	God makes himself known through his word.

APPLY

A Give **two** Sikh beliefs about God.

B Read the following explanation of why the Mool Mantra is important. **Improve it** by adding more detail about the content of the Mool Mantra, and why this makes it important.

The Mool Mantra is said daily in Sikh prayers. It is also recited in worship. The first words of the Mool Mantra are used as a symbol of the Sikh religion.

3.2 God as Creator

RECAP

Essential information:

- ☐ Sikhs believe God created and sustains everything.
- ☐ God is uncreated; he has no limits and is different from his creation.
- ☐ God is present in every human being as the soul or divine spirit.

God the Creator

- There are no creation stories in Sikhism. Sikhs accept scientific views about how life was created (such as the theory of evolution), but believe all creation happens through God's will.`
- Sikhs believe God was present before creation when there was nothing else.
- God wills the universe to exist and gives order to everything.
- Sometimes the world is described as God's 'pastime' or his 'play'. This shows the greatness of God compared to the world humans live in.

> "He established the earth, the sky and the air."
>
> *Guru Granth Sahib 1399*

God's relationship to the universe

God as separate from the universe	God shown in and through the universe
God is beyond human understanding and human language, although human qualities are used to try to describe him.	Sikhs believe that every part of the universe reveals God.
God is limitless, timeless and spaceless (he has no limits and does not occupy time or space).	God's presence is in every human. Sikhs look into their hearts and souls as well as the created universe to find God.
Sikhs use the word 'nirgun' (meaning without qualities or form) to describe God in this way.	Sikhs use the word 'sargun' (meaning with qualities or form) to describe God in this way.
Sikhs believe God has never assumed a physical form.	God directs and sustains the universe in a kindly way.
God is transcendent: beyond and outside life on earth and the universe. "He is the Perfect Transcendent Lord, from the very beginning, and throughout the ages." *Guru Granth Sahib 397*	As God created everything, he is everywhere. "Sing the Praise of the One, the Immaculate Lord; He is contained within all." *Guru Granth Sahib 706*

Story from Sikh tradition

Guru Nanak once made a long journey to the city of Makkah. He fell asleep with his feet pointing towards the holy shrine there, the Ka'aba. A watchman found him and kicked him, asking how he could dare to point his feet towards the shrine as this was disrespectful. Guru Nanak replied, 'Kindly turn my feet in the direction where God is not.'

This story shows the Sikh belief that God is everywhere.

TIP

You can use this story in your exam without explaining it all. Just refer to it as the story about Guru Nanak visiting Makkah.

APPLY

A Explain **two** Sikh beliefs about God as Creator.

B 'Sikhs see God as transcendent.'

Evaluate this statement using **two** arguments to support the statement and **two** arguments to support a different point of view.

RECAP

Essential information:

- [ ] The aim of life for Sikhs is to become one with God.
- [ ] There are five basic Sikh virtues: **truthful living**, compassion, contentment, humility and love.

Union with God

- Sikhs believe God has given humans an opportunity to become reunited with him.
- Life is seen as a cycle of birth, death and rebirth moving towards a blissful, perfect existence with God.
- Sikhs hope to make good spiritual progress during a lifetime, but accept it may take several lifetimes to be liberated and united with God.
- As humans are not perfect, they cannot become one with God without also accepting his grace and mercy.

The five virtues

Virtue	What this means
Truthful living	God is truth, so to get close to God Sikhs should lead a truthful life. This includes telling the truth, being realistic, working honestly, acting fairly and treating everyone equally. Justice is linked to truthful living as it recognises the rights of all people and works to protect them. "Truth is higher than everything; but higher still is truthful living." *Guru Granth Sahib 62*
Compassion	God is compassionate and merciful; he looks with kindness and goodness on everything. Sikhs should show compassion by being aware of the needs of others, responding to suffering and vulnerability, and being careful and kindly in speech. Being compassionate also requires patience, which includes being tolerant of others, forgiving faults and weaknesses, and being prepared to make sacrifices for others.
Contentment	Sikhs should focus on God and not on material possessions. They are encouraged to accept the life God has given them and to try to do God's will. Sikhs believe contentment leads to happiness by removing worry about the future. This attitude can be practised by focusing on God and not on the self.
Humility	Sikhs should not consider themselves important because God is the ultimate reality. In contrast to God's greatness, humans should be humble. To do this, Sikhs should be self-disciplined, pray regularly and bring God to mind. This self-control is linked to temperance, which means thinking and speaking in moderation.
Love	Sikhs believe God is loving and so they must also be full of love. Sikhs should accept everyone they come into contact with and treat them with kindness and respect. Part of a Sikh's loving response to God is to serve others and show love to them.

Wisdom and courage

Wisdom and courage are two other important virtues for Sikhs to develop. **Wisdom** means understanding the five basic virtues and putting them into practice in daily life.

Courage means staying true to what is right, even when it is extremely difficult. Some of the Gurus showed courage in sacrificing their lives for their beliefs, and for the right of others to practise their faith.

TIP
Learn the five virtues so you can use them to give extra detail in exam answers.

APPLY

 State **two** of the Sikh virtues.

B 'Truthful living is the most important virtue.'

Give arguments to support a different point of view.

3.4 Karma, rebirth and mukti

RECAP

Essential information:

- ☐ Sikhs believe in **reincarnation**, which means that when a human dies their soul is reborn into another body.
- ☐ **Karma** is the consequences of a person's actions. Sikhs believe it determines what happens to them in the future.
- ☐ **Mukti** is the final goal for Sikhs, when the individual soul rejoins God.

Rebirth

Rebirth is part of the cycle of birth, death and being reborn. Sikhs believe this cycle of reincarnation repeats itself until the soul is liberated or freed from the cycle and becomes united with God.

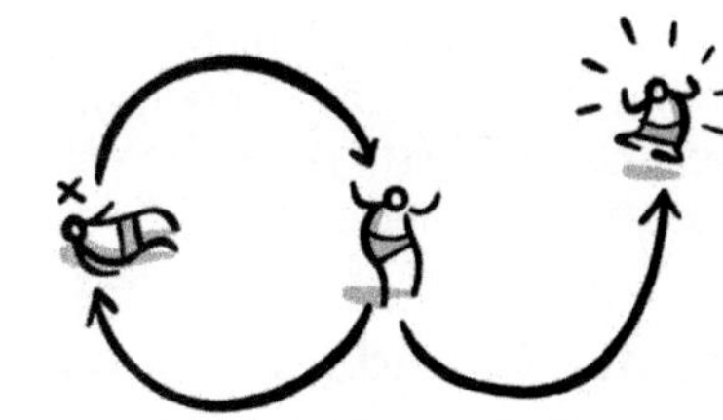

Sikhs believe that all animals have souls as well as humans. At death the soul changes its form of life and is reborn into a new stage of its existence. The goal is to achieve liberation from rebirth.

Karma

> "The body is the field of karma in this age; whatever you plant, you shall harvest."
>
> *Guru Granth Sahib 78*

- Sometimes karma is described as 'destiny' because it refers to what will happen in the future.
- Sikhs believe that when a person is reborn, what they have done in their previous life (their karma) affects their new life and future.
- Good actions in a previous life mean rebirth as a human is more likely. Once born as a human, a person can make further progress towards liberation by doing good actions to build up good karma, and by receiving God's grace.
- For every bad deed, there will be suffering in a future life.
- Sikhs can rid themselves of bad karma by meditating on God's name, hearing his word and serving others.

Story from Sikh tradition

A proud man thought he understood all about karma. → He saw a blind man struggling up some steps. He thought, 'he deserves to be blind. He must have refused to see something important in a past life.' → The blind man laughed and told the man he was right. He had refused to see the things he could do to help others and forgot that God is in everyone. → The blind man told the proud man that he was doing the same thing – judging rather than helping and being proud rather than kind.

Mukti

Mukti:

- Means 'freedom', 'liberation', 'release' and sometimes 'salvation'
- The final goal for Sikhs; when a soul rejoins God and becomes reunited with him
- May be achieved while someone is alive (jivan mukti)
- Can be achieved by removing all barriers to God, e.g. by not giving in to temptation to do wrong things
- Sikhs need to go through several stages to reach mukti
- Impossible to describe but thought to be ultimate bliss, happiness, contentment and peace

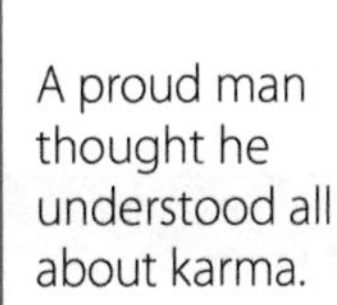

TIP

You do not need to retell the whole story in your exam. You can refer to it briefly as the story of the proud man and the blind man.

APPLY

A Give **two** meanings of 'mukti'.

B 'Human beings cannot change their karma.'

Write a paragraph disagreeing with this statement.

3.5 The five stages of liberation

RECAP

Essential information:

- ☐ Sikhs believe there are five stages (**khands**) that will lead a person to God.
- ☐ The five khands are piety, knowledge, effort, grace and truth.
- ☐ There are five evils that take people away from God: anger, lust, greed, worldly attachment and pride.

The stages of liberation

The five khands are like stages of a journey towards God. It will usually take more than one lifetime to pass through them. Sikhs believe that God intends humans to live as part of a community (rather than withdrawing from the world) and it is through daily life that God is revealed. The five stages of **liberation** from the cycle of birth, death and rebirth can be passed through while living a normal life centred on God.

The five khands

Piety (dharam khand)
All human beings are born into the stage of piety, giving them the opportunity to show commitment and devotion to God.

Knowledge (gian khand)
Knowledge is gained by devoting time to God and learning about him.

Effort (saram khand)
In devoting themselves to God, a person has made the effort to 'tune in' to God and develop their personality and gifts as far as they can.

Grace (karam khand)
This is only reached when God takes part in a person's development. It results in the person being at peace with themselves and God.

Truth (sach khand)
This final stage involves finding God in his completeness. It cannot be described, only experienced.

> "By the Grace of the Holy, let your mind be imbued with the Lord's love."
>
> *Guru Granth Sahib 866*

Barriers to mukti

For Sikhs, illusion, self-centredness and the five evils prevent them from moving closer to God. The **illusion** that things in life are permanent prevents them from seeing the truth. **Self-centredness** (sometimes called ego) prevents them from getting close to God and obeying his will.

The five evils	
Anger	This causes someone to stop thinking and to act without balance. Anger can lead to hatred, which is not acceptable when directed at a person whom God created.
Lust	Uncontrolled lust results in weakness and encourages wrongdoing, untruthfulness and unreliability. Sikhs see sex within marriage as good, but outside marriage as something that leads people away from God.
Greed	This results in a desire to possess more than one needs. It is selfish and self-centred. It ignores the principles of equality and justice and is focused on material things.
Worldly attachment	This is connected to greed. It leads to wanting relationships and possessions.
Pride	This is being proud of things or characteristics which are not important (such as intelligence or material wealth). It makes people feel more important than others and leads to jealousy and rivalry.

APPLY

A State **two** of the five khands.

B 'The five evils are not relevant in today's world.'

Write an argument against this statement.

3.6 The importance of being God-centred

RECAP

Essential information:

- [ ] Sikhs aim to be **gurmukh** (God-centred), with their minds centred on God at all times.
- [ ] People who are **manmukh** (man-centred) are centred on themselves and their own desires.
- [ ] **Haumai** is a quality similar to pride that prevents individuals from understanding their dependence on God and from seeking liberation.

Gurmukh and manmukh

Gurmukh (God-centred)	Manmukh (Man-centred)
Aims to have their mind centred on God at all times.	Centres their mind on themselves and their own desires.
Lives in accordance with Sikh teaching and meditates on the name of God.	Controlled by the five evils and the illusion that temporary things are important and permanent.
Free from attachment, pride and ego.	Attached to worldly wealth and things that will not last.
Does good because it is good – not for any other motive.	Not aware of the needs of others.
Becoming a perfect person as God intended.	Their attitudes and actions prevent them from being liberated and achieving mukti.
"The Gurmukh acts in harmony with God's Will; the Gurmukh finds perfection." *Guru Granth Sahib 1058*	"The foolish self-willed manmukh does not remember the Lord, and shall regret and repent hereafter." *Guru Granth Sahib 441*

Haumai

- Haumai can mean pride, self-reliance or egotism.
- Although self-reliance can sometimes be seen as a good thing, Guru Nanak taught that this quality can stop individuals from understanding their dependence on God.
- Trying to affect what happens in the present or future without listening to or obeying God prevents release from rebirth.
- Haumai is sometimes described as a spiritual disease that produces confusion and brings suffering.
- The only way to overcome it is to become gurmukh, to remember God and forget self.

> "Egotism [haumai] is opposed to the Name of the Lord"
>
> *Guru Granth Sahib 560*

Story from Sikh tradition

Guru Nanak and a disciple arrived in a village, knocked on a door and asked where the inn was. The man shut the door in their faces saying, 'Go away'. They went to several other houses, but everyone was rude and unwelcoming.

→ Guru Nanak walked to the next village. A man offered them food and drink and arranged somewhere for them to stay the night. As they talked to other people, they were all welcoming and friendly. They had a good night's sleep.

→ As they left the village next morning, Guru Nanak said to his disciple, 'I hope that village is uprooted and scattered.' He meant that if this happened, welcoming and generous people would be scattered across the world.

APPLY

A Give **two** ways a gurmukh could be described.

B **Develop** this argument to oppose the statement, 'Self-reliance is a good character trait.'

Self-reliance or haumai is bad for Sikhs because it can stop them from depending on God. If they don't listen to God then they won't be able to achieve mukti.

3.7 The oneness of humanity and the equality of all

RECAP

Essential information:

- ☐ Guru Nanak strongly believed that God is One and there are many ways of approaching him.
- ☐ Sikhs believe in the **oneness of humanity** and do not feel the need to convert others to Sikhism.
- ☐ Sikh belief in the **equality of all** led Guru Nanak to introduce the langar.

TIP

The langar is the community kitchen in each gurdwara. 'Langar' also refers to the free meals served by the kitchen.

The oneness of humanity and the equality of all

- Sikhs believe there are many paths to God and each individual can find their way with the support of their community and God's grace.
- Sikhism is a tolerant and inclusive faith; Sikhs are expected to honour and protect the rights of others to practise their faith.
- God created and is within all people. Respecting this equality means living and working in peace and harmony with others.
- Any man or woman can be initiated into the **Khalsa** and become **amritdhari** Sikhs.
- Both men and women within Sikhism take part in worship, read the Guru Granth Sahib, play music and cook and serve the langar.

> "All are made of the same clay; the light within all is the same."
>
> *Guru Granth Sahib 96*

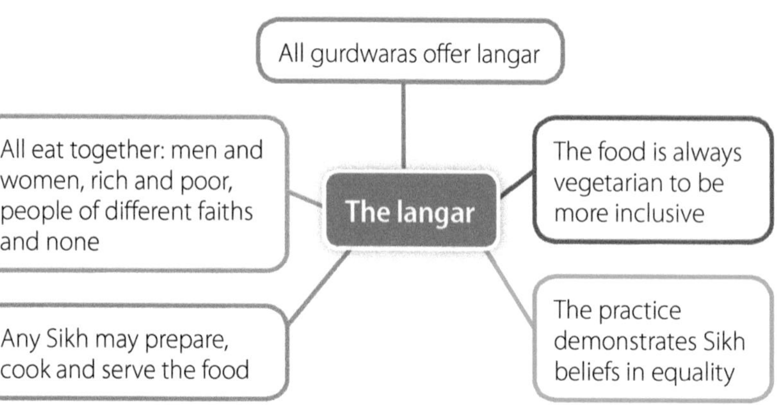

All gurdwaras offer langar
All eat together: men and women, rich and poor, people of different faiths and none
The langar
The food is always vegetarian to be more inclusive
Any Sikh may prepare, cook and serve the food
The practice demonstrates Sikh beliefs in equality

The five Ks

Amritdhari Sikhs are required to wear the five Ks.

Kesh (uncut hair)	Sikhs believe their hair is a gift from God and should not be cut. It is covered with a turban to keep it clean. (The turban is not one of the five Ks.)
Kangha (wooden comb)	Carried to keep the kesh tidy and remind Sikhs of the need to keep their body and mind in a healthy state.
Kara (steel bracelet)	A circle symbolises the unbreakable bond with God. It is like a slave bangle so acts as a reminder to do God's will. Steel is also a symbol of strength and integrity.
Kachera (cotton underwear)	A reminder of the traditional role of Sikhs as soldiers, being prepared to act quickly and with dignity and modesty. It is also a reminder of the need for self-control and chastity.
Kirpan (small sword)	A sign that Sikhs are soldiers in the army of God and should fight for justice and protect the weak. The sword should not be used in anger.

APPLY

A State **two** of the five Ks.

B 'Equality of all is an important belief within Sikhism.'

Write an argument **in support of this view**. Include **religious teaching**.

3.8 Equality and Guru Nanak

RECAP

Essential information:

- ☐ Guru Nanak was the founder of the Sikh faith.
- ☐ Guru Nanak saw a vision at the river Bain, after which he was changed and taught others about God.
- ☐ Guru Nanak taught about the importance of equality between men and women. He also developed the **langar** to offer hospitality to all.

Guru Nanak's life

Guru Nanak was born in 1469 in the Punjab. His family were Hindus, but at 13 years old he rejected taking part in the sacred thread ceremony initiating him into Hinduism. His father worked for Muslims and he had Muslim and Hindu friends. He married when he was a teenager and later had two sons.

One day Guru Nanak went down to wash at the river Bain, but did not return. Three days later he reappeared but seemed to be in a trance. Later he told people he had a vision and had been in God's court.

> "My Lord and Master has summoned me, His minstrel, to the True Mansion of His Presence."
>
> *Guru Granth Sahib 150*

Guru Nanak changed. He gave up his job and gave all his belongings to the poor.

Guru Nanak is said to have travelled widely across India and the Middle East preaching about God. He always showed great respect to those of other religions. In about 1520 he settled in Kartapur and this new town became a Sikh community, working, praying and learning together. He developed the idea of a free kitchen (a langar) to provide hospitality for everyone.

> "The philosophy behind the Guru's kitchen/eating house is two fold: to provide training to the Sikhs in voluntary service and to help banish all distinction of high and low, touchable and untouchable from the Sikhs' minds."
>
> *Rehat Maryada, article 21*

Guru Nanak's teaching on equality

- Guru Nanak taught that all humanity is created by God and is equal.
- He believed in the equality of men and women and that they could play an equal part in worship and within the Sikh community. He said, 'From woman, man is born; within woman, man is conceived, to woman he is engaged and married [...] So why call her bad?' (Guru Granth Sahib 473).
- He established the langar, in which men and women prepared, cooked and served free food and all ate together. This practice continues today in all gurdwaras around the world.

APPLY

A Explain **two** of Guru Nanak's teachings on equality.

B **Unscramble the arguments** below referring to the statement, 'Equality is the most important Sikh teaching.' Decide which arguments could be used to support the statement and which could be used against it. **Write a paragraph** to explain whether you agree or disagree with the statement, having evaluated both sides of the argument.

1. Guru Nanak taught about the equality of men and women.	4. By establishing the langar, Guru Nanak showed that all were equal.
2. Guru Nanak saw a vision at the river Bain after which he taught people about God.	5. Guru Nanak taught that people should focus on God and be gurmukh.
3. Guru Nanak taught that all humanity is created by God and is equal.	6. Guru Nanak taught that God is everywhere in the story about when he slept with his feet facing Makkah.

RECAP

Essential information:

- [ ] After Guru Nanak died, the Sikhs were led by nine other Gurus. The tenth Guru, Guru Gobind Singh, declared that after his death the Guru Granth Sahib would be the 'living Guru'.
- [ ] Guru Gobind Singh established the Khalsa (the body of committed Sikhs) in 1699 at the festival of Vaisakhi.
- [ ] Members of the Khalsa are known as amritdharis.

Guru Gobind Singh

- Guru Gobind Singh was nine years old when he became the tenth Guru, after his father, Guru Tegh Bahadur, was martyred for refusing to become a Muslim.
- He declared the Guru Granth Sahib to be the final Guru. Sikh communities today now use exact copies of it as Guru Gobind Singh established it.
- The dramatic way in which he established the Khalsa (described in the story below) demonstrated the importance of commitment and equality.

Story from Sikh tradition

Guru Gobind Singh explained to the Sikhs who had come to celebrate Vaisakhi that the community needed to go forward with unity and strength. He challenged the crowd, drawing his sword and asking, 'Who will die for God and his Guru?'

One Sikh came forward and was led into the Guru's tent. There was a swish of a sword and a thud and the Guru emerged with blood on his sword.

The Guru asked the same question again and another person came forward. This happened three more times, with the same noise and the Guru coming out with blood on his sword.

The Guru then came out of the tent with the five volunteers all dressed identically in special clothes. They were then given **amrit** (a mixture of water and sugar crystals) prepared by the Guru and his wife in an iron bowl, stirred with a two-edged sword. Guru Gobind Singh and his wife Mata Sahib Kaur were also initiated.

The five men (the Panj Piare) all came from different backgrounds but were treated equally because of their commitment to God. They left their jobs to be 'saint-soldiers' who would defend the faith and work for justice and equality.

The names Singh and Kaur

Men and women are initiated into the Khalsa through the Amrit Sanskar ceremony, and then become known as amritdharis. Guru Gobind Singh said that after a woman is initiated, she should take the name 'Kaur' meaning 'princess' (showing the value of women in Sikhism). Men should take the name 'Singh' meaning 'lion' (representing strength and courage in upholding the faith). These common last names were intended to eliminate caste names and emphasise the equality of all.

APPLY

A Give **two** ways Guru Gobind Singh strengthened Sikhism.

B 'Guru Gobind Singh was more important than Guru Nanak in developing Sikhism.'

Write a paragraph arguing for this statement and a paragraph arguing against it.

3.10 Equality in the Guru Granth Sahib and in Sikhism today

RECAP

Essential information:

- ☐ The Guru Granth Sahib was completed in 1604 and installed in the Golden Temple in Amritsar.
- ☐ It is considered to be the final, 'living Guru'.
- ☐ The importance of equality is emphasised in the Guru Granth Sahib and in Sikhism today.

The Guru Granth Sahib

- Guru Nanak wrote many hymns and the two Gurus that succeeded him collected them together.
- These were incorporated into the Guru Granth Sahib, which also contains the hymns of the first four Gurus; writings of saints (including Hindu and Muslim writers whose ideas about God were similar to the Sikhs'); and writings from the two last human Gurus.
- The Guru Granth Sahib is written on 1430 pages, and the words are always written on the same pages and lines on all copies of the scriptures.
- Guru Gobind Singh chose the Guru Granth Sahib to be the final and eternal Guru – 'the living Guru' that would teach and lead the Sikh community.
- It is written in Gurmukhi, a new writing script meaning 'from the mouth of the Guru'.
- The Spirit of the Gurus is considered to be present whenever Sikhs meet before the Guru Granth Sahib.

Equality in Sikhism today

> “All beings and creatures are His, He belongs to us all.”
>
> *Guru Granth Sahib 425*

> “God's Kingdom is steady, stable and eternal. There is no second or third status; all are equal there.”
>
> *Guru Granth Sahib 345*

TIP

You could use these quotes in your exam to show how equality is very important in Sikhism.

- All gurdwaras have a langar, which accepts people of every race, gender, class and religion.
- Men and women play equally important roles in worship and performing sewa (selfless service).
- Sikh men and women share in the bringing up of children and doing both paid and voluntary work in the community.

APPLY

A Give **two** ways that equality is demonstrated in Sikhism today.

B Mark these statements about the Guru Granth Sahib as **true or false**. Then use the correct statements to **create a paragraph** explaining why the Guru Granth Sahib is considered a vital part of the Sikh faith.

1. The Guru Granth Sahib was written entirely by Guru Nanak.
2. It was written in Punjabi.
3. It is considered to be the final and eternal Guru.
4. It contains poems and hymns from several of the first ten Gurus.
5. It contains some writings from Muslim and Hindu saints, demonstrating the inclusivity of the faith.
6. The Guru Granth Sahib contains no teachings on equality.
7. The Spirit of the Gurus is considered to be present whenever Sikhs meet before the Guru Granth Sahib.

RECAP

Essential information:

- ☐ **Sewa** means selfless service and is a way of life for Sikhs.
- ☐ Sikhs must serve others without any thought of personal gain.
- ☐ There are three kinds of sewa: tan (physical sewa), man (mental sewa) and dhan (material sewa).

Different types of sewa

Examples of sewa

Dhan (material sewa)

- Using material wealth to help others
- Giving a tenth of income (dasvandh) to the Sikh community
- Giving money to charities

Tan (physical sewa)

- Preparing, cooking and serving food in the langar
- Cleaning the gurdwara
- Helping with gardening

Man (mental sewa)

- Reading the Guru Granth Sahib
- Teaching people
- Using skills to organise, communicate or inspire others

The importance of sewa

“Through selfless service, eternal peace is obtained.”

Guru Granth Sahib 125

“One who performs selfless service, without thought of reward, shall attain his Lord and Master.”

Guru Granth Sahib 286

Sikhs believe that sewa:

- is an important way of worshipping and serving God.
- helps lead them to God and to become gurmukh.
- helps lead them away from pride, greed and self-centredness.
- helps them develop humility, compassion and love.
- demonstrates belief in the equality of all people; when serving others, there can be no distinctions of class, creed, race, age or gender.

TIP

If you can't remember the exact quote in the exam, you can put it in your own words, introducing it with a phrase such as, 'The Guru Granth Sahib teaches that...'

APPLY

A State **two** kinds of sewa.

B Here are some arguments that could be used to evaluate the statement, 'Sewa is the best way for Sikhs to demonstrate equality.' **Sort** them into arguments in support of the statement and arguments in support of different views. Use the arguments to **write a conclusion** where you explain why you agree or disagree with the statement.

1. Serving others with no distinctions of race, class etc. demonstrates equality.	4. Teaching is a type of mental sewa that shows children are as important as adults.
2. The word 'Sikh' means learner or disciple. This shows that all members of Sikhism need to learn more about their faith.	5. The Guru Granth Sahib contains writings of Muslim and Hindu saints, showing they were also important and valued.
3. Material sewa is the only practical way for most Sikhs to help people in other countries and show they are valued.	6. Both men and women are admitted to the Khalsa, showing they are treated equally.

3.12 The role and importance of the sangat

RECAP

Essential information:

- ☐ The **sangat** is the community of Sikhs coming together in the presence of the Guru Granth Sahib.
- ☐ The sangat consists of amritdhari Sikhs, believers born into Sikh families, and believers who do not come from Sikh families (**sahajdharis**).
- ☐ The role of the sangat is represented by the Khanda symbol.

The sangat

The sangat originally referred to the groups of disciples established by Guru Nanak. Today it refers to a gathering of Sikhs where the Guru Granth Sahib is present (usually in the gurdwara).

- Meets as a community for learning, prayer or a ceremony.
- Those present may chant hymns, listen to musicians praising God, listen to a talk, or discuss local or community issues.
- Offers opportunities for sewa, e.g. by preparing langar or looking after people's shoes while they worship.
- Being part of the sangat is an important way to develop spiritual and moral values.

Amritdhari Sikhs and sahajdharis

Most people in the sangat are born into Sikh families but are not amritdharis. Some people in the sangat do not come from Sikh families: these believers are known as sahajdharis.

Amritdhari Sikhs	Sahajdharis
Once initiated into the Khalsa, amritdhari Sikhs are expected to offer daily prayers, wear the five Ks, pay tithes, take the names Singh or Kaur, and practise the Sikh virtues. They should be strictly vegetarian and obey the code of conduct in the Rehat Maryada. Tobacco, alcohol and illegal drugs are forbidden.	These Sikhs believe in the ten Gurus and the Guru Granth Sahib but were not born into Sikh families. They have no other religion but have not undergone initiation into the Khalsa.

The Nishan Sahib and the Khanda

Gurdwaras always have a flag outside called the Nishan Sahib. The symbol on the flag is called the Khanda and represents some of the most important values in Sikhism.

The Khanda includes three symbols:

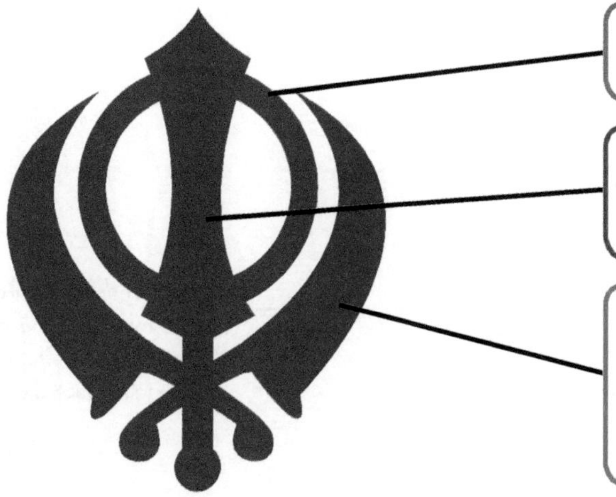

Chakra: a circle, which is a symbol of the One God who has no beginning or end.

Khanda: a double-edged sword that is finely balanced. It represents a balance between divine justice on one side, and freedom and authority on the other.

Two kirpans: two swords symbolising political power (Miri) – a reminder of the need to defend the faith – and spiritual authority (Piri), a symbol of God's truth. This reminds Sikhs of the importance of balancing spiritual growth alongside physical skills.

APPLY

A Explain **two** of the symbols included in the Khanda.

B 'Being part of the sangat is essential for Sikhs wanting to progress in their faith.'

Write a paragraph setting out the arguments in support of this view.

3 Exam practice

Test the 1 mark question

1 Which **one** of the following means pride or ego?

A Haumai B Gurdwara C Mukti D Gurmukh **[1 mark]**

2 Which **one** of the following is the Sikh declaration of faith?

A Kesh B Mool Mantra C Guru Granth Sahib D Sangat **[1 mark]**

Test the 2 mark question

3 Give **two** ways in which the langar demonstrates equality in Sikhism. **[2 marks]**

1) ______

2) ______

4 Name **two** of the five evils. **[2 marks]**

1) ______

2) ______

TIP

If a question asks you to name something then you only have to give short answers – don't waste time writing in full sentences.

Test the 4 mark question

5 Explain **two** types of service that Sikhs may offer. **[4 marks]**

• **Explain one type.**	*Sikhs can offer tan (physical) sewa.*
• Develop your explanation with more detail/an example/ reference to a religious teaching or quotation.	*This involves using the body to help others, for example by preparing and cooking the meal in the langar.*
• **Explain a second type.**	*Another way to serve is by doing mental sewa (man).*
• Develop your explanation with more detail/an example/ reference to a religious teaching or quotation.	*This type of sewa means using mental skills to help others, for example teaching the Guru Granth Sahib.*

6 Explain **two** requirements for how amritdhari Sikhs should live. **[4 marks]**

• **Explain one requirement.**	
• Develop your explanation with more detail/an example/ reference to a religious teaching or quotation.	
• **Explain a second requirement.**	
• Develop your explanation with more detail/an example/ reference to a religious teaching or quotation.	

TIP

You can develop your answer by explaining why amritdhari Sikhs follow certain practices.

7 Explain **two** Sikh beliefs about being gurmukh. **[4 marks]**

Test the 5 mark question

8 Explain **two** Sikh beliefs about the five khands.
Refer to sacred writings or another source of Sikh belief and teaching in your answer. **[5 marks]**

• **Explain one belief.**	*Sikhs believe there are five stages (khands) they can pass through which will lead them to God.*
• Develop your explanation with more detail/an example.	*The five khands are piety, knowledge, effort, grace and truth.*
• **Explain a second belief.**	*Sikhs believe that God needs to take part in the development of an individual. This is the stage of grace.*
• Develop your explanation with more detail/an example.	*God, through his love, enables spiritual growth and strength.*
• Add a reference to sacred writings or another source of Sikh belief and teaching. If you prefer, you can add this reference to your first belief instead.	*Guru Granth Sahib 866 describes the stage of grace when it says, 'By the grace of the Holy, let your mind be imbued with the Lord's love'.*

TIP
You could choose to develop a point by explaining your reference to sacred writings or another source of Sikh belief and teaching.

9 Explain **two** Sikh beliefs about karma.
Refer to sacred writings or another source of Sikh belief and teaching in your answer. **[5 marks]**

• **Explain one belief.**	
• Develop your explanation with more detail/an example.	
• **Explain a second belief.**	
• Develop your explanation with more detail/an example.	
• Add a reference to sacred writings or another source of Sikh belief and teaching. If you prefer, you can add this reference to your first belief instead.	

10 Explain **two** Sikh beliefs about the nature of God.
Refer to sacred writings or another source of Sikh belief and teaching in your answer. **[5 marks]**

Test the 12 mark question

11 'Equality is the most important Sikh belief.'

Evaluate this statement. In your answer, you should:

- refer to Sikh teaching
- give reasoned arguments to support this statement
- give reasoned arguments to support a different point of view
- reach a justified conclusion.

[12 marks]
[+3 SPaG marks]

REASONED ARGUMENTS IN SUPPORT OF THE STATEMENT ● **Explain why some people would agree with the statement.** ● Develop your explanation with more detail and examples. ● Refer to religious teaching. Use a quote or paraphrase or refer to a religious authority. ● **Evaluate the arguments.** Is this a good argument or not? Explain why you think this.	*Some people say equality is the most important Sikh belief as it is referenced in so many aspects of Sikh belief and practice. For example, sewa provides an opportunity to serve others without distinctions of class, gender, race, belief etc. Also, in the Khalsa there is equality between men and women. Both can take part in worship and working in the langar. This view is supported by the quote from the Guru Granth Sahib, 'The God-conscious looks upon all alike, like the wind which blows equally on the king and the poor beggar.'*
REASONED ARGUMENTS SUPPORTING A DIFFERENT POINT OF VIEW ● **Explain why some people would agree with the statement.** ● Develop your explanation with more detail and examples. ● Refer to religious teaching. Use a quote or paraphrase or refer to a religious authority. ● **Evaluate the arguments.** Is this a good argument or not? Explain why you think this.	*Others would argue the most important belief in Sikhism is in God. Sikhs believe the teaching in the Mool Mantra about the existence and nature of God was the first teaching of Guru Nanak after he had become enlightened. Without belief in God, the rest of Sikh teaching is irrelevant. The Mool Mantra opens with 'One Universal Creator God', showing that belief in God is key to Sikhism.*
CONCLUSION ● **Give a justified conclusion.** ● Include your own opinion together with your own reasoning. ● **Include evaluation.** Explain why you think one viewpoint is stronger than the other or why they are equally strong. ● Do not repeat arguments you have already used without explaining why they apply to your reasoned opinion/conclusion.	*In conclusion, I think belief in God has to be more important than belief in equality because the teaching on equality comes from Guru Nanak and Guru Gobind Singh, for whom belief in God was the basis of their teaching and practice and so was more important. The Guru Granth Sahib teaches that 'All beings and creatures are His; He belongs to all'. The basis of equality is that all creatures belong to God. Without God, the teaching becomes meaningless.*

TIP

This answer is strong because it uses references to sacred writings in each paragraph to support the arguments.

12 'Service to others is the most important Sikh belief.'

Evaluate this statement. In your answer, you should:

- refer to Sikh teaching
- give reasoned arguments to support this statement
- give reasoned arguments to support a different point of view
- reach a justified conclusion.

[12 marks]
[+3 SPaG marks]

REASONED ARGUMENTS IN SUPPORT OF THE STATEMENT ● **Explain why some people would agree with the statement.** ● Develop your explanation with more detail and examples. ● Refer to religious teaching. Use a quote or paraphrase or refer to a religious authority. ● **Evaluate the arguments.** Is this a good argument or not? Explain why you think this.	
REASONED ARGUMENTS SUPPORTING A DIFFERENT POINT OF VIEW ● **Explain why some people would agree with the statement.** ● Develop your explanation with more detail and examples. ● Refer to religious teaching. Use a quote or paraphrase or refer to a religious authority. ● **Evaluate the arguments.** Is this a good argument or not? Explain why you think this.	
CONCLUSION ● **Give a justified conclusion.** ● Include your own opinion together with your own reasoning. ● **Include evaluation.** Explain why you think one viewpoint is stronger than the other or why they are equally strong. ● Do not repeat arguments you have already used without explaining why they apply to your reasoned opinion/conclusion.	

13 'Achieving mukti in Sikhism is not very difficult.'

Evaluate this statement. In your answer, you should:

- refer to Sikh teaching
- give reasoned arguments to support this statement
- give reasoned arguments to support a different point of view
- reach a justified conclusion.

[12 marks]
[+3 SPaG marks]

Check your answers using the mark scheme on pages 158–159. How did you do?
To feel more secure in the content you need to remember, re-read pages 48–59.
To remind yourself of what the examiner is looking for in your answers, go to pages 7–13.

4 Sikhism: Practices

4.1 The gurdwara

RECAP

Essential information:

- [ ] The **gurdwara** is the Sikh place of worship; it literally means 'the door of the Guru'.
- [ ] A gurdwara is a place where the Guru Granth Sahib is installed and treated with respect. It is often a separate building for public worship, but it could be a room in a home.
- [ ] The gurdwara is open to all, whatever their nationality, religion or class.

Outside the gurdwara

- Gurdwaras that have been purpose-built for Sikh worship often have a dome and external decorations.
- There will be a Sikh flag (Nishan Sahib) outside. This is usually yellow with a Khanda symbol in blue on it, flying from a flagpole wrapped in yellow cloth.

Inside the gurdwara

There are two main areas in the gurdwara: the prayer hall (Darbar Sahib) and the langar.

The manji is a small bed on which the Guru Granth Sahib is placed during the day.

The prayer hall has a raised platform or 'throne' (**takht**) at one end. The takht will usually be covered in fine cloth and surrounded with flowers. There may be a Khanda symbol or Ik Onkar symbol. In worship, readings from the Guru Granth Sahib take place from the takht; this shows honour and respect to the Guru Granth Sahib.

There is usually a domed structure over the takht called the **palki**. A large canopy of decorated cloth is placed over the palki near the ceiling.

In front of the platform, there is space for Sikhs to give offerings of money and food. There will also usually be a bowl containing karah parshad for the congregation.

- Elsewhere in the hall, there may be another raised area for musicians.
- The room might be decorated with pictures of the Gurus or verses from the scriptures.
- Everyone sits on the floor below the level of the Guru Granth Sahib.

TIP

Look at some pictures or virtual tours of gurdwaras online. This will give you a better understanding of how the gurdwara is used.

APPLY

A State **two** features of a gurdwara.

B 'Equality with others is the most important Sikh teaching demonstrated in the gurdwara.'

Decide which of the following arguments agree with this statement and which support a different point of view. **Write a conclusion** evaluating these points of view and explaining which you think is strongest.

1. The langar, which is part of the gurdwara, feeds everyone whatever their faith, race, gender or age.	4. Everyone sits below the level of the Guru Granth Sahib to show great respect to it.
2. Everyone sits on the floor. No person is considered more important than any other.	5. The 'throne' (takht) is similar to the honoured seat that would have been offered to the human Gurus, showing how important the Guru Granth Sahib is in Sikhism.
3. The Guru Granth Sahib takes the central place in the prayer hall, showing its importance to Sikhs.	6. The gurdwara is open to all, whatever their nationality, religion or class.

RECAP

Essential information:

- [ ] The Guru Granth Sahib contains the writings of many of the Gurus, as well as other wise and holy people.
- [ ] It is the eleventh Guru (the Eternal Living Guru) and is shown great respect.
- [ ] The akhand path is a continuous ceremonial reading of the whole Guru Granth Sahib.

How do Sikhs show their respect for the Guru Granth Sahib?

- It is called Sahib, which is a term of respect.
- All printed copies are identical. This shows respect by ensuring the words (and their layout) do not change and are kept completely accurate.
- Sikhs sit on the floor in the gurdwara so they are lower than the Guru Granth Sahib.
- They do not point their feet to the holy book when sitting down.
- Worshippers bow to the Guru Granth Sahib when entering the gurdwara.
- **Rumallas** (decorated cloths) are used to cover the Guru Granth Sahib when it is not being read.
- A **chauri** (fan) is waved over the Guru Granth Sahib as a sign of respect.
- At the end of worship, the Guru Granth Sahib is wrapped in a clean cloth and carried on the head of a Khalsa Sikh to its rest room. The following morning, it will be brought back to the prayer hall in the same way, and the **Ardas** prayer will be said.

The importance of the Guru Granth Sahib

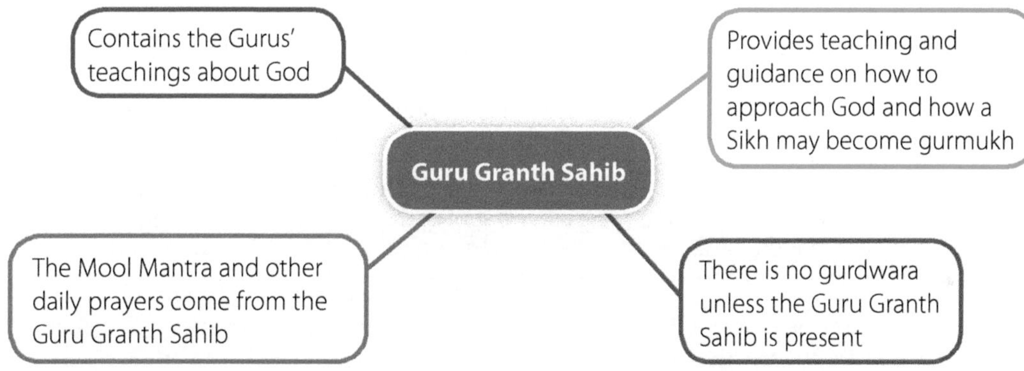

Guru Granth Sahib
Contains the Gurus' teachings about God
Provides teaching and guidance on how to approach God and how a Sikh may become gurmukh
The Mool Mantra and other daily prayers come from the Guru Granth Sahib
There is no gurdwara unless the Guru Granth Sahib is present

The akhand path

The akhand path is a continuous reading of the Guru Granth Sahib (all 1430 pages), which is usually completed within 48 hours. Readers take turns to read and they must be clear, accurate and not too fast. Karah parshad is distributed just before an akhand path begins and immediately after it ends.

An akhand path usually takes place before a festival begins and at times of great joy or sorrow, such as before a marriage. It is seen as a blessing and helps Sikhs to develop a closer relationship with the Guru Granth Sahib, by meditating as they listen.

APPLY

A Explain **two** ways that Sikhs show respect to the Guru Granth Sahib.

B 'The Guru Granth Sahib is the highest authority in Sikhism.'

Why might Sikhs agree with this statement? **List the arguments to support it.**

RECAP

Essential information:

- ☐ Sikh worship (**diwan**) can include services in the gurdwara, private prayer, meditation, and serving others.
- ☐ The most important part of worship is keeping God in mind.
- ☐ Services in the gurdwara can include prayers, hymn singing, readings from the Guru Granth Sahib, and a sermon or talk.

Worship in the gurdwara

> "Worship in adoration that True Lord; everything is under His Power."
>
> *Guru Granth Sahib 521*

Sikhs standing in prayer in the gurdwara

Where does Sikh worship happen?	Worship can happen anywhere as Sikhs believe God is present throughout the universe. However, special reverence is shown to God in gurdwaras and many Sikhs attend services here.
What does worship include?	Worship can include listening, meditating, singing, reciting, working and serving people.
How do Sikhs show respect?	Before entering the prayer hall in a gurdwara, Sikhs remove their shoes and cover their heads. They wash their hands and may wash their feet as well. As they enter the prayer hall, they walk towards the Guru Granth Sahib, bow and touch the floor. They may offer money to the gurdwara. Worshippers sit on the floor below the Guru Granth Sahib.
How do Sikhs worship in the gurdwara?	All services of worship begin and end with the Ardas prayer, during which Sikhs stand. After this prayer at the start of the service, a reading is given at random (**hukam**) from the Guru Granth Sahib. The service also includes hymns (**kirtan**), prayers and sometimes a sermon or talk.
Who leads worship?	The worship is led by any Sikh, male or female, who is known to be knowledgeable.
What music is used in worship?	Hymn singing (kirtan) is based on shabads (verses) from the Guru Granth Sahib. It is considered to nourish the soul and encourages Sikhs to focus on God. Ragis are musicians who sing or play accompaniment for kirtan. Common instruments used are harmoniums and tabla (drums).
How is the end of the service marked?	Karah parshad is given to everyone. This is a sweet food made of semolina, butter, sugar, flour and water. This symbolises equality of all and it means that no one leaves the presence of God 'empty-handed'.

APPLY

A Explain **two** ways Sikhs show respect in worship services.

B 'Attending services in the gurdwara is the best way for Sikhs to worship.'

Give a developed argument to support this statement. Then give a developed argument to support a **different point of view**.

TIP

Remember that Sikhs can worship in a variety of ways, including private prayer and performing sewa.

4.4 The langar

RECAP

Essential information:

- [ ] The langar was established in the fifteenth century by Guru Nanak, as a way to demonstrate his belief in equality.
- [ ] '**Langar**' describes both the kitchen where meals are prepared and the meals that are served there.
- [ ] In Sikh gurdwaras, langar food is served free to all.

Origins of the langar

- Guru Nanak established the langar to show in a practical way his belief in equality, by inviting people from different castes to eat together. After he founded a Sikh community in Kartapur, he worked on the farm to provide food for the langar.
- The second Guru (Guru Angad) continued the langar and it was run by his wife, Mata Khivi. Everyone who came was given the best possible food and treated with great respect. This led Sikhs to gain a reputation for showing hospitality and kindness to all.
- It is believed that the last Guru, Guru Gobind Singh, said as he was dying, 'Keep the langar ever open.' This showed he believed the practice to be a central part of the Sikh faith.

The langar today

Today, some gurdwaras serve langar every day of the year, while others serve food on certain days of the week or for particular festivals. The food is simple and vegetarian. It is prepared and served by Sikh volunteers as part of sewa, and paid for by voluntary contributions. The food is served free to all regardless of faith, race, gender or background.

Some large gurdwaras might serve thousands of meals a day. For example, the Guru Singh Sabha Gurdwara in London serves around 5000 meals each day of the week and 10,000 at weekends. Many gurdwaras run food banks and programmes to feed the homeless as part of their langar.

> "The Langar – the Kitchen of the Guru's Shabad has been opened, and its supplies never run short."
>
> *Guru Granth Sahib 967*

The importance of the langar

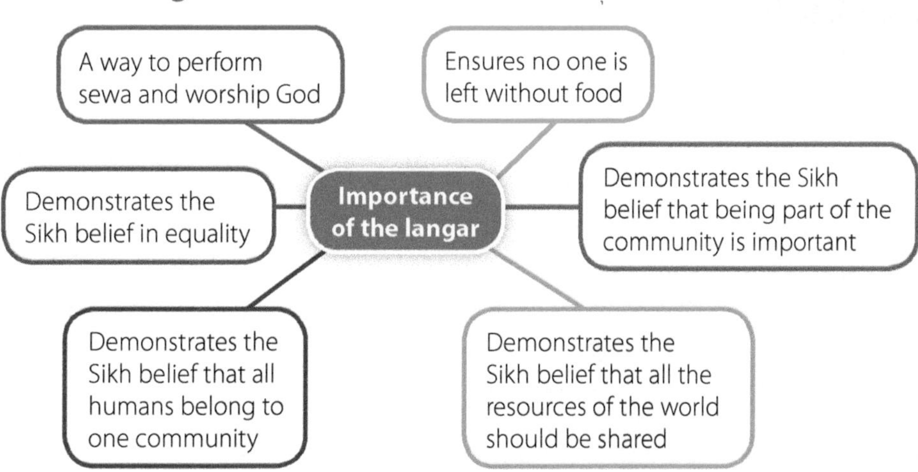
Importance of the langar
A way to perform sewa and worship God
Ensures no one is left without food
Demonstrates the Sikh belief in equality
Demonstrates the Sikh belief that being part of the community is important
Demonstrates the Sikh belief that all humans belong to one community
Demonstrates the Sikh belief that all the resources of the world should be shared

APPLY

A Explain **two** reasons why the langar is important within Sikhism.

B 'The langar demonstrates the Sikh belief in the importance of community.'

Give arguments to support this statement.

4.5 Prayer in the home and meditating on God's name

RECAP

Essential information:

- ☐ Sikhs are expected to remember God at all times, which includes reciting daily prayers at home.
- ☐ Sikhs have three responsibilities: meditating on the name of God (**nam japna**); doing honest work while remembering God; and sharing all they have and giving to charity.

Prayer at home

- Some Sikhs have a copy of the Guru Granth Sahib at home, which is treated in a special way. It has a room or an area of the house to itself and is treated with respect in the same way as in the gurdwara.
- Most Sikhs do not have a copy of the Guru Granth Sahib, and instead use a prayer book called a **gutka**. This is also treated with great respect. It is wrapped in a special cloth and Sikhs wash their hands before picking it up.

Daily prayer routine

Guru Ram Das set out a routine for prayer. Sikhs are expected to grow in self-discipline and commitment as they follow this guidance to become gurmukh (centred on God).

Morning	• Sikhs should bathe to remind them that God is all around them. This helps them to prepare for meditation and separates it from other tasks. • At dawn, Sikhs should recite the **Japji** prayer (given by Guru Nanak) and the Jap and Swayyas prayers (written by Guru Gobind Singh). • Some Sikhs also use a mala (prayer beads with 108 knots) to meditate on the name of God. They pass the beads through their fingers as they repeat 'Waheguru'. • Some Sikhs may attend morning worship at the gurdwara before work.
Evening	• At dusk, the Rahiras prayer should be recited. • When going to bed, the Sohila prayer should be recited.

Ideally, God should be remembered throughout the day – not just in the daily prayers or communal worship. Sikhs can do this by meditating on the name of God – by quietly reciting God's name to themselves. Sikhs believe the more they focus on God, the more selfless they will become, making practices like sewa and giving to charity easier.

> "One who meditates on my Lord… that GurSikh becomes pleasing to the Guru's Mind."
>
> *Guru Granth Sahib 305*

TIP
You could use this quote in your exam to show that Sikhs should keep God in mind at home (and throughout the day) by meditating on his name.

APPLY

 **A** Explain **two** ways that Sikhs pray as part of their daily routine.

B 'All Sikhs should focus on prayer if they want to please God.'

Evaluate this statement.

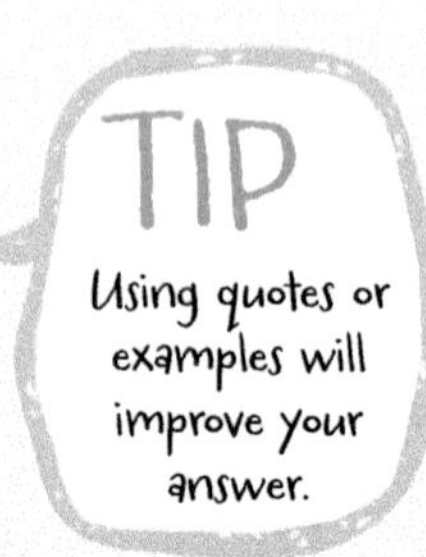

TIP
Using quotes or examples will improve your answer.

4.6 The role of the gurdwara in the Sikh community

RECAP

Essential information:

- [ ] Each gurdwara has a number of facilities that help serve the sangat (Sikh community) as well as the local community.
- [ ] A **granthi** is a trained Sikh who organises and conducts services and ceremonies in the gurdwara.

The gurdwara

Most of the cleaning, maintenance and organisation of a gurdwara is done by Sikh volunteers as a part of sewa. The gurdwara is funded by donations from Sikhs.

Gurdwaras are places of worship, but also have other facilities to help serve Sikhs and the local community.

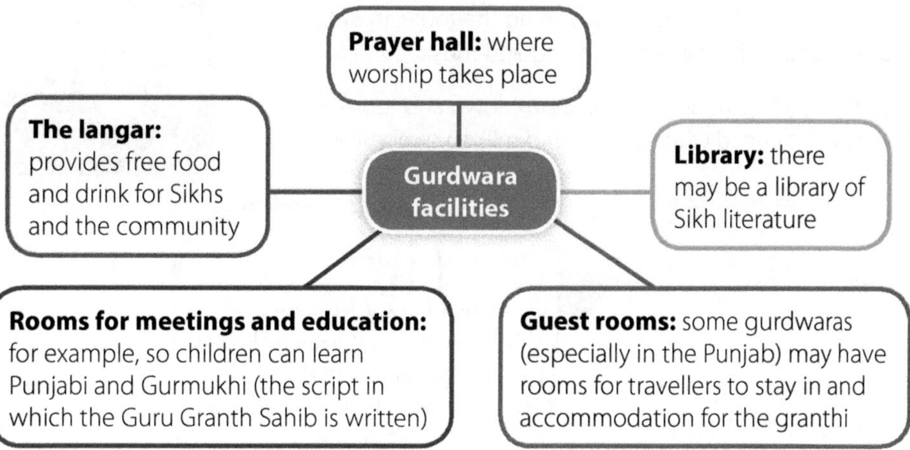

Gurdwara facilities
Prayer hall: where worship takes place
The langar: provides free food and drink for Sikhs and the community
Library: there may be a library of Sikh literature
Rooms for meetings and education: for example, so children can learn Punjabi and Gurmukhi (the script in which the Guru Granth Sahib is written)
Guest rooms: some gurdwaras (especially in the Punjab) may have rooms for travellers to stay in and accommodation for the granthi

The granthi

Who can be a granthi?	Granthis are amritdhari Sikhs (members of the Khalsa). They are expected to live according to the Sikh Code of Conduct (the Rehat Maryada) and show devotion to God and humility. Depending on their duties, a granthi may have another job as well. Some may be paid a small salary in addition to free accommodation and food.
How does a granthi train for their role?	There are several places of training; the most famous is the Shahid Sikh Missionary College at Amritsar in the Punjab. In the UK, Sikhs often appoint a granthi who has trained in the Punjab. There is no ceremony of ordination because granthis are not priests and do not have a higher status than other Sikhs.
What does a granthi do?	• Their most important role is to take care of the Guru Granth Sahib and arrange the ceremonies to bring it from the rest room to the prayer hall in the morning and return it in the evening. • They also arrange the daily religious services. • They may lead kirtan (hymn singing). • They conduct rites of passage, such as weddings and funerals. • They are responsible for performances of the akhand path (continuous readings of the Guru Granth Sahib). • They teach and advise community members. • Granthis who live on the premises of the gurdwara may be responsible for its maintenance and security.

APPLY

A Give **two** of the granthi's roles.

B 'The most important role of the gurdwara is to provide a space for listening to the Guru Granth Sahib being read.'

Evaluate this statement.

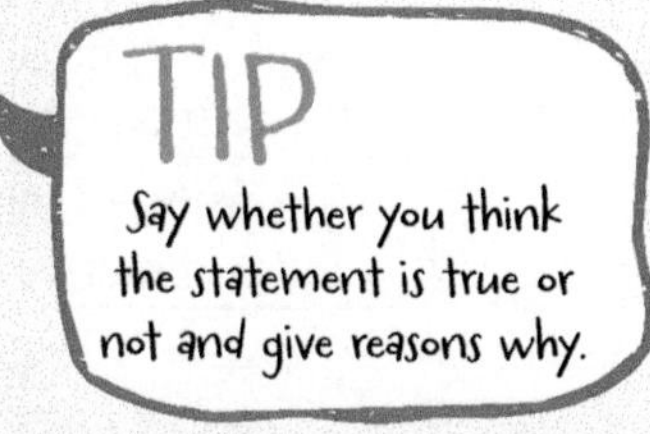

TIP
Say whether you think the statement is true or not and give reasons why.

4.7 The festival of Vaisakhi (Baisakhi)

RECAP

Essential information:

- ☐ **Vaisakhi** is normally celebrated on 13 or 14 April.
- ☐ Vaisakhi was originally a wheat harvest festival.
- ☐ Guru Gobind Singh (the tenth Guru) established the Khalsa at Vaisakhi, and this is now remembered in celebrations today.

Celebrations at Vaisakhi

During Vaisakhi, every gurdwara holds an akhand path (a continuous reading of the Guru Granth Sahib) followed by an act of worship.

Sikh musicians celebrating at Vaisakhi

Processions are held in many towns in Britain and elsewhere. The Guru Granth Sahib is carried on a decorated float, accompanied by Sikhs singing and dancing. Free sweets and soft drinks are given away from stalls lining the route. In India, large fairs are organised with sports, martial arts, dancing and music.

At each gurdwara, the Sikh flag (the Nishan Sahib) is taken down and replaced with a new one. The flagpole is cleaned with yoghurt and milk to symbolise purity and cleanliness.

Other customs include:

- reciting the Ardas prayer
- holding large community meals
- performing kirtan
- sending Vaisakhi cards to friends and family
- wearing new clothes (especially children)
- voting for elected committees for the gurdwara.

TIP

Watch some videos online of Vaisakhi celebrations both in the UK (for example in Leicester) and in the Punjab to get a better idea of what the festival involves.

The importance of Vaisakhi

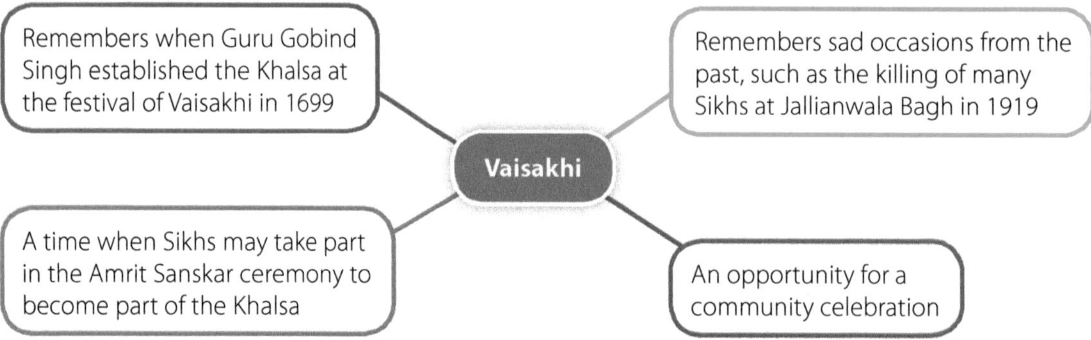

Remembers when Guru Gobind Singh established the Khalsa at the festival of Vaisakhi in 1699
Remembers sad occasions from the past, such as the killing of many Sikhs at Jallianwala Bagh in 1919
Vaisakhi
A time when Sikhs may take part in the Amrit Sanskar ceremony to become part of the Khalsa
An opportunity for a community celebration

APPLY

 Explain **two** ways Vaisakhi is celebrated.

 'Celebrating Vaisakhi helps Sikhs remember the establishment of the Khalsa.'

Identify which of the following statements agree with this statement and which agree with a different point of view. Then **write a concluding paragraph** setting out your point of view and the reasons for it.

1. Ceremonies to become amritdhari Sikhs remind participants of the actions of Guru Gobind Singh.	4. Families celebrate Vaisakhi by sending cards and buying new clothes.
2. A continuous reading of the Guru Granth Sahib reminds Sikhs of those who wrote it and their actions.	5. Amritdhari Sikhs are committed to the faith, and can show this by attending the gurdwara service and serving others in the langar at Vaisakhi.
3. The festival is celebrated with fairs, processions and community meals.	6. Vaisakhi is an opportunity to have fun by watching sporting competitions and listening to music.

4.8 The festival of Divali

RECAP

Essential information:

- ☐ **Divali** is held in October or early November and is a celebration of freedom.
- ☐ Sikhs remember Guru Hargobind and Bhai Mani Singh at Divali.
- ☐ Light is an important symbol in the festival to represent the victory of good over evil.

Celebrations at Divali

Divali celebrations
Each gurdwara holds an akhand path
Many Sikhs travel to the Golden Temple in Amritsar to celebrate
Street processions are held
Langars are held, some in the open air
Homes are cleaned, decorated and lit up with lamps and lights
Presents are given, especially to children
There are bonfires and firework displays

Guru Hargobind and Bhai Mani Singh

At Divali, Sikhs remember Guru Hargobind (the sixth Guru) and Bhai Mani Singh (a granthi at the Golden Temple). The festival celebrates freedom and remembers the courage of Sikhs prepared to stand up for their faith in the face of persecution and adversity. It is also a time to celebrate equality and the promotion and protection of religious faith.

Guru Hargobind	Bhai Mani Singh
• In 1619, Guru Hargobind and 52 Hindu princes were imprisoned in the town of Gwalior by the Mughal authorities for political reasons. • The emperor investigated the charges against Guru Hargobind, decided they were false and ordered him to be released. • He refused to leave unless the Hindu princes were released too. • The emperor said that any prince who could hold onto the Guru's clothes as he left would be allowed to leave. • The Guru put on his cloak that had 52 tassels, and with the Hindu princes each holding a tassel, the Guru led them to freedom. • The Guru became known as 'Bandi Chhor' (the deliverer from prison) and the day became known as 'Bandi Chhor Divas' (freedom day).	• Bhai Mani Singh gained permission for a gathering of Sikhs to celebrate Bandi Chhor Divas at the Golden Temple in 1737, in return for a large tax which the emperor demanded. • He then discovered that the emperor was intending to kill many Sikhs at this gathering and cancelled the meeting. • The emperor ordered his death.

TIP

You can use this story as a source of wisdom and authority in your exam to show how freedom of religious faith is important to Sikhs today.

APPLY

A Explain **two** ways Sikhs celebrate Divali.

B 'Divali celebrations demonstrate important Sikh beliefs.'

Evaluate this argument in support of this view and explain your reasoning.

During Divali, Sikhs remember the release of Guru Hargobind and the 52 princes and the martyrdom of Bhai Mani Singh. Many Sikhs go to the Golden Temple for Divali, which is where Bhai Mani Singh tried to celebrate freedom day. Also many Sikhs hold a langar which demonstrates their belief in equality by serving food to all.

RECAP

Essential information:

- ☐ **Gurpurbs** are celebrations which take place on anniversaries – usually the birth or death of one of the Gurus.
- ☐ The four gurpurbs that are widely celebrated are the birthdays of Guru Nanak and Guru Gobind Singh, and the martyrdoms of Guru Arjan and Guru Tegh Bahadur.

Gurpurb celebrations

Many local communities will organise a procession to carry the Guru Granth Sahib. It is sometimes carried on a float with Khalsa members on either side. In front will be five Sikhs representing the first five members of the Khalsa (the Panj Piare). Celebrations might also involve:

- kirtan
- local competitions
- presents and cards
- special langars.

Gurdwaras will hold an akhand path before each gurpurb. Langar and karah parshad are available throughout this time as people come and go. Worship includes singing hymns composed by the Guru whose anniversary is being celebrated, and listening to songs and talks about the life of the Guru.

The main differences between gurpurb celebrations in India and Great Britain are:

India	Britain
Celebrations take place on the actual anniversary date. If this is a weekday then schools may close.	Gurpurbs are usually celebrated at the weekend.
There may be large processions with firework displays and fairs.	Celebrations are usually quieter and more local, often centred on the gurdwara.

Two gurpurbs

Guru Nanak's birthday	The martyrdom of Guru Tegh Bahadur
Guru Nanak founded Sikhism so this is the most important of the gurpurbs. • Candles are lit in the gurdwara as well as in homes, shops and offices. • Processions and firework displays take place. • In the Punjab, children are given new clothes and have a holiday from school.	In 1675, Guru Tegh Bahadur tried to persuade the emperor to stop the persecution of Sikhs that was happening at the time. He was arrested with three other Sikhs, who were executed in front of him. Like them, he refused to become a Muslim and was executed too.

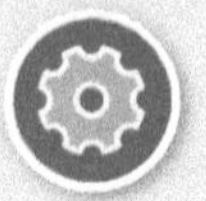

APPLY

A Give **two** ways that gurpurbs are celebrated.

B 'The gurpurbs are a time for solemn remembering of the Gurus rather than fun.'

Do you think Sikhs would agree with this statement? **Explain your reasoning.**

4.10 Pilgrimage to the Golden Temple

RECAP

Essential information:

- [ ] Many Sikhs make a pilgrimage to **Harimandir Sahib**, the Golden Temple. This historical gurdwara is the most famous place of worship for Sikhs.
- [ ] Pilgrimage to historical gurdwaras can encourage spiritual reflection and help Sikhs to learn more about the history of their faith.

TIP

A historical gurdwara is a Sikh place of worship that is linked to an important event in Sikh history, such as an event in the life of one of the ten Gurus.

The Golden Temple

- The Golden Temple is in the city of Amritsar in the Punjab. It is surrounded by a pool of fresh water.
- The gurdwara has four entrances to symbolise that people from all four corners of the world are welcome.
- At the northern entrance steps go up and then down again into the temple, symbolising the need to be humble and respectful in the presence of the Guru Granth Sahib.
- Inside the temple, the original Adi Granth (the first version of the holy book compiled by Guru Arjan) is installed on a takht (throne) under a jewelled canopy.
- A continuous reading of the Guru Granth Sahib is performed every day.

The Akal Takht is a building that faces onto the causeway leading to the Golden Temple. It is where the spiritual leader of the Sikhs works and is the centre of religious government. It also houses the rest room for the Guru Granth Sahib, which is taken across the causeway every morning to the Golden Temple and returned in the evening.

Visiting the Golden Temple

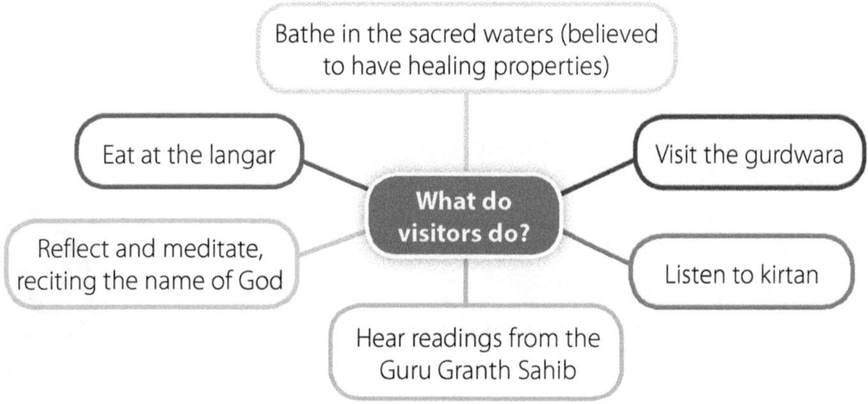
What do visitors do?
Bathe in the sacred waters (believed to have healing properties)
Eat at the langar
Visit the gurdwara
Reflect and meditate, reciting the name of God
Listen to kirtan
Hear readings from the Guru Granth Sahib

The importance of pilgrimage

The Gurus taught that ceremonies and rituals – such as bathing in the pool at the Golden Temple – will do nothing if people are not clean inside. Putting effort into understanding God and having the right state of mind are most important. Sikhs who go on pilgrimage believe the effort required and the time given to spiritual reflection deepen their faith and understanding.

Pilgrims may also visit other historical gurdwaras to understand more about the beginnings of their faith. One of these places is Goindval, where Guru Amas Das built a deep well with 84 steps going into it. Sikhs sometimes recite the Japji on each of the steps as they go down to bathe. As always, the emphasis is not on the ritual but on focusing on God's name.

> "There is no sacred shrine equal to the Guru."
> *Guru Granth Sahib 1328*

APPLY

A Explain **two** reasons why the Akal Takht is important in Sikhism.

B 'Going on pilgrimage is the best way for a Sikh to become more holy.'

Develop two arguments against this view.

4.11 Birth and naming ceremonies

RECAP

Essential information:

- ☐ About two weeks after the birth of a child, the family go to the gurdwara for a naming ceremony.
- ☐ The naming ceremony is a time to celebrate and give thanks to God for the birth of a child.

The naming ceremony in the gurdwara

The naming ceremony is usually part of the normal service of worship in the gurdwara (though it can also be held at home if the mother is ill or there is no gurdwara nearby).

- As usual in a worship service, everyone bows before the Guru Granth Sahib and makes offerings of food or money.
- The parents take karah parshad to share with the congregation (or money to pay for it). They may also offer something special to the gurdwara, such as a rumalla (highly decorated cloth used to cover the Guru Granth Sahib).
- The Mool Mantra is said in thanks for the new life.
- Hymns of joy and thanksgiving are said or sung.
- The baby is given a spoonful of amrit (a mixture of sugar and water).
- The granthi recites the first five verses of the Japji as they stir the amrit with a khanda (two-edged sword).
- The granthi then dips the sword into the amrit and touches the baby's tongue and head with it.
- The rest of the amrit is given to the mother to drink.

> "The True Guru has truly given a child."
>
> *Guru Granth Sahib 396*

The naming of a child

Choosing the name	After the ceremony with amrit, the granthi opens the Guru Granth Sahib at random and reads out the top section of the left-hand page. The first letter of the first word gives the first letter of the child's name. The parents then choose a name beginning with this letter.
Announcing the name	The granthi announces the name and says a blessing. The congregation sings Anand Sahib and offers a prayer of thanksgiving. They say prayers for the child and share out karah parshad.
Sikh surnames	Some Sikhs use their family name as a surname, but others follow Guru Gobind Singh's practice of calling all women 'Kaur' (princess) and men 'Singh' (lion). The Guru introduced this practice to prevent discrimination based on what caste a person was from, to demonstrate the Sikh belief in the equality of all.

APPLY

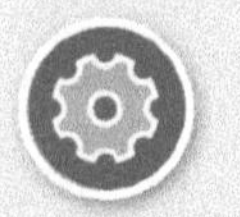

A Give **two** actions in a Sikh naming ceremony.

B 'Sikh ceremonies associated with birth remind Sikhs of the importance of God.'

Give arguments to support this statement.

4.12 The initiation ceremony (Amrit Sanskar)

RECAP

Essential information:

- ☐ Sikhs who are prepared to be fully committed to the Sikh faith take part in the **Amrit Sanskar** ceremony.
- ☐ Sikhs who have undergone the ceremony are members of the Khalsa.
- ☐ They wear the five Ks and follow the rules in the Rehat Maryada.

Initiation into the Khalsa

Both men and women can become members of the Khalsa. Once they have been through the Amrit Sanskar ceremony they are known as amritdhari. Sikhs need to be old enough to recognise the importance and seriousness of the responsibilities they are taking on, so they wait until their late teens or even adulthood to be initiated.

Sikhs who have not yet become amritdhari are known as sahajdhari. They believe in the teachings of Sikhism but may choose not to wear all five Ks or strictly follow the Sikh Code of Conduct.

> "Today you are reborn in the true Guru's household."
>
> *Rehat Maryada, article 24*

How do Sikhs prepare for the ceremony?	The person being initiated must bathe, wash their hair, cover their head and wear clean clothes. They also wear the five Ks.
Who is present?	At least six other amritdhari Sikhs must be present. Five represent the first Panj Piare and the sixth – the granthi – reads the Guru Granth Sahib.
What happens at the ceremony?	• The person is asked whether they want to be initiated and if they understand what is involved. • Each one of those representing the Panj Piare recites a prayer and uses a khanda to stir the amrit. • The granthi opens the Guru Granth Sahib at random and reads a hymn. • The person drinks amrit from the bowl five times, saying, 'The Khalsa belongs to God, victory belongs to God.' • The Panj Piare sprinkle amrit on the person's eyes and hair five times. • The person recites the Mool Mantra. • If the person being initiated does not yet have a Sikh name, they are given one. • Everyone eats a share of karah parshad.

Requirements for members of the Khalsa

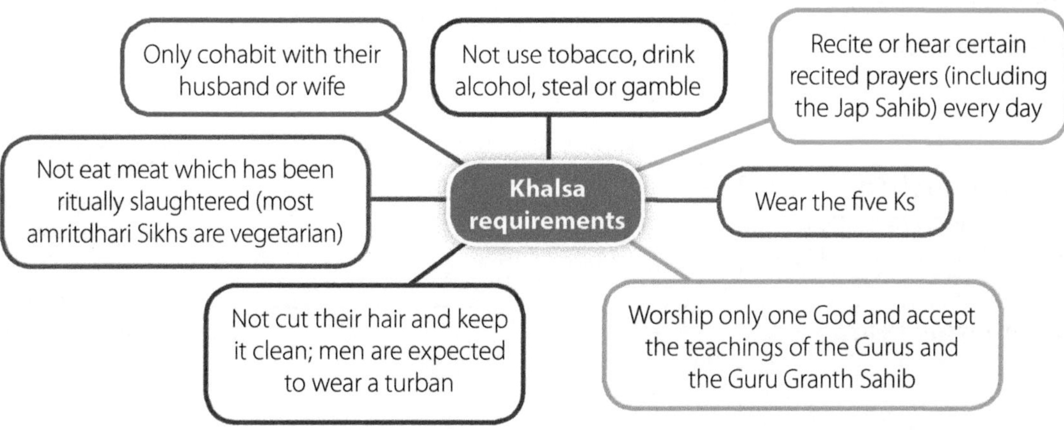

Khalsa requirements
Only cohabit with their husband or wife
Not use tobacco, drink alcohol, steal or gamble
Recite or hear certain recited prayers (including the Jap Sahib) every day
Not eat meat which has been ritually slaughtered (most amritdhari Sikhs are vegetarian)
Wear the five Ks
Not cut their hair and keep it clean; men are expected to wear a turban
Worship only one God and accept the teachings of the Gurus and the Guru Granth Sahib

APPLY

A Explain **two** elements of the Amrit Sanskar ceremony.

B 'The Amrit Sanskar ceremony is the most important event in a Sikh's life.'

Write a paragraph supporting this viewpoint.

TIP
Think about what the ceremony represents, and how a Sikh's daily life changes after the ceremony.

Test the 1 mark question

1 Which **one** of the following is the initiation ceremony in Sikhism?

A Amrit Sanskar B Mool Mantra C Mukti D Sahajdhari Sikh **[1 mark]**

2 Which **one** of the following means meditating on the name of God?

A Harimandir Sahib B Manmukh C Karma D Nam japna **[1 mark]**

Test the 2 mark question

3 Name **two** Sikh festivals. **[2 marks]**

1) __________

2) __________

4 Give **two** features of a gurdwara. **[2 marks]**

1) __________

2) __________

Test the 4 mark question

5 Explain **two** contrasting ways in which Sikhs show respect for the Guru Granth Sahib. **[4 marks]**

• **Explain one way.**	*Sikhs show respect in their posture, by sitting on the floor when they worship.*
• Develop your explanation with more detail/an example/ reference to a religious teaching or quotation.	*This means they are at a lower level than the Guru Granth Sahib, which sits on a raised platform in the prayer hall.*
• **Explain a second way.**	*Worshippers wave a fan over the Guru Granth Sahib.*
• Develop your explanation with more detail/an example/ reference to a religious teaching or quotation.	*Honoured teachers would been offered this service in India to provide cool air and keep the flies away.*

6 Explain **two** contrasting ways in which Sikhs pray. **[4 marks]**

• **Explain one way.**	
• Develop your explanation with more detail/an example/ reference to a religious teaching or quotation.	
• **Explain a second way.**	
• Develop your explanation with more detail/an example/ reference to a religious teaching or quotation.	

TIP

Here the question asks for 'contrasting' ways, so they must be different to each other. For example, you could contrast private and communal prayer.

7 Explain **two** contrasting ways in which Sikhs celebrate gurpurbs in India and Great Britain. **[4 marks]**

Test the 5 mark question

8 Explain **two** ways in which Sikh birth and naming ceremonies are important.
Refer to sacred writings or another source of Sikh belief and teaching in your answer. **[5 marks]**

• **Explain one way.**	*Sikh birth and naming ceremonies are an important way to give thanks to God for the birth of a child.*
• Develop your explanation with more detail/an example.	*The Mool Mantra is said in thanksgiving for the new life.*
• **Explain a second way.**	*Another reason the ceremony is important is that the child is named in the ceremony.*
• Develop your explanation with more detail/an example.	*The child's parents choose a name based on the first letter of a word from the Guru Granth Sahib.*
• Add a reference to sacred writings or another source of Sikh belief and teaching. If you prefer, you can add this reference to your first belief instead.	*The Guru Granth Sahib contains a hymn of joy for the birth of a child: 'The true Guru has truly given a child.' This shows how important it is that there is gratitude for the new life.*

TIP

Make sure your reference to sacred writings or another source of Sikh belief and teaching is relevant to the question. It should support one of the points you have already made.

9 Explain **two** ways in which Sikhs worship in the gurdwara.
Refer to sacred writings or another source of Sikh belief and teaching in your answer. **[5 marks]**

• **Explain one way.**	
• Develop your explanation with more detail/an example.	
• **Explain a second way.**	
• Develop your explanation with more detail/an example.	
• Add a reference to sacred writings or another source of Sikh belief and teaching. If you prefer, you can add this reference to your first belief instead.	

10 Explain **two** ways in which Sikhs celebrate festivals.
Refer to sacred writings or another source of Sikh belief and teaching in your answer. **[5 marks]**

Test the 12 mark question

11 'The most important duty of a Sikh is to become a member of the Khalsa.'

Evaluate this statement. In your answer, you should:

- refer to Sikh teaching
- give reasoned arguments to support this statement
- give reasoned arguments to support a different point of view
- reach a justified conclusion.

[12 marks]
[+3 SPaG ma

REASONED ARGUMENTS IN SUPPORT OF THE STATEMENT ● **Explain why some people would agree with the statement.** ● Develop your explanation with more detail and examples. ● Refer to religious teaching. Use a quote or paraphrase or refer to a religious authority. ● **Evaluate the arguments.** Is this a good argument or not? Explain why you think this.	*Initiation into the Khalsa demonstrates that a Sikh is prepared to be fully committed to their faith and so many would say this is their most important duty. Other duties follow on from this, for example wearing the five Ks and following the rules of the Khalsa. The Rehat Maryada explains the importance of membership of the Khalsa, saying 'Today you are reborn in the true Guru's household.'* *Membership of the Khalsa includes the expectation that a number of prayers are said or heard every day. Being a member of the Khalsa shapes a Sikh's commitment to God and their behaviour and patterns of life.*
REASONED ARGUMENTS SUPPORTING A DIFFERENT POINT OF VIEW ● **Explain why some people would support a different view.** ● Develop your explanation with more detail and examples. ● Refer to religious teaching. Use a quote or paraphrase or refer to a religious authority. ● **Evaluate the arguments.** Is this a good argument or not? Explain why you think this.	*Others might argue that worship is a more important duty than undergoing the Amrit Sanskar ceremony to join the Khalsa. Guru Granth Sahib 521 says, 'Worship in adoration that True Lord', showing that worship is an important duty that all Sikhs should carry out. It helps all Sikhs to become closer to God and give thanks to God.* *Another duty that all Sikhs should follow is performing sewa. This selfless service is central to Sikhism. Some might say it is more important than becoming a member of the Khalsa because it strengthens the Sikh community and helps other people in a practical way.*
CONCLUSION ● **Give a justified conclusion.** ● Include your own opinion together with your own reasoning. ● **Include evaluation.** Explain why you think one viewpoint is stronger than the other or why they are equally strong. ● Do not repeat arguments you have already used without explaining why they apply to your reasoned opinion/conclusion.	*I think that undergoing the Amrit Sanskar ceremony is very important, but not more important than worship and sewa for Sikhs.* *Worship especially should be central to all that Sikhs do by keeping the name of God in their minds. All other duties follow from this. Even the Amrit Sanskar ceremony acknowledges the importance of worship when Sikhs taking part in it are told 'You are to worship none except the One Timeless Being'.*

TIP

It can be helpful to include some new information in the conclusion which backs up your opinion.

12 'Remembering the name of God in daily life is more important than worship at the gurdwara.'

Evaluate this statement. In your answer, you should:

- refer to Sikh teaching
- give reasoned arguments to support this statement
- give reasoned arguments to support a different point of view
- reach a justified conclusion.

[12 marks]
[+3 SPaG marks]

REASONED ARGUMENTS IN SUPPORT OF THE STATEMENT ● **Explain why some people would agree with the statement.** ● Develop your explanation with more detail and examples. ● Refer to religious teaching. Use a quote or paraphrase or refer to a religious authority. ● **Evaluate the arguments.** Is this a good argument or not? Explain why you think this.	
REASONED ARGUMENTS SUPPORTING A DIFFERENT POINT OF VIEW ● **Explain why some people would support a different view.** ● Develop your explanation with more detail and examples. ● Refer to religious teaching. Use a quote or paraphrase or refer to a religious authority. ● **Evaluate the arguments.** Is this a good argument or not? Explain why you think this.	
CONCLUSION ● **Give a justified conclusion.** ● Include your own opinion together with your own reasoning. ● **Include evaluation.** Explain why you think one viewpoint is stronger than the other or why they are equally strong. ● Do not repeat arguments you have already used without explaining why they apply to your reasoned opinion/conclusion.	

13 'The best way for Sikhs to become gurmukh is to make a pilgrimage to the Golden Temple.'

Evaluate this statement. In your answer, you should:

- refer to Sikh teaching
- give reasoned arguments to support this statement
- give reasoned arguments to support a different point of view
- reach a justified conclusion.

[12 marks]
[+3 SPaG marks]

Check your answers using the mark scheme on page 159. How did you do?
To feel more secure in the content you need to remember, re-read pages 64–75.
To remind yourself of what the examiner is looking for in your answers, go to pages 7–13.

5 Relationships and families

5.1 Religious teachings about human sexuality

RECAP

Essential information:

- ☐ **Human sexuality** refers to how people express themselves as sexual beings.
- ☐ Many Christians and Sikhs believe that **heterosexual** relationships within marriage are the ideal.
- ☐ Christian and Sikh teaching do not condemn a person's sexual orientation.

You might be asked to compare beliefs on same-sex relationships between Christianity (the main religious tradition in Great Britain) and another religious tradition.

Attitudes towards sexual relationships

	Christianity	Sikhism and other views
General attitudes towards sexual relationships 	• The Christian Church teaches that sex expresses a deep, loving, life-long union that first requires the **commitment of marriage**. • Not all Christians agree with this, but all are against unfaithfulness. • The Bible teaches that heterosexual relationships are part of **God's plan** for humans. • Genesis 1:28 and 2:24 say that a man and woman should be united together and 'increase in number'.	• For Sikhs, sex is a **wonderful creative act** and a **means of spiritual growth**. • The Guru Granth Sahib compares the soul's relationship with God to the union between husband and wife, describing it as joyous and infinitely pleasurable. • Sikhs believe it is important to **remain chaste** before marriage since the body contains the divine spark of God.
Views on same-sex relationships 	• Some Christians oppose same-sex relationships because they believe this goes against God's plan. • The Catholic Church teaches that sex between members of the same sex is a sinful activity. "Do not have sexual relations with a man as one does with a woman; that is detestable." *Leviticus 18:22* [NIV] • The Church of England welcomes same-sex couples living in committed, celibate relationships, but does not allow same-sex marriage in church. Some other Churches do. • Some Christians think loving, faithful same-sex relationships are just as holy as heterosexual ones.	• The Guru Granth Sahib does not mention same-sex relationships, but does encourage heterosexual marriage. • Many Sikhs believe that because of this, same-sex marriage is wrong as heterosexual marriage is intended by God. "[same-sex marriage] is unnatural and ungodly, and the Sikh religion cannot support it." *Manjit Singh Kalkatta* • Some Sikhs accept same-sex marriage as a valid way to express love and commitment. • Many people in Britain today believe that people in same-sex relationships should have the same rights as those in heterosexual relationships, including the right to marry.

APPLY

A Write down **two** contrasting religious beliefs about same-sex relationships. **Develop** both beliefs by explaining in more detail, adding an example, or referring to a relevant religious teaching or quotation.

B 'Sex has been devalued in British society.'

Develop the answer below to support this statement. Refer to one religious argument and one non-religious argument.

"Nowadays many people in Britain have lots of different sexual partners."

5.2 Sexual relationships before and outside marriage

RECAP

Essential information:

- ☐ **Sex before marriage** is sex between two unmarried people. It is common in British society, but is forbidden in Sikhism and goes against the beliefs of many Christians.
- ☐ **Sex outside marriage** is sex between two people where one or both of them is married to someone else. This is also called **adultery**.
- ☐ Most religious and non-religious people believe sex outside marriage is wrong.

Sexual relationships before marriage

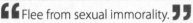

Sex before marriage is now widely accepted in British society, although it is against the beliefs of many religious people.

Christian views

- For many Christians, sex expresses a deep, lifelong union that requires the commitment of marriage. It should not be a casual, temporary pleasure.
- Anglican and Catholic Churches teach that sex before marriage is wrong.
- Some liberal Christians think sex before marriage can be a valid expression of love, particularly if the couple are intending to get married or have a life-long commitment.
- Christians believe it is wrong to use people for sex, to spread sexually transmitted infections or to risk pregnancy outside of marriage.

> "Flee from sexual immorality."
> *1 Corinthians 6:18* [NIV]

Sikh views

- The Rehat Maryada says that anyone who has sex before or outside marriage is not a true Sikh.
- Sikhism teaches that premarital sex lowers one's self-esteem and respect for others, who hold God's divine spark within them.
- Family honour and modesty is important within Sikhism.

You might be asked to compare beliefs on sexual relationships before marriage between Christianity (the main religious tradition in Great Britain) and another religious tradition.

Sexual relationships outside marriage

All religions generally teach that adultery is wrong as it involves lies, secrecy and the betrayal of trust. Most non-religious people are against adultery for similar reasons.

Christian views

- Christians are against adultery as it breaks the marriage vows they make before God, and threatens the stable relationship needed for their children's security.
- Jesus once forgave a woman caught committing adultery, but ordered her to leave her life of sin (John 8:1–11).
- Adultery is forbidden in one of the Ten Commandments.

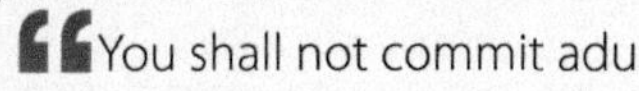

> "You shall not commit adultery."
> *Exodus 20:14* [NIV]

Sikh views

- Adultery is considered a serious sin. It is one of the four misdeeds (kurahat) that members of the Khalsa must not commit.
- The kachera (underwear worn by men and women, and one of the five Ks) reminds Sikhs they must be faithful and sexually pure in marriage.

> "The blind fool abandons the wife of his own home, and has an affair with another woman."
> *Guru Granth Sahib 1165*

APPLY

A Here are two religious beliefs about sexual relationships outside of marriage (adultery). **Develop** one of the points by referring to a relevant religious teaching or quotation.

"Christians think sex outside of marriage (adultery) is wrong because it breaks the vows couples make at their wedding."

"Sex outside marriage is forbidden in Sikhism."

B Give **two** points in support and **two** points against the statement, 'It is not always wrong to have sex before marriage.' **Develop** one of them by adding more detail or an example.

5.3 Contraception and family planning

RECAP

Essential information:

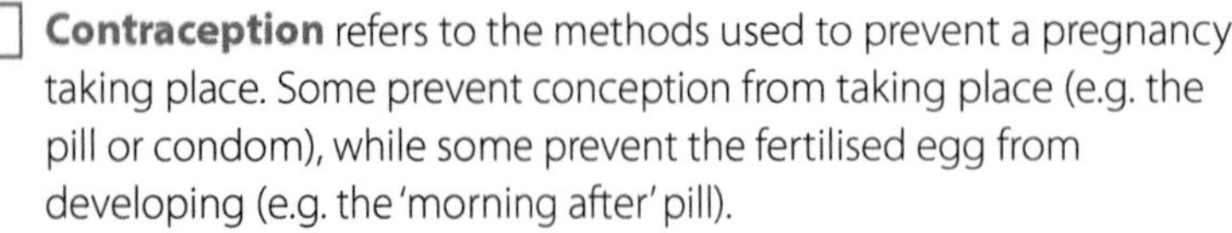

- ☐ **Contraception** refers to the methods used to prevent a pregnancy taking place. Some prevent conception from taking place (e.g. the pill or condom), while some prevent the fertilised egg from developing (e.g. the 'morning after' pill).
- ☐ **Family planning** is controlling how many children couples have and when they have them.
- ☐ There is widespread acceptance of contraception in Britain among non-religious people.

You might be asked to compare beliefs on contraception between Christianity (the main religious tradition in Great Britain) and another religious tradition.

Religious and non-religious attitudes

Group	Beliefs	Favoured methods
Catholics	• Artificial contraception goes against natural law and the purpose of marriage. • Sex should always be open to creating new life. • Family planning should only involve natural methods of contraception.	The rhythm method (avoiding sex at fertile times of the month).
Anglicans and Non-conformists	• Contraception is allowed for couples to develop their relationship before having children, to space out pregnancies, to avoid harming the mother's health, or to limit the number of children in a family so they can all be cared for. • In 1930 the Church of England approved artificial contraception used 'in the light of Christian principles'. • Christians who believe life begins at the moment of conception are against methods that prevent the fertilised egg from developing, as this is seen as causing an abortion and a form of murder.	A preference among some for contraception that prevents conception from taking place.
Sikhs	• There is no specific guidance about contraception in the Sikh scriptures. • Most Sikhs accept family planning that uses artificial contraception as morally responsible behaviour, but believe contraception should not be used to prevent having children altogether. • Some Sikhs disagree with the use of contraception as they believe sex is a God-given gift that should be used to have children. These Sikhs are against forms of contraception such as the morning after pill as it is seen as killing life.	A preference among some for contraception that prevents conception from taking place.
Non-religious people in British society	• There is widespread acceptance of artificial contraception to help family planning. • Many people think it is responsible to use contraception to prevent unwanted pregnancies, control population growth, and prevent the spread of sexually transmitted diseases.	Any type of contraception.

APPLY

A Give **two** religious beliefs about the use of contraception.

B 'The Christian Church should not take a view on family planning.'

Evaluate this argument against the statement.

"The Christian Church is right to have a view on family planning as it believes marriage is a sacred bond and children are a gift from God to a married couple. If people selfishly prevent having children, they are going against the purpose of marriage."

TIP

The word 'Give' means you can simply write down two different beliefs. There is no need to go into any detail.

5.4 Religious teachings about marriage

RECAP

Essential information:

- [ ] **Marriage** is a legal union between a man and a woman (or in some countries, including the UK, two people of the same sex) as partners in a relationship.
- [ ] Different religious and non-religious groups vary in their views about the purpose and nature of marriage, and whether **same-sex marriage** is acceptable.
- [ ] **Cohabitation** refers to a couple living together and having a sexual relationship without being married. It is common in Britain today, but not all Christians agree with it.

The purpose and nature of marriage

What is marriage?

Non-religious views

- A legal union between two people in a relationship.
- A serious, lifelong commitment made in public to another person.
- Provides legal and financial benefits.

Sikh views

- A religious act and an opportunity to become one spirit within two bodies.

> "They alone are called husband and wife, who have one light in two bodies."
> *Guru Granth Sahib 788*

- A union witnessed by God, shown by the presence of the Guru Granth Sahib at the ceremony.
- Sikhs are expected to marry; they believe it is the way God intended them to live.
- As long as both man and woman profess the Sikh faith, they may be married in the Anand Karaj ceremony.

Christian views

- A gift from God and part of the natural law.
- A covenant (agreement) before God in which the couple promises to live faithfully together till death.
- A unique relationship between a man and woman that allows for the possibility of creating new life.
- A spiritual bond of trust that reflects the love of Christ for the Church.
- The proper place to enjoy sex, raise children in a religious faith, and provide a secure, stable environment for family life.

> "The Church sees marriage between a man and woman as central to the stability and health of human society." *House of Bishops of the General Synod of the Church of England*

Cohabitation

- In Britain many couples cohabit before they get married, or without ever getting married.
- They may want to see if the relationship will work before getting married, or may not believe it is necessary to get married.
- **Catholic and Orthodox Churches** oppose cohabitation as they believe sex should only take place within marriage.
- Many **Anglican and Protestant Christians** accept that although marriage is best, people may cohabit in a faithful, loving and committed way without being married.
- **Sikhs** do not approve of cohabitation because they believe a sexual relationship should only take place within marriage.

TIP

Cohabitation is one example of people having contrasting beliefs within a religion. Remember that not all people who belong to the same religion have the same beliefs.

APPLY

A Here is a religious belief about the nature of marriage. **Develop** this by referring to the main religious tradition in the UK and another religious tradition.

"Marriage is God's gift to human beings."

B 'Marriage gives more stability to society than cohabitation.'

Evaluate this statement by giving arguments for and against it.

5.5 Divorce and remarriage

RECAP

Essential information:

- ☐ In the UK, **divorce** (legal ending of a marriage) is allowed after one year if a marriage cannot be saved. **Remarriage** is when someone marries again while their former husband or wife is still alive.
- ☐ Some religious groups oppose divorce and remarriage, while others may disapprove but accept they are sometimes the best way to reduce people's suffering.

Reasons for divorce

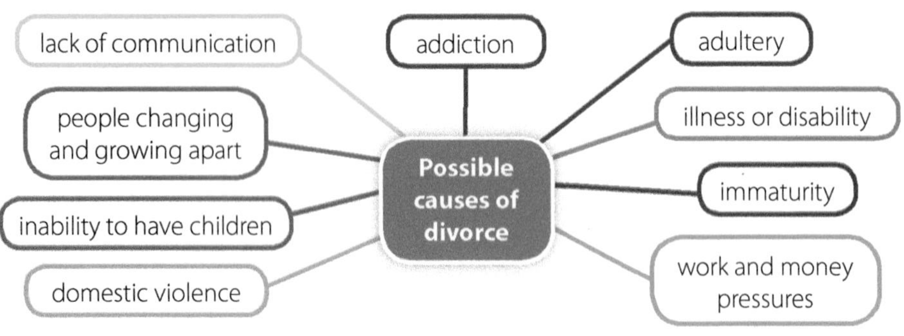

Christian and Sikh views on divorce and remarriage

Christian views	Sikh views
• Some Christians believe the **sanctity of the marriage vows** means they must be kept no matter what. • The Catholic Church teaches that **marriage is a sacrament** that is permanent, lifelong and cannot be dissolved by civil divorce. Catholics can separate but not remarry while their partner is still alive. • Other Christians believe that sometimes divorce is the **lesser of two evils** and should be allowed for compassionate reasons. • Protestant Churches (e.g. Methodists) accept civil divorce and allow remarriage in church under certain conditions. Divorced Anglicans can remarry in church with the bishop's permission. • These Christians think the Church should **reflect God's forgiveness** and allow couples a second chance for happiness. • Jesus taught that anyone who divorced and remarried was **committing adultery** (Mark 10:11–12). • But Matthew 5:32 says, 'If a man divorces his wife for any cause other than unchastity (unfaithfulness) he involves her in adultery'.	• Sikhs believe **marriage should be for life**. The Rehat Maryada teaches that, in general, no Sikh should marry for a second time if their spouse is alive. • A couple's family and community will try to help them mend their relationship. If this is not possible, **Sikhs reluctantly accept civil divorce**. • Grounds for divorce include adultery, desertion, insanity and change of religion. • The Rehat Maryada says that widows and widowers may remarry if they find someone suitable.  TIP Note that Mark 10:11–12 suggests divorce is always wrong, but Matthew 5:32 suggests it is acceptable in cases of unfaithfulness.

Christian and Sikh responses to couples having marriage problems

- Christian churches may offer counselling, prayer and sacraments to support the couple.
- They may refer the couple to outside agencies such as Relate and ACCORD.
- Christians may be encouraged to bring forgiveness and reconciliation into their marriage.
- Sikhs may be supported by their family and community to resolve their differences.

APPLY

 Explain **two** reasons why couples get divorced.

 'Divorce is never right.'

Write a paragraph to explain whether you agree or disagree with this statement. Then write a paragraph from another point of view.

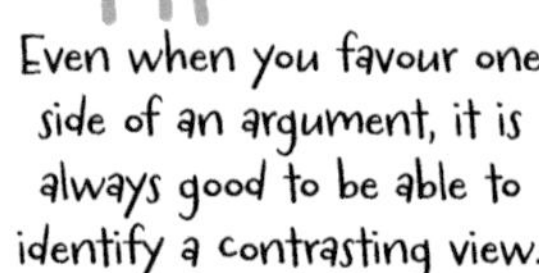

TIP
Even when you favour one side of an argument, it is always good to be able to identify a contrasting view.

5.6 Religious teachings about the nature of families

RECAP

Essential information:

- ☐ There are different types of **families** (people related by blood, marriage or adoption) in Britain, including nuclear families, extended families, and families with same-sex parents.
- ☐ In most families, parents and children are expected to fulfil certain roles and obligations to each other. For example, parents are expected to care for their children, and children are expected to obey their parents.

Types of family

Nuclear family	**Extended family**
 • Two parents and their children. • The most common family type in the West. • For Christians, it fulfils God's plan for a man and woman to be united together and increase in number (Genesis 1:28 and 2:24).	 • Includes grandparents and other relatives as well. • In Biblical times, many people lived in extended families for extra support. • Extended families are still common in Sikh communities.
Families with same-sex parents	**Polygamous families**
• When a same-sex couple raise children together. • Some Christians and many Sikhs disapprove of same-sex parents as they believe children should grow up with a male and female role model as parents. • Other Christians think it is more important for children to be in a secure and loving family regardless of the gender of their parents.	• When a person has two or more husbands or wives. • Illegal in the UK. • For Christians, it goes against God's plan for marriage to be between one woman and one man, and can lead to sexual immorality (1 Corinthians 7:2). • Sikh couples are expected to be monogamous (to only have one husband or wife).

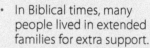

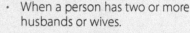

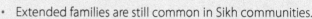

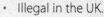

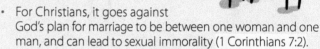

Role of parents and children

In Christianity and Sikhism, parents and children are expected to fulfil certain roles or duties.

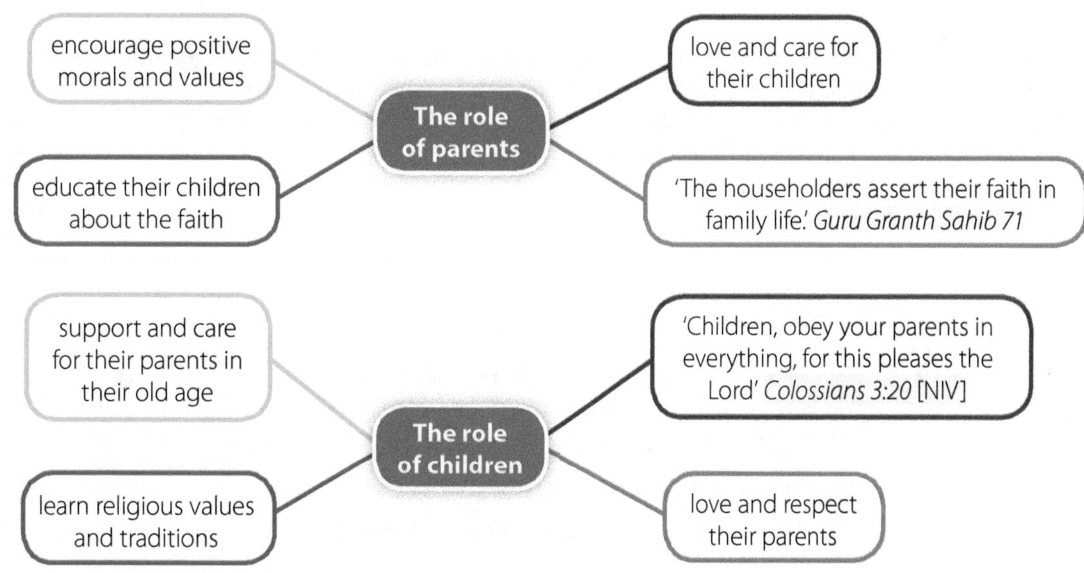

APPLY

A Give **two** religious beliefs about the nature of the family.

B 'It is more important for children to grow up in a loving, secure family than in a family with traditional heterosexual parents.'

List arguments for and against the statement. Include religious views.

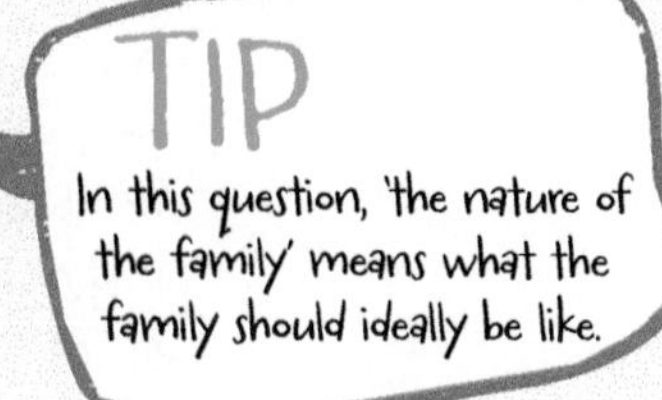

TIP
In this question, 'the nature of the family' means what the family should ideally be like.

5.7 Religious teachings about the purpose of families

RECAP

Essential information:

- ☐ The family is the main building block of society where **procreation** (bringing babies into the world) takes place.
- ☐ Happy, healthy families create **stability** for their members and society, helping to **protect children** and keep them safe from harm.
- ☐ For Christians and Sikhs, another purpose of the family is to **educate children in their faith** (bringing up children according to the religious beliefs of the parents).

The purpose of families

Procreation

- An important purpose of the family for many Sikhs and Christians (especially Catholics).
- In Sikh and Christian families, grown up children have a duty to care for elderly relatives.

> "Honour your father and mother."
> *Exodus 20:12* [NIV]

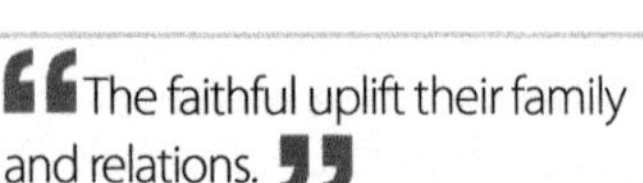

> "The faithful uplift their family and relations."
> *Guru Granth Sahib 3*

Stability and the protection of children

- Families provide secure, stable environments for children to grow up in.
- Families offer mutual support and protection for their members.

> "Children thrive, grow and develop within the love and safeguarding of a family. Within the family we care for the young, the old and those with caring needs."
> *The Church of England website*

Educating children in a faith

- **Christian** parents are expected to be good role models and teach their children Christian values.
- They should teach children about the faith and nurture their spiritual lives, which they may do through daily prayer.
- Some parents send their children to faith schools or groups run by their church for religious education.
- In **Sikhism**, the mother has a very strong role in educating her children in the faith.
- The Rehat Maryada states that, 'It is a Sikh's duty to get his children educated in Sikhism.'
- Sikh parents hope children will follow their example in practising the faith, such as rising early to meditate on the name of God.
- Amritdhari Sikhs initiate their children into wearing the five Ks.

APPLY

A Here are two religious beliefs about the role of parents in a religious family. **Develop** both points by explaining in more detail, adding an example, and referring to a relevant quotation from scripture or sacred writings.

"Sikhs are expected to educate their children in their faith."

"Christian parents bring their children up in their faith."

B **Evaluate** this argument to support the statement, 'Families should do more for their elderly relatives in Britain today.'

"When children leave home and move away from their parents, they may not realise the difficulties this can cause when their parents become old and infirm. If they live far away, they may not be able to do very much for their elderly relatives. Christians, though, believe they must 'Honour their father and mother' so they should still try to support elderly family members financially, take the time to chat online so they still feel part of the family, and keep their parents in their prayers."

TIP

The 'purpose of families' means what families are for, or why families are needed in society.

5.8 Religious attitudes to gender equality

RECAP

Essential information:

- [ ] **Gender equality** means that men and women should be given the same rights and opportunities as each other.
- [ ] Issues standing in the way of gender equality include **gender prejudice** (holding biased opinions about people based on their gender), **sexual stereotyping** (having a fixed idea or image of how men and women will behave), and **gender discrimination** (acting against someone on the basis of their gender).

Gender discrimination and prejudice

The Sex Discrimination Act in 1975 made gender discrimination illegal in the UK. Despite this, it still occurs today.

Views on gender prejudice and discrimination, and the roles of men and women, vary between people based on their religious and personal beliefs.

Examples of gender prejudice and discrimination

- in Catholicism, women are not allowed to be ordained as priests
- in traditional Indian culture, women are expected to do most of the household chores
- in the UK, some women are paid less than men for doing the same jobs
- in the UK, women make up roughly half the workforce, but men hold a higher proportion of senior positions

In the UK	Christian views	Sikh views
• In the past, men had more power and rights than women. • Traditional roles involved men working to support the family, and women caring for the home and raising children. • Today, most people in the UK are against gender prejudice and discrimination, but it still occurs. • The roles of men and women have become more flexible, and childcare is often shared more equally between parents. • Who takes on what role in a family may be decided by financial considerations or the different skills of the parents.  	• Christians believe all people are created equal in the image of God (Genesis 1:27). "There is neither Jew nor Gentile, neither slave nor free, nor is there male and female, for you are all one in Christ Jesus." *Galatians 3:28* [NIV] • The command to love one's neighbour means discrimination is wrong. • Jesus treated women with respect and welcomed them as disciples. • Some traditional Christians think husbands should rule over their wives, based on a literal interpretation of Genesis 3:16. • Most Christians today see marriage as an equal partnership.	• In Sikh teachings, women and men are equal before God, who is beyond gender. • Guru Nanak spoke up on behalf of women, describing them as vessels who carry the next generation and the culture and values of the community. "Without woman, there would be no one at all." *Guru Granth Sahib 473* • Sikh men are taught to treat all women with respect and consideration. • Equality is important in Sikh family life (e.g. both parents share chores), and in worship (e.g. both men and women can lead services). • Amritdhari Sikh women use the name 'Kaur' (meaning 'princess'), which frees them from taking their husband's name when marrying.

APPLY

A Give **two** religious reasons why gender equality is important.

B 'Men and women do not have equal rights.'

Develop this argument in support of the statement by explaining in more detail, adding an example and referring to a religious teaching or quotation.

"Despite the Sex Discrimination Act making gender discrimination illegal, women still get paid less than men for similar jobs. Often women face unfair questions at interviews. Looking at big businesses, there are still many more men than women in top positions. Even some religions expect women to stay at home and look after children."

Test the 1 mark question

1 Which **one** of the following is **not** a reason why some marriages fail?

A Domestic violence B Adultery C Addiction D Stability **[1 mark]**

2 Which **one** of the following describes a nuclear family?

A A couple, children and grandparents B A couple and their children

C A couple, children, aunts and uncles D A couple without children **[1 mark]**

Test the 2 mark question

3 Give **two** religious beliefs about gender equality. **[2 marks]**

1) ______

2) ______

4 Give **two** religious beliefs about cohabitation. **[2 marks]**

1) ______

2) ______

Test the 4 mark question

5 Explain **two** contrasting beliefs in contemporary British society about sex before marriage.
In your answer you should refer to the main religious tradition of Great Britain and one or more other religious traditions. **[4 marks]**

• **Explain one belief.**	*Some Christians accept that couples may have sex before getting married.*
• Develop your explanation with more detail/an example/reference to a religious teaching or quotation.	*They think that as long as the couple are faithful to each other, it is acceptable.*
• **Explain a second contrasting belief.**	*Sikhs consider marriage the only place for a sexual relationship and so sex before marriage is forbidden.*
• Develop your explanation with more detail/an example/reference to a religious teaching or quotation.	*The Rehat Maryada says that anyone who has sex before marriage is not a true Sikh.*

TIP
Remember the main religious tradition of Great Britain is Christianity.

6 Explain **two** contrasting religious beliefs about divorce.
In your answer you must refer to one or more religious traditions. **[4 marks]**

• **Explain one belief.**	
• Develop your explanation with more detail/an example/reference to a religious teaching or quotation.	
• **Explain a second contrasting belief.**	
• Develop your explanation with more detail/an example/reference to a religious teaching or quotation.	

TIP
You can answer this question from the perspective of two denominations of Christianity or from two religions.

7 Explain **two** contrasting religious beliefs about human sexuality.
In your answer you must refer to one or more religious traditions. **[4 marks]**

Test the 5 mark question

8 Explain **two** religious beliefs about the nature of marriage.

Refer to sacred writings or another source of religious belief and teaching in your answer. **[5 marks]**

● **Explain one belief.**	*Christians believe that marriage is a unique relationship between a man and a woman that involves their ability to create new life in the form of children.*
● Develop your explanation with more detail/an example.	*They believe that God planned marriage from the beginning of creation when he told the first parents to be fruitful and increase in number, meaning to have children.*
● **Explain a second belief.**	*Sikhs believe that marriage is the only appropriate place for a sexual relationship.*
● Develop your explanation with more detail/an example.	*They believe that premarital sex can lower a person's self-respect and respect for others.*
● Add a reference to sacred writings or another source of religious belief and teaching. If you prefer, you can add this reference to your first belief instead.	*Christian beliefs about marriage being a unique relationship between a man and a woman partly stem from this passage in the Bible: 'That is why a man leaves his father and mother and is united to his wife, and they become one flesh.' (Genesis 2:24)*

TIP

There is no need to put the exact reference in your answer as long as you quote or paraphrase the passage.

9 Explain **two** religious beliefs about the purpose of families.

Refer to sacred writings or another source of religious belief and teaching in your answer. **[5 marks]**

● **Explain one belief.**	
● Develop your explanation with more detail/an example.	
● **Explain a second belief.**	
● Develop your explanation with more detail/an example.	
● Add a reference to sacred writings or another source of religious belief and teaching. If you prefer, you can add this reference to your first belief instead.	

10 Explain **two** religious beliefs about the role of children in a religious family.

Refer to sacred writings or another source of religious belief and teaching in your answer. **[5 marks]**

Test the 12 mark question

11 'The love and care parents show in bringing up their children is all that matters; the sex of the parents is unimportant.'

Evaluate this statement. In your answer you:

- should give reasoned arguments in support of this statement
- should give reasoned arguments to support a different point of view
- should refer to religious arguments
- may refer to non-religious arguments
- should reach a justified conclusion.

[12 marks]
[+3 SPaG ma

REASONED ARGUMENTS SUPPORTING A DIFFERENT POINT OF VIEW ● **Explain why some people would support a different view.** ● Develop your explanation with more detail and examples. ● Refer to religious teaching. Use a quote or paraphrase or a religious authority. ● **Evaluate the arguments.** Is this a good argument or not? Explain why you think this.	*It is true that the love and care parents show in bringing up their children is the most important thing for a good family life. Without love and care, children would grow up deprived of stability and security. But the statement says 'the sex of the parents is unimportant' and that is where people may have different views.* *Some Christians disapprove of same-sex parents because they think God made people male and female so that they would 'be fruitful and increase in number' (Genesis 1:28). Same-sex couples cannot do this naturally.* *Many Sikhs think the ideal for children is to grow up with a male and female role model as parents, as the Gurus showed. They believe same-sex parents could not set good examples for their children.*
REASONED ARGUMENTS IN SUPPORT OF THE STATEMENT ● **Explain why some people would agree with the statement.** ● Develop your explanation with more detail and examples. ● Refer to religious teaching. Use a quote or paraphrase or a religious authority. ● **Evaluate the arguments.** Is this a good argument or not? Explain why you think this.	*On the other hand, many liberal Christians think that it is more important that children are raised in a secure and loving family regardless of the gender of their parents. There is nothing to say same-sex parents are not religious even if particular faiths disapprove of their relationships. Many can still bring their children up to love God or live spiritual and morally good lives.*
CONCLUSION ● **Give a justified conclusion.** ● Include your own opinion together with your own reasoning. ● **Include evaluation.** Explain why you think one viewpoint is stronger than the other or why they are equally strong. ● Do not just repeat arguments you have already used without explaining how they apply to your reasoned opinion/conclusion.	*In conclusion, I think that whether parents are good at bringing up children depends on the individuals and not on their gender. Some heterosexual couples spoil their children or even abuse them which does not show good parenting. Many children live in single-parent families so do not have the benefit of a male and female role model anyway. The most important thing any family should have is love, and this is at the heart of all religions.*

TIP

In this answer the stud begins by presenting different point of view followed by argument supporting the stateme It doesn't matter whic order the arguments appear in, as long as yo remember to include both sides.

TIP

Religious attitudes to sor issues vary within religion well as between religions, helps to say 'some Christi or 'liberal Christians' to sh you understand that not Christians share the same views.

12 'Marriage is the proper place to enjoy a sexual relationship.'

Evaluate this statement. In your answer you:

- should give reasoned arguments in support of this statement
- should give reasoned arguments to support a different point of view
- should refer to religious arguments
- may refer to non-religious arguments
- should reach a justified conclusion.

[12 marks]
[+3 SPaG marks]

REASONED ARGUMENTS IN SUPPORT OF THE STATEMENT ● **Explain why some people would agree with the statement.** ● Develop your explanation with more detail and examples. ● Refer to religious teaching. Use a quote or paraphrase or a religious authority. ● **Evaluate the arguments.** Is this a good argument or not? Explain why you think this.	
REASONED ARGUMENTS SUPPORTING A DIFFERENT VIEW ● **Explain why some people would support a different view.** ● Develop your explanation with more detail and examples. ● Refer to religious teaching. Use a quote or paraphrase or a religious authority. ● **Evaluate the arguments.** Is this a good argument or not? Explain why you think this.	
CONCLUSION ● **Give a justified conclusion.** ● Include your own opinion together with your own reasoning. ● **Include evaluation.** Explain why you think one viewpoint is stronger than the other or why they are equally strong. ● Do not just repeat arguments you have already used without explaining how they apply to your reasoned opinion/conclusion.	

TIP

When evaluating a statement like this one, do not simply list what different people think about the issues, for example 'Christians would agree that the best place to enjoy sex is in marriage. Sikhs think...' Remember to explain the reasons why they hold these opinions and to add an evaluation of how convincing you find these views to be.

13 'It is wrong for religious couples to use artificial contraception within marriage.'

Evaluate this statement. In your answer you:

- should give reasoned arguments in support of this statement
- should give reasoned arguments to support a different point of view
- should refer to religious arguments
- may refer to non-religious arguments
- should reach a justified conclusion.

[12 marks]
[+3 SPaG marks]

Check your answers using the mark scheme on pages 159–160. How did you do?
To feel more secure in the content you need to remember, re-read pages 80–87.
To remind yourself of what the examiner is looking for, go to pages 7–13.

6 Religion and life

6.1 The origins of the universe and the value of the world

RECAP

Essential information:

- ☐ The **Big Bang theory** suggests there was a massive expansion of space that set the creation of the universe in motion. This theory is accepted by most Christians and Sikhs.
- ☐ Christians also use the Genesis creation stories to explain the origins of the universe, which they believe was created by God.
- ☐ Sikhs likewise believe that God created the universe.

The Big Bang theory

The Big Bang theory is currently the leading scientific explanation for how the universe began. It suggests the following events happened to form the universe as we know it today:

The universe started with a tiny, dense collection of mass → A massive expansion of space took place and the condensed matter was flung in all directions → As the universe expanded and cooled, the matter became stars grouped into galaxies → The universe has continued to expand over billions of years to form the cosmos as we know it today

Religious views on the origins of the universe

Christian views	Sikh views
• Christians believe the universe was **designed and made by God** out of nothing. • The creation story in Genesis 1 says that God made the universe and all life in it in six days (see page 17). • Some **Fundamentalist Christians** believe the creation story describes exactly how the universe was created. Others believe the six days describe six longer periods of time. • **Liberal Christians** do not believe the Genesis creation story is a literal account of what actually happened. They believe the creation story is symbolic, with the main message being that God created the universe. They might look to science to understand how God did this.	• Sikhs believe the universe and everything in it was **made by Waheguru (God)**. • Before Waheguru's creation, he was all that existed. There was 'utter darkness' for a very long time (Guru Granth Sahib 1035). • Then God spoke and his word created everything. • This means the whole of creation belongs to God, who is in charge of all life. • The Guru Granth Sahib supports the idea of an expanding universe and so does not conflict with the Big Bang theory.

The value of the world

Christians view the earth as a priceless gift from God, loaned to humans as a result of his love. The beauty of the world can give a sense of **awe** and **wonder**, and devout respect for God's power of creation.

Sikhs value the world because God not only created everything in it, but he also rejoices in it and cares for it.

APPLY

A Give **two** contrasting beliefs about how the universe was created.

B 'The Big Bang theory explains how God created the universe.'

Develop one argument that agrees with this statement and one argument that disagrees with it.

RECAP

Essential information:

- ☐ Most Christians believe God gave humans the responsibility to care for the world and protect the environment. This idea is known as stewardship.
- ☐ Sikhs believe God has a divine presence in all of creation, so the world is sacred and should be treated with respect.
- ☐ The overuse of natural resources (particularly those that are non-renewable) is a problem in the world today.

The duty of humans to protect the world

Christian beliefs about how people should interact with the environment stem from the ideas of stewardship and dominion.

Stewardship means Christians have a duty to look after the environment on behalf of God. This is implied in Genesis 2:15, when God puts Adam into the Garden of Eden to 'work it and take care of it'.

- This responsibility has been passed down to the rest of humanity, which means it is the role of all humans to look after the world for God. If they use the world wrongly, they are destroying what belongs to God.
- In return for caring for the world, humans may use it to sustain life.

> "Rule over the fish in the sea and the birds in the sky and over every living creature that moves on the ground."
>
> *Genesis 1:28* [NIV]

Genesis 1:28 teaches that God gave humans **dominion** (power and authority) over the world. A minority of Christians interpret this as meaning that humans can do whatever they want with the world. But most Christians want to care for the world as God's stewards.

For **Sikhs**, the Guru Granth Sahib explains that the world is priceless because it was created by God, who watches over his creation with care and kindness.

Sikhs believe there is a divine spark in every living thing, so the whole of nature should be treated with respect. Humans have been given the task of stewardship and living in harmony with the environment.

Sikhs do not believe that humans have dominion over nature or are superior to it.

> "The Lord infused His Light into the dust and created the world, the universe. The sky, the earth, the trees and the water – all are the Creation of the Lord."
>
> *Guru Granth Sahib 723*

The use of natural resources

- **Natural resources** are materials found in nature (such as oil and trees) that can be used by people to make more complex products.
- Some natural resources (such as oil and gas) are non-renewable, which means they will eventually run out. Once they do, human society may have to adapt considerably in order to live without them.
- Reducing the use of natural resources, recycling more, using renewable energy sources (which do not run out), and helping to protect the environment are all ways that people can help to preserve the world for future generations.

APPLY

A **Explain** why it is important to develop renewable energy sources.

B 'Stewardship is more likely to encourage people to look after the earth than dominion.'

Give **two** arguments that agree with this statement and **develop** each one.

TIP
Remember that 'stewardship' and 'dominion' have specific religious meanings in the context of Christianity.

6.3 Pollution

RECAP

Essential information:

- [ ] The overuse of non-renewable resources, pollution and deforestation are major threats to life on earth.
- [ ] Christians and Sikhs show their concern by taking action to help to protect the earth.

Abuse of the environment

Many Christians and Sikhs are concerned that human practices such as pollution and deforestation are contributing to an environmental crisis, and have the potential to threaten the stability of the environment for future generations.

Overuse of natural resources	Pollution	Deforestation
Oil, gas, copper, zinc and many rare minerals are being used up quickly. Future generations will have fewer resources to use.	Pollution of the air, sea, rivers and land is putting animal and human life at risk, for example by killing marine life or causing acid rain.	Clearing areas of forest for housing and agriculture, and cutting down trees for wood, is contributing to climate change.

Religious views about pollution

Christians want to reduce pollution. They might base their views on the following beliefs and teachings:

- The world is on loan to humans, who have been given the responsibility by God to look after it (Genesis 1:28).
- Pollution is not loving towards others – Jesus teaches Christians to 'love your neighbour' (Luke 10:27).

> "The earth is the Lord's and everything in it." *Psalms 24:1* [NIV]

Sikhs believe that people who are conscious of God and his creation are motivated to look after the environment. As God is in all of creation, seeking to live in harmony with it and promote **sustainable development** is very important.

Examples of action that has been taken by Christians or Sikhs to help tackle pollution include the following:

- **Pope Francis has called on everyone to take action** to help protect the environment.
- In his open letter, 'On the Care of Our Common Home', he stressed the need to reduce pollution, use renewable energy and recycle more.

- **Some Christian groups work in their local communities** to clean up the environment, for example by litter-picking.
- Religious believers might also **join secular environmental organisations** such as Greenpeace and Friends of the Earth, which aim to tackle pollution on a wider scale.

- **EcoSikh** is a charity that seeks to encourage ecological action and awareness among the Sikh community.
- The charity encourages gurdwaras in India to become more sustainable.
- It also promotes Sikh Environment Day on 14 March.

APPLY

A Explain **two** religious beliefs about why polluting the earth is wrong.

B 'Individual people cannot do anything to solve the global problem of pollution.'

Improve this argument against the statement by **developing** the points made, for example by adding examples and referring to religious teachings.

"Individual people can help to clean up their local environment, and if everyone does this then an impact will be felt worldwide. Also, individual people can donate to charities that have the resources to tackle pollution on a global scale."

6.4 The use and abuse of animals

RECAP

Essential information:

- ☐ Many Christians believe animals should be treated kindly, but humans are more important.
- ☐ Sikhs believe it is important to treat animals well because they have souls and are part of God's creation.

Religious attitudes towards animals

Christians believe animals were created by God for humans to use and care for. Many believe humans are more important than animals as they were created in the image of God, but animals should still be treated kindly.

Sikhs believe that animals have souls. They are part of the cycle of birth, death and rebirth that all souls go through before they become one with God. All animals are believed to be sentient, feeling beings and should be treated with compassion and respect.

You might be asked to compare beliefs on animal experimentation between Christianity (the main religious tradition in Great Britain) and another religious tradition.

Animal experimentation

Scientists use animals to test new products such as cosmetics, medicines and food, to make sure they are safe for human use.

Christian views	Sikh views
• Most Christians believe that if testing is proved to be necessary, and the welfare of the animals is considered, it is justified to ensure human safety. • Many believe animals can be used to help save human lives.	• Most Sikhs oppose animal experimentation unless it is vital for medical research and is done as humanely as possible. • Sikhs believe taking part in animal experimentation for non-essential reasons (like testing cosmetics) could negatively affect a person's karma.

The use of animals for food

Vegetarians do not eat meat or fish, while **vegans** also do not eat animals or food produced by animals (such as eggs). Vegans also try not to use products that have caused harm to animals (such as leather).

Christian views	Sikh views
• Christianity has no rules about eating meat. • Romans 14:3 says Christians should be sensitive to the beliefs of others about what they wish to eat. • Most Christians eat meat. They believe God gave humans animals to use for food. “Everything that lives and moves about will be food for you.” *Genesis 9:3* [NIV] • Some vegetarians and vegans point out that if crops were grown on land currently used to raise animals for meat, there would be much more food to go round, and this would please God.	• Most Sikhs are vegetarian and do not eat meat, fish or eggs. • The Guru Granth Sahib forbids killing living beings. • Vegetarian food is always served in the langar and at Sikh religious events. “Show kindness and mercy to all beings.” *Guru Granth Sahib 508*

APPLY

A Explain **two** religious reasons why some people do not eat meat.

B 'Experimenting on animals is wrong because it is cruel.'

Develop this point of view and elaborate it with religious teachings. Make sure to explain how the teachings are relevant to the argument.

6.5 The origins of human life

RECAP

Essential information:

- [ ] **The theory of evolution** is the theory that higher forms of life have gradually developed (evolved) from lower ones.
- [ ] Many Christians think it is possible to believe both the creation stories in Genesis and the theory of evolution.
- [ ] Sikhs believe that God oversees the natural process of evolution, and that life came about due to God's will.

The theory of evolution

In 1859, in a book called *On the Origin of Species by Means of Natural Selection*, Charles Darwin put forward the theory of evolution. Darwin suggested that as the earth cooled, conditions became right to support life. Simple organisms then evolved over many years into other species:

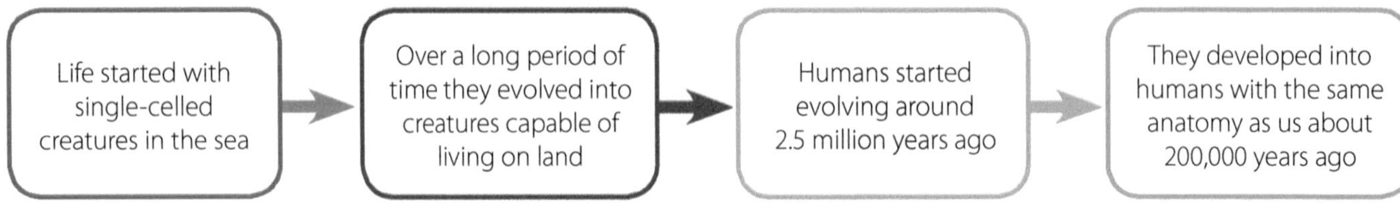

Life started with single-celled creatures in the sea
Over a long period of time they evolved into creatures capable of living on land
Humans started evolving around 2.5 million years ago
They developed into humans with the same anatomy as us about 200,000 years ago

Creatures were able to change or **adapt** into their environment and thrived. This is called survival of the fittest.

Christian beliefs about the origins of life

- Genesis 1 says that **God created all life**, with human life being created last.
- Genesis 2 tells how **God created the first man**, Adam, from the soil and breathed life into him.
- Some time later, while Adam was asleep, God took one of his ribs and used it to **create a woman**, Eve. Eve was created to help Adam, and to live in a close relationship with him and with God.

Many Christians do not believe this to be literally true (although some do). Instead they interpret the story as showing that humans are special to God because they were created in his image.

Fundamentalist Christians do not believe in the theory of evolution. They believe God created each species separately. Some believe life was created exactly as described in Genesis 1 and 2.

The **majority of Christians** accept the theory of evolution but believe that God is the creator: he started the process and evolution explains how life developed afterwards.

Sikh views on the origins of life

- The question of how and when humans came into existence is not an important question for Sikhs.
- More important is the belief that **God created every living thing**.
- Sikhs believe a person's soul has undergone a **long cycle of birth, death and rebirth**, evolving from more primitive forms of life until it received the gift of a human form.

> "Without God, there is nothing at all."
> *Guru Granth Sahib 485*

APPLY

A. Explain **one** scientific teaching and **one** religious teaching about the origins of life.

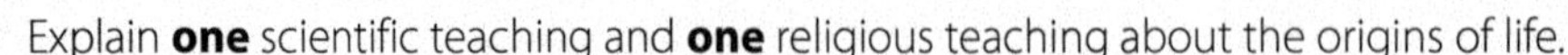

B. Choose one of the theories about the origin of life and give your opinion on whether you agree with it. Write **two developed reasons** to support your opinion.

RECAP

Essential information:

- [ ] Abortion is legal in the UK provided doctors agree it meets certain criteria.
- [ ] Christians generally oppose abortion, although some agree with it in certain situations (such as if the child would have a very poor quality of life).
- [ ] Sikhs are against abortion as it interferes with God's creative work. They believe life is a gift from God and begins at conception.

You might be asked to compare beliefs on abortion between Christianity (the main religious tradition in Great Britain) and another religious tradition.

Abortion in the UK

- **Abortion** is the deliberate removal of a foetus from the womb in order to end a pregnancy.
- In the UK, an abortion can take place in a licensed clinic if two doctors agree there is a risk to the physical or mental health of the mother, the baby, or existing children in the family.
- Abortion can only happen during the first 24 weeks of pregnancy unless the mother's life is in danger or the foetus is severely deformed. In these cases there is no time limit.

Christian and Sikh attitudes towards abortion

Christian views	Sikh views
• Christians believe in the **sanctity of life**. This means human life is sacred as it is made in the image of God. All human life should be valued and respected. • Many Christians who believe **life begins at the moment of conception** think abortion is wrong, as it is taking away life that is given by God. • However, some Christians think **abortion is sometimes acceptable**, e.g. if the pregnancy is the result of rape or the child would have a very poor quality of life.	• Sikhism teaches that life **begins at conception** and ending it deliberately is a sin. • An abortion is **only acceptable** if the **mother's life is at risk** or the pregnancy was the **result of rape**. • Despite these teachings, aborting female embryos has been a widespread practice in many Indian communities (including the Punjabi Sikh community) due to financial concerns.  The Lord infused His Light into you, and then you came into the world. ” *Guru Granth Sahib 921*

Further arguments for and against abortion

Religious and non-religious people might also be pro-choice (for abortion) or pro-life (against abortion) for the following reasons:

For	Against
• Pro-choice groups believe the mother's life is more important. • The mother has to carry the baby, give birth to it and bring it up, so she should have the right to choose whether to continue with the pregnancy. • Life doesn't start until birth (or from the point when the foetus can survive outside the womb), so abortion does not involve killing. • It is cruel to allow a severely disabled child to be born.	• Pro-life groups argue that as life begins at conception, abortion is a form of murder. • It is possible for disabled children to enjoy a good quality of life, so they should be allowed to live. • Unwanted children can be adopted into families that will care for them. • Those who choose abortion can suffer from depression and guilt afterwards.

APPLY

A Explain **two** religious teachings that may be used to argue against abortion.

B 'If the child's quality of life is not going to be good, abortion is the best option.'

Write a developed argument to support this statement, and a developed argument to support a different point of view.

TIP

The commandment 'do not kill' is often used when discussing Christian views on abortion. If you use it as part of an answer, you should explain it is only relevant if someone believes that life begins at conception or some point before an abortion happens.

6.7 Euthanasia

RECAP

Essential information:

- ☐ **Euthanasia** is the painless killing of a patient who is suffering from an incurable and painful illness, or who is in an irreversible coma.
- ☐ Christians generally oppose euthanasia, although some may agree with it when it seems to be the most loving and compassionate action to take.
- ☐ Sikhs oppose euthanasia because they believe life is sacred and God should decide when to end it.

You might be asked to compare beliefs on euthanasia between Christianity (the main religious tradition in Great Britain) and another religious tradition.

What is euthanasia?

Euthanasia involves taking deliberate steps to end a person's life, for example by giving them life-ending medication. **This is illegal in the UK**. There are three different types of euthanasia:

Voluntary: the ill person asks for their life to be ended because they don't want to live any more

Involuntary: the person is capable of expressing a choice but is not given the opportunity to do so

Non-voluntary: the person is unable to express a choice, for example a baby or a person in a coma

- Doctors can decide to withhold treatment if it is in the patient's best interests, for example by not resuscitating a person after a heart attack or by withdrawing food. This would not be considered euthanasia as it is allowing death to take place rather than actively ending a life.
- Some countries in Europe allow euthanasia under certain strict criteria.

Christian and Sikh attitudes towards euthanasia

Christian views	Sikh views
• Many Christians believe euthanasia is a form of murder and **interferes with God's plan** for a person's life. • They believe that euthanasia is **against the sanctity of life,** and **only God has the right to take away life**. • They might argue that if euthanasia were legal, the very old **could feel pressure to end their lives** in order not to burden their family. • They might argue that **suffering brings people closer to God** and helps them to understand Jesus' suffering. • The Salvation Army has said that euthanasia and assisted suicide 'undermine human dignity and are morally wrong'. • Some Christians support euthanasia when it seems the **most loving thing to do**. • They may argue that as **God gave people free will** they should be able to choose when to end their lives.	• Sikhism teaches that no person has the right to decide to end a life prematurely because the **timing of birth and death is decided by God**. • A person may be suffering as a result of bad actions in this life or previous lives. **Escaping this suffering through euthanasia would mean suffering in the next life**. • Sikhs believe instead they should **pray for courage and strength** to endure suffering. • **Caring for others is a duty and part of sewa;** the Gurus started hospitals for the sick and dying so they could be cared for.

APPLY

A **Explain** one argument in favour of euthanasia. Then explain a Christian or Sikh teaching that opposes euthanasia.

B 'Euthanasia should be allowed in the UK.'

Explain your opinion and include your reasoning. **Refer to religious teachings** as part of your answer.

TIP

You can use the Christian teaching 'love your neighbour' in a discussion of euthanasia. However, to use it most effectively, consider to whom an action is most loving and to whom it may not be loving.

6.8 Death and the afterlife

RECAP

Essential information:

- [ ] Christians and Sikhs both believe death is not the end.
- [ ] Many Christians believe that after death they are judged by God and spend eternity in heaven or hell.
- [ ] Sikhs believe in reincarnation and that after death they are reborn. Rebirths then continue until they achieve union with God.

Christian beliefs about death and the afterlife

Christians believe Jesus' resurrection is evidence for an afterlife. Many Christians believe that after death, they are **judged by God** and will either be **eternally with God** (heaven) or **eternally without God** (hell). The desire to be close to God motivates them to **have faith in Jesus** and **follow his teachings**.

Further beliefs about the afterlife include the following:

- Catholics believe in a middle stage called purgatory, where souls are purified to allow them into heaven.
- Some Christians believe judgement happens as soon as a person dies.
- Others believe Jesus will return on a future Day of Judgement when all souls will be judged.
- Some believe people will be in heaven in their physical bodies, while others believe it is just their souls that enter heaven.
- Some believe that God, who is the source of all good, would not condemn people to hell and that all go to heaven. Others believe that all who go to hell deserve their fate.

> "For God so loved the world that he gave his one and only Son, that **whoever believes in him shall not perish but have eternal life.**"
>
> *John 3:16* [NIV]

TIP

Christian beliefs about the afterlife are discussed in more detail on pages 20–21.

Sikh beliefs about death and the afterlife

- Sikhs believe the soul is **immortal** and goes through numerous life forms until it is purified to become one again with God.
- After death, the soul goes from one body to the next (**reincarnation**); this happens many times as part of the cycle of samsara (the cycle of birth, death and rebirth).
- **Good merit or karma** brings about a better spiritual understanding and a **closer relationship with God**. This can be achieved by meditating on God and purifying the soul.
- **When a righteous person dies**, they may enter into union with God and **escape the samsara cycle**.
- Failing to worship God and purify the soul results in **more reincarnations**.

> "The blind and ignorant fools do not serve the True Guru; how will they find the gate of salvation? **They die and die, over and over again, only to be reborn, over and over again.**"
>
> *Guru Granth Sahib 115*

TIP

For more on how a person's karma affects their future rebirth, see page 51.

APPLY

A Explain **two** religious teachings about the afterlife.

B 'Beliefs about the afterlife should motivate religious believers to spend their lives helping others.'

By referring to two different religions, **develop** an argument to support this statement. Then develop an argument which supports a different point of view.

Test the 1 mark question

1 Which **one** of the following is the meaning of the term euthanasia?

A A type of abortion
B A method of animal testing
C A painless death
D A scientific view about the origin of the earth **[1 mark]**

2 Which **one** of the following is the leading scientific theory for how life on earth developed?

A Sustainable development
B The sanctity of life
C The cycle of samsara
D The theory of evolution **[1 mark]**

Test the 2 mark question

3 Give **two** religious reasons for reducing pollution. **[2 marks]**

1) ____________________

2) ____________________

4 Give **two** religious beliefs about the treatment of animals. **[2 marks]**

1) ____________________

2) ____________________

TIP

Here the beliefs are 'contrasting' because one is against euthanasia and one is for euthanasia. But you could also give two beliefs that are both for or against euthanasia, but for different reasons. If the reasons are different enough, this would still count as giving 'contrasting' beliefs.

Test the 4 mark question

5 Explain **two** contrasting beliefs in contemporary British society about euthanasia.
In your answer you should refer to the main religious tradition of Great Britain and one or more other religious traditions.

• **Explain one belief.**	*Some Christians agree with euthanasia as they believe it may be the most compassionate action.*
• Develop your explanation with more detail/an example/reference to a religious teaching or quotation.	*They might argue that this is a demonstration of Jesus' teaching to love your neighbour.*
• **Explain a second contrasting belief.**	*Sikhs oppose euthanasia because they believe God should decide when someone dies.*
• Develop your explanation with more detail/an example/reference to a religious teaching or quotation.	*Sikhs believe instead someone who is suffering should pray for the strength to keep going.*

6 Explain **two** contrasting religious beliefs about animal experimentation. In your answer, you must refer to one or more religious traditions. **[4 marks]**

• **Explain one belief.**	
• Develop your explanation with more detail/an example/reference to a religious teaching or quotation.	
• **Explain a second contrasting belief.**	
• Develop your explanation with more detail/an example/reference to a religious teaching or quotation.	

7 Explain **two** similar religious beliefs about the value of the world.

In your answer, you must refer to one or more religious traditions. **[4 marks]**

Test the 5 mark question

8 Explain **two** religious beliefs about what happens when a person dies.

Refer to sacred writings or another source of religious belief and teaching in your answer. **[5 marks]**

• **Explain one belief.**	*Christians believe in the resurrection of the dead.*
• Develop your explanation with more detail/an example.	*Christians believe Jesus' resurrection proved there is life after death because he came back to life after being crucified, so those who believe in him can also have eternal life in heaven.*
• **Explain a second belief.**	*Sikhs believe that when people die they will be reborn into a new body.*
• Develop your explanation with more detail/an example.	*The kind of rebirth that someone can expect depends upon their karma and whether they have purified their soul.*
• Add a reference to sacred writings or another source of religious belief and teaching. If you prefer, you can add this reference to your first belief instead.	*The Christian belief in resurrection is supported by John 11 in the Bible: 'Jesus said to her, "I am the resurrection and the life. He who believes in me will live, even though he dies; and whoever lives and believes in me will never die"' (John 11:25–26).*

TIP

There is no need to include the exact Bible reference and doing so will not earn you any additional marks.

9 Explain **two** religious beliefs about the duty of human beings to protect the earth.

Refer to sacred writings or another source of religious belief and teaching in your answer. **[5 marks]**

• **Explain one belief.**	
• Develop your explanation with more detail/an example.	
• **Explain a second belief.**	
• Develop your explanation with more detail/an example.	
• Add a reference to sacred writings or another source of religious belief and teaching. If you prefer, you can add this reference to your first belief instead.	

10 Explain **two** religious beliefs about the origins of the universe.

Refer to sacred writings or another source of religious belief and teaching in your answer. **[5 marks]**

Test the 12 mark question

11 'Religious believers should not eat meat.'

Evaluate this statement. In your answer you:

- should give reasoned arguments in support of this statement
- should give reasoned arguments to support a different point of view
- should refer to religious arguments
- may refer to non-religious arguments
- should reach a justified conclusion.

[12 marks]
[+3 SPaG ma

REASONED ARGUMENTS IN SUPPORT OF THE STATEMENT ● **Explain why some people would agree with the statement.** ● Develop your explanation with more detail and examples. ● Refer to religious teaching. Use a quote or paraphrase or a religious authority. ● **Evaluate the arguments.** Is this a good argument or not? Explain why you think this.	*Eating meat involves the killing of animals to provide the meat. This is seen by many religious believers as cruel and unnecessary, and they are quite happy to be vegetarians. For example, Sikhs agree with this statement as they believe that all creation has a divine presence and each animal has a soul. The Guru Granth Sahib forbids killing living things.* *This is why most Sikhs are vegetarian and all the food served in the langar is vegetarian.* *Some people might argue that Christians should not eat meat because it means that overall there is less food to go round (as animals take up more resources and land to farm than crops), which contributes to poverty and suffering that is not pleasing to God.*
REASONED ARGUMENTS SUPPORTING A DIFFERENT VIEW ● **Explain why some people would support a different view.** ● Develop your explanation with more detail and examples. ● Refer to religious teaching. Use a quote or paraphrase or a religious authority. ● **Evaluate the arguments.** Is this a good argument or not? Explain why you think this.	*Most Christians do eat meat because they believe it is a good source of protein or they like the taste of it. Although they believe animals should not be treated cruelly, they believe they were created by God for human use. In Genesis it says that after the flood, God told Noah that animals could be used for food. Also in the New Testament it implies that Jesus ate fish and saw nothing wrong with fishing as an occupation. Although some Christians choose to be vegetarian, the majority believe it is acceptable to eat meat as humans have been given the power to rule over animals (Genesis 1:28).*
CONCLUSION ● **Give a justified conclusion.** ● Include your own opinion together with your own reasoning. ● **Include evaluation.** Explain why you think one viewpoint is stronger than the other or why they are equally strong. ● Do not just repeat arguments you have already used without explaining how they apply to your reasoned opinion/conclusion.	*So there is a difference of opinion concerning whether it is right to eat meat. Although I can see why some people prefer not to kill animals, I believe meat is important for a balanced diet. Also many farmers would lose their livelihoods if people stopped eating meat. In my opinion it would be unfair on religious believers if they were prevented from enjoying meat. I can see that if your religion opposes eating meat then you would need to keep the rules of your faith. However, within Christianity this does not apply as God expressly gave Noah permission to eat meat.*

TIP
The Sikh content above is an excellent chain of reasoning. It starts with an introductory statement, leading to an opinion, followed by development of the point that refers to religious teachings.

TIP
This is a good conclusion because it includes reference to the arguments already made and supports them with more reasoning, not just the same as before.

12 'Abortion should not be allowed.'

Evaluate this statement. In your answer you:

- should give reasoned arguments in support of this statement
- should give reasoned arguments to support a different point of view
- should refer to religious arguments
- may refer to non-religious arguments
- should reach a justified conclusion.

[12 marks]
[+3 SPaG marks]

REASONED ARGUMENTS IN SUPPORT OF THE STATEMENT • **Explain why some people would agree with the statement.** • Develop your explanation with more detail and examples. • Refer to religious teaching. Use a quote or paraphrase or a religious authority. • **Evaluate the arguments.** Is this a good argument or not? Explain why you think this.	
REASONED ARGUMENTS SUPPORTING A DIFFERENT VIEW • **Explain why some people would support a different view.** • Develop your explanation with more detail and examples. • Refer to religious teaching. Use a quote or paraphrase or a religious authority. • **Evaluate the arguments.** Is this a good argument or not? Explain why you think this.	
CONCLUSION • **Give a justified conclusion.** • Include your own opinion together with your own reasoning. • **Include evaluation.** Explain why you think one viewpoint is stronger than the other or why they are equally strong. • Do not just repeat arguments you have already used without explaining how they apply to your reasoned opinion/ conclusion.	

13 'Humans should use the earth's resources however they wish.'

Evaluate this statement. In your answer you:

- should give reasoned arguments in support of this statement
- should give reasoned arguments to support a different point of view
- should refer to religious arguments
- may refer to non-religious arguments
- should reach a justified conclusion.

[12 marks]
[+3 SPaG marks]

Check your answers using the mark scheme on pages 160–161. How did you do?
To feel more secure in the content you need to remember, re-read pages 92–99.
To remind yourself of what the examiner is looking for, go to pages 7–13.

7 The existence of God and revelation

7.1 The Design argument

RECAP

Essential information:

- ☐ The **Design argument** says that because everything in the universe is so intricately made, it must have been created by God. Therefore God exists.
- ☐ Over the centuries, there have been several different ways of illustrating the Design argument in order to explain it.
- ☐ There are a number of objections to this argument.

Did God create the universe?

- **Christians** believe that God created the universe.
- Because everything in the universe is so intricate and complex, God must have designed it.
- Genesis 1 supports this view.

Atheists, who don't believe in God, believe the life on earth was not created, but instead evolved naturally.

Agnostics believe there is not enough evidence that God exists or that he created the universe.

- **Sikhs** believe that God created everything.
- The precision, order and complexity in the world could not have happened by chance; it must be the result of an intelligent designer (God).
- Guru Nanak taught that creation and its creator are inseparable, just as the ocean is made of individual drops of water. God designed and is present in everything.

Different versions of the Design argument

William Paley	Isaac Newton	Thomas Aquinas	F. R. Tennant
 Paley argued that the workings of a watch are so intricate they must have been designed by a watchmaker. Something so complex cannot be produced by chance. Similarly, the universe is so complex and intricate that it must have been designed by God.	 Newton argued that the human thumb, which permits delicate movement such as tying shoelaces, must have been designed, and that such design could only be achieved by God.	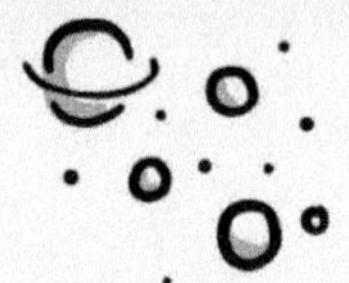 Aquinas argued that only an intelligent being could keep everything in the universe in regular order. The fact that the planets rotate in the solar system without colliding is because of God.	Tennant put forward the idea that as everything is just right for humans to develop, it must have been designed. He referred to the strength of gravity being absolutely right, and the force and speed of the explosion caused by the Big Bang being perfect to sustain life.

Objections to the Design argument

- Natural selection happens by chance. Species 'design' themselves through the process of evolution, not through a designer God.
- If God is good, and he designed the universe, why is there so much suffering?
- The order in the universe, which is necessary to support life, makes it look as though it is designed. In reality, the order and structure in nature is imposed by humans to help explain it.

APPLY

A Choose **two** arguments in favour of the Design argument and summarise their main points.

B 'The Design argument proves that God exists.'

Write two developed arguments in response to this statement, one in agreement and one against.

TIP

You should learn the strengths and weaknesses of the Design argument and be prepared to argue the case for each, regardless of what you believe.

7.2 The First Cause argument

RECAP

Essential information:

- [ ] The **First Cause argument** states there has to be an uncaused cause that made everything else happen.
- [ ] Thomas Aquinas put forward an argument which he said proved the existence of God.
- [ ] There are a number of objections to this argument.

TIP

This five-point chain of reasoning gives a simple overview of the First Cause argument. Try to remember it so you can use it to explain the First Cause argument in your exam.

What is the First Cause argument?

Some Christians argue in favour of the First Cause argument. Their chain of reasoning runs like this:

Everything that exists or begins to exist must have a cause → As the universe exists and had a beginning, it too must have a cause → There must be something existing with no cause, which is eternal, to cause everything else to exist → The eternal first cause can only be God → This means God must exist

- The key assumption in the First Cause argument is that the **universe had a starting point**.
- Many scientists believe the universe started with the Big Bang.
- Christians, Sikhs and other theists would argue that God caused the Big Bang.
- They would argue that if the universe was eternal, there would be no adequate explanation for its existence, so it must have had a cause.

Thomas Aquinas' First Cause argument

Aquinas argued that everything in the universe is caused to exist. Nothing can become something by itself, and nothing equals nothing and remains nothing unless something is added. As nothing can cause itself to exist, either there is:

- an infinite chain of effects preceded by causes, or
- a first cause that is itself uncaused by anything else (God).

> "The entire creation came from God."
> *Guru Granth Sahib 294*

> "In the beginning, God created the heavens and the earth."
> *Genesis 1:1* [NIV]

Objections to the First Cause argument

- If everything that exists has a cause, who or what caused God?
- If God is eternal then the universe could be eternal as well.
- The idea that everything has a cause does not necessarily mean the universe has to have a cause as well (or that the cause must be God).
- The Big Bang was a random event and had nothing to do with God.
- Religious creation stories about how God brought the universe into being, such as the ones in Genesis, are myths. The truth they tell is spiritual, not literal.

APPLY

A Give **two** points that contribute to the First Cause argument.

B 'The First Cause argument proves that God exists.'

Write a developed argument to oppose this statement.

7.3 The argument from miracles

RECAP

Essential information:

- ☐ **Miracles** are seemingly impossible events that cannot be explained by natural or scientific laws, and are thought by Christians to be the action of God.
- ☐ Some Christians and Sikhs think miracles prove God's existence. They show God's love and help to strengthen a believer's faith.
- ☐ Atheists and agnostics argue that miracles may be lucky coincidences or have scientific explanations that we don't yet know about.

You might be asked to compare beliefs on miracles between Christianity (the main religious tradition in Great Britain) and another religious tradition.

Different attitudes to miracles

Christians	Atheists and agnostics	Sikhs
• If there is no scientific explanation for an event, it must be caused by something outside nature, i.e. God. • The fact that some people convert to Christianity after experiencing a miracle is proof of God's existence. • 69 healing miracles have officially been recognised by the Catholic Church as taking place at Lourdes (a pilgrimage site in France). • Jesus performed miracles.	• Miracles are no more than lucky coincidences. • They may have scientific explanations we don't yet know about. • Some miracles are deliberately made up for fame or money. • Miracle healings may be the result of mind over matter or misdiagnosis.	• According to Sikh tradition, the Gurus experienced miracles. E.g. Guru Nanak disappeared in the river Bain for three days. • Guru Nanak said only God could perform miracles. • Sikhs believe supernatural powers might be possible but should not be used selfishly or to convert people to a religion. Guru Arjan and Guru Tegh Bahadur were put to death for refusing to perform miracles.

Examples of miracles

Here are three examples of religious miracles, one from Christianity and two from Sikhism:

- In 1902, the French woman Marie Bailly was diagnosed with tubercular peritonitis, which made her abdomen swell and meant she couldn't eat.
- She asked to visit Lourdes, but on arrival was so ill she had to be taken to hospital, where doctors told her she was dying.
- She returned to Lourdes, where holy water was poured on her abdomen and she prayed to Mary.
- She returned to good health.

- Guru Nanak was sitting under a reetha tree and was asked for some food. The fruit of the reetha or soapnut tree is normally bitter. However, when Guru Nanak told his friend Mardana to pick the fruit, it was sweet. The fruit was only sweet on the side on which they were sitting – it remained bitter on the other side of the tree.
- Guru Nanak and his companions were thirsty and asked a farmer who owned a well at the top of the hill for some water. The farmer refused. Guru Nanak dug into the ground at the bottom of the hill and miraculously found a spring. The farmer was furious and pushed a huge boulder down the hill. The Guru stretched out his hand and miraculously stopped the boulder.

TIP

Memorise at least one example of a miracle, as you may be required to write about it in your exam.

APPLY

A **Explain** how some theists use miracles to prove their faith in God.

B Finish the argument below. Then **write a reasoned argument** to express a different point of view.

"When atheists argue against miracles I believe they are right because..."

7.4 Further arguments against the existence of God

RECAP

Essential information:

- [ ] Some people use science and the existence of **evil** (the opposite of good) and **suffering** (when people have to live with unpleasant conditions) to question the existence of God.
- [ ] They argue that God was invented to explain what science couldn't, and a good and all-powerful God would not create a world with evil and suffering in it.
- [ ] Christians and Sikhs respond by saying there does not have to be a conflict between religion and science, and that evil and suffering exist because of free will.

How science may challenge belief in God

Arguments against the existence of God	Christian and Sikh responses
• Some atheists think religious beliefs, especially about God, were invented by people to answer questions about the universe that in the past could not be explained. • Similarly, questions about hardship and suffering, such as disease or the failure of crops, could best be explained as punishment by God for wrongdoing. • Science can now answer many questions that in the past couldn't be answered without the idea of God. • In the future, science will be able to answer all questions, so the idea of God is no longer necessary or helpful. • The fact that science is close to creating human life provides further evidence there is no God.	• Many **Christians** see no conflict between science and religion, as they believe the Genesis creation stories should not be interpreted literally. • This means they can accept scientific theories about the origins of the universe. "The big bang […] does not contradict the divine act of creation. Rather, it requires it." *Pope Francis* • Fundamentalist Christians argue it is wrong to change religious truths to fit scientific laws, which they believe other Christians are doing when they view the creation stories as myths. • **Sikhs** believe science and religion are complementary and both show divine truth. • Sikhs believe scientific theories about the origins of life and the universe support teaching in the Guru Granth Sahib.

Evil and suffering as an argument against the existence of God

Atheists argue that the existence of evil and suffering proves God does not exist:

God is believed to be all-knowing, all-powerful and all-loving → If this is true, God should be aware of evil → If God is aware of evil, he should want to use his powers to prevent the effects of it → God doesn't do this, so he doesn't exist

Christian responses	Sikh responses
• Suffering and evil are a result of free will. • They were brought into God's perfect world by Adam and Eve, who used their free will to disobey God. • Giving humans the ability to choose what they do gives them the power to make bad choices. • If there was nothing bad in the world, no one would be able to exercise compassion, learn from their mistakes, or actively choose good over bad.	• Suffering is often the result of a person's own actions or moral choices. • God does not cause or want suffering, but permits it to test people's faith and courage. • God has reasons for allowing evil that humans cannot know. • If God constantly intervened to prevent evil then humans would not be free.

APPLY

A Explain **two** reasons why atheists might believe that evil and suffering prove God doesn't exist, and **two** ways that Christians or Sikhs might counter their reasoning.

B **Write two logical chains of reasoning**, one to agree that science is correct in challenging the existence of God, and the other to disagree.

TIP

Remember that a logical chain of reasoning can express an opinion, give a reason to support the opinion, and further develop the reason, possibly using religious arguments to elaborate it.

7.5 Special revelation and enlightenment

RECAP

Essential information:

- ☐ For Christians and Sikhs, **special revelation** is when God makes himself known through direct personal experience.
- ☐ **Enlightenment** is a goal for Sikhs and can be reached through prayer, meditation and following a religious way of life.

You might be asked to compare beliefs on visions between Christianity (the main religious tradition in Great Britain) and another religious tradition.

Special revelation

- **Christians** and **Sikhs** believe they cannot fully understand God, but they can know something of his nature and purpose through revelations.
- Special revelation is when a person experiences God directly in a particular event.
- Examples from the Bible include Moses receiving the Ten Commandments from God, or Mary finding out from the angel Gabriel that she would give birth to Jesus.
- **Sikhism** began with a special revelation of God to Guru Nanak.
- Sikh scriptures describe God's self-revelation through the words of the Gurus, which have come directly from God.

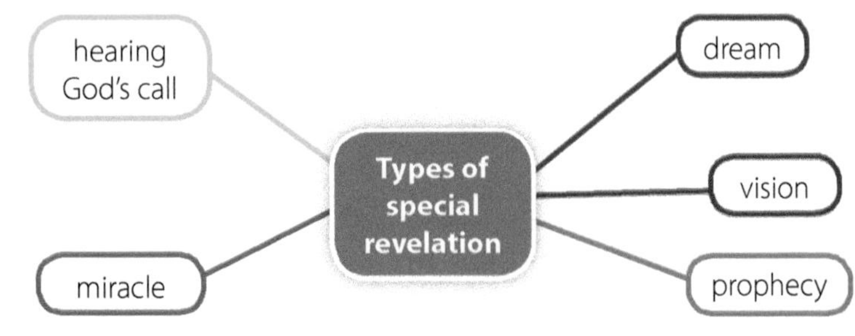

> "By myself I do not know even how to speak; I speak all that the Lord commands."
>
> *Guru Granth Sahib 763*

Visions

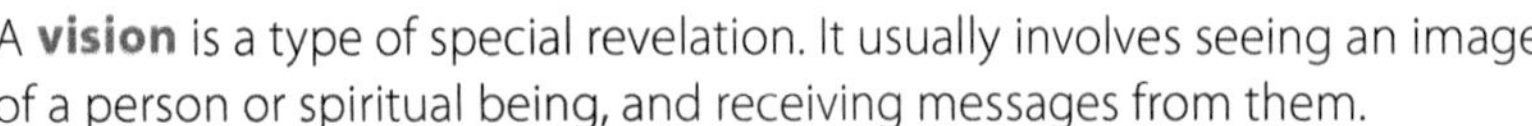

A **vision** is a type of special revelation. It usually involves seeing an image of a person or spiritual being, and receiving messages from them.

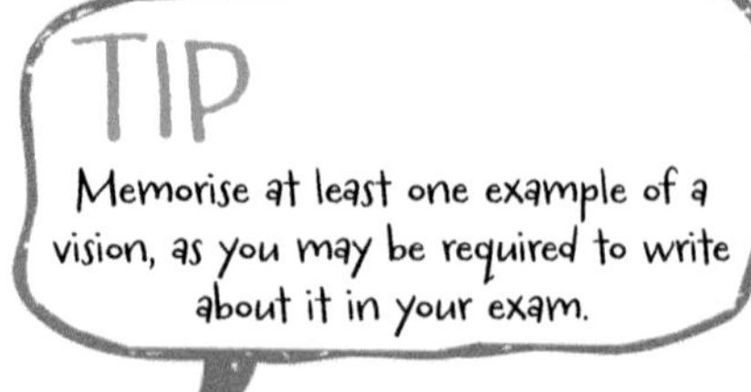

TIP
Memorise at least one example of a vision, as you may be required to write about it in your exam.

Here are two examples of visions, one from Christianity and one from Sikhism:

- Acts 9:1–19 describes a vision that persuaded Saul, a Jew, to convert to Christianity.
- Saul was travelling to Damascus when he experienced a blinding light and was spoken to by Jesus.
- Afterwards he committed himself to the Christian faith (whose followers he had previously persecuted).

- Guru Nanak disappeared one day when bathing in the river Bain.
- He claimed he was in a divine trance where he was sitting in God's own presence.
- God gave him a cup of nectar and said, 'I am with you. Go and repeat My Name, and teach others to do the same.'
- Guru Nanak responded with the words of the Mool Mantra.
- God looked on him with infinite kindness and said, 'My name is God, and you are the divine Guru.'

Enlightenment

Enlightenment is a goal for Sikhs, Hindus and Buddhists. For Sikhs and Hindus, it means escaping the cycle of birth, death and rebirth to achieve union with God. For Buddhists (who do not believe in God), the goal is to reach an understanding of ultimate reality. Enlightenment can be achieved through prayer, meditation and following a religious way of life.

APPLY

A Using one detailed example, **explain** the meaning of special revelation.

B 'Those who see visions are only hallucinating.'

Write a detailed argument that shows what you think about this statement.

7.6 General revelation

RECAP

Essential information:

- ☐ **General revelation** is coming to understand God or the nature of reality through ordinary, common events that can be experienced by everyone.
- ☐ Coming to know the divine through observing the natural world or by reading scripture are two examples of general revelation.

Examples of general revelation

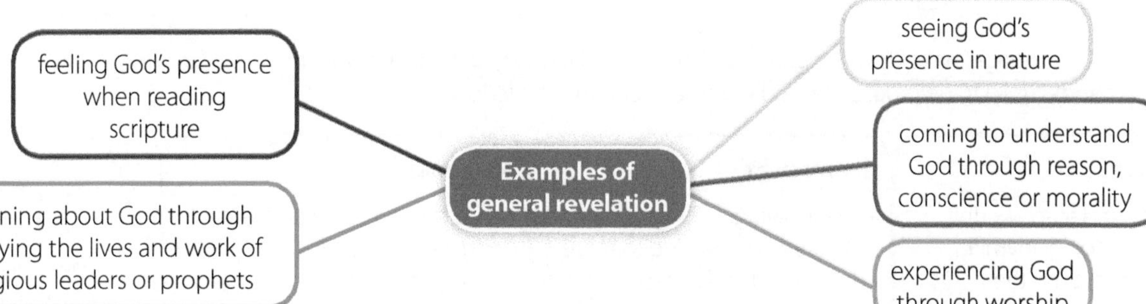

Examples of general revelation
feeling God's presence when reading scripture
learning about God through studying the lives and work of religious leaders or prophets
seeing God's presence in nature
coming to understand God through reason, conscience or morality
experiencing God through worship

Nature as a way of understanding the divine

- Many Christians and Sikhs believe they can gain insight into God through the natural world.
- E.g. they believe God is revealed through his creation to be creative, clever and powerful.
- This may lead to awe and wonder at God's power, which may result in stronger faith.
- Atheists and humanists might argue that observing nature can give them a greater understanding of the world but not of God.

> You might be asked to compare beliefs on nature as general revelation between Christianity (the main religious tradition in Great Britain) and another religious tradition.

> "The heavens declare the glory of God; the skies proclaim the work of his hands [...] night after night they reveal knowledge." *Psalms 19:1–2* [NIV]

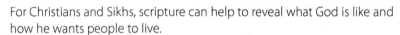

Scripture as a way of understanding the divine

For Christians and Sikhs, scripture can help to reveal what God is like and how he wants people to live.

There are different ways to interpret scripture:

Christians	Atheists	Sikhs
• **Fundamentalist Christians** believe the Bible contains God's actual words. These must not be changed or questioned. • **Liberal Christians** believe the Bible was inspired by God but the words must be seen in their original context and understood differently in today's world.	• The Bible consists of the authors' opinions rather than the word of God. • Scripture does not prove God is real or reveal anything about God.	• The Guru Granth Sahib is a special revelation of God to the Gurus, but it can reveal truths about God to anyone who reads it. • The Guru Granth Sahib describes how to become a person of truth by meditating on God's name and living a moral life.

APPLY

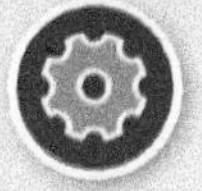

A Explain **two** ways in which Christians or Sikhs believe general revelation helps them to understand God.

B 'It is impossible to believe that ancient texts, written such a long time ago, can help people to believe in God today.'

Evaluate this statement.

7.7 Different ideas about the divine

RECAP

Essential information:

- [ ] Christians and Sikhs believe it is impossible to describe or understand God fully, but there are certain words or qualities that can be used to give humans some idea of what God is like.
- [ ] Christians and Sikhs view God as being omnipotent, omniscient, personal, immanent and transcendent.

Descriptions of God's nature

The limitations of language make describing an unseen, infinite God very difficult. However, certain terms can be used to help describe God's nature, including the following:

Omnipotent

- Almighty and all-powerful.
- Capable of doing anything (including creating the universe).

Omniscient

- All-knowing.
- Aware of everything that has happened in the past, present or future.

Personal

- Has human characteristics, e.g. being merciful and compassionate.
- People can have a relationship with God through prayer.

Transcendent

- Is beyond and outside life on earth.
- Not limited by the world, time or space.
- Does not act within the world or intervene in people's lives.

Immanent

- Is present in the universe and involved with life on earth.
- Acts in history and influences events.
- People can experience God in their lives.

Impersonal

- Has no human characteristics.
- Is unknowable and mysterious.
- Is more like an idea or a force than a person.

TIP

You could be examined about any of these terms, so make sure you understand all of them.

Can God be immanent, transcendent, personal and all-powerful?

Christians believe God is immanent, transcendent, personal and all-powerful. This is because:

- God's **immanence** means he is involved in life on earth. He is revealed in Jesus and in the work of the Holy Spirit on earth.
- But God is also the **transcendent** creator of the universe.
- God is **personal** because he allows followers to join in a relationship with him and cares about them on an individual level.
- But he is also seen to be **all-powerful** and acts throughout the universe.

Sikhs believe...

- God is referred to as Waheguru (Wonderful Lord)
- God is beyond human understanding
- God is referred to as brother, father, mother, friend, lover and husband (all personal terms)
- God is immanent within creation but not contained in creation
- God is transcendent because he is truth (satnam)

> "The Cherisher Lord is so very merciful and wise; He is compassionate to all."
>
> *Guru Granth Sahib 249*

APPLY

A Give **two** terms to describe God's nature and explain what they mean.

B 'It is not possible to fully express God's nature in words.'

Write two developed points of view about this, one in favour and one that expresses a different opinion.

TIP

In your answer you could compare Christian or Sikh ideas about the nature of God with how atheists view God.

7.8 The value of revelation and enlightenment

RECAP

Essential information:

- ☐ Theists believe that revelation and enlightenment are valuable sources of knowledge about the divine.
- ☐ Revelations are difficult to prove because they are subjective, personal experiences.
- ☐ What some theists may regard as revelations, non-theists may understand in other ways.

The value of revelation

For some **Christians** and **Sikhs**, revelation can:

- provide proof of God's existence
- help to start a religion
- enable believers to have a relationship with God
- help believers to understand how God wants them to live.

For Sikhs, God's revelation to Guru Nanak (see page 55) led him to start the Sikh religion and, through his teachings, lay the foundation for his followers to live an ethical life.

Revelation: reality or illusion?

Revelation cannot be proved, so how can believers have confidence in a revelation? They may ask themselves:

Question	Explanation and examples
Does their revelation match the real world?	• The more the revelation aligns with what actually happens, the more likely it is to be real. • E.g. a revelation that claims people can fly is unlikely to be believed. A revelation that claims the water in a holy place can cure people, and it then does, is more likely to convince believers.
Does it fit with other revelations accepted by a religion?	• If it contradicts a long-held belief of a religion, it is less likely to be accepted as a true revelation. • However, beliefs may change over time (e.g. about slavery or same-sex relationships), so this is not always the case.
Does it change the faith or the life of a person?	• E.g. Nicky Cruz, a gang leader in New York in the 1950s, was converted to Christianity through the teaching of a Christian street preacher called David Wilkerson, whose words and example came as a revelation to Cruz. For him, this was true.
How can different religions have different revelations? They can't all be correct.	• Atheists might argue that the existence of conflicting revelations proves they cannot all be real. • Different interpretations of revelations can also lead to conflicting ideas about the divine. • Theists might reply by saying that different religions offer different paths to the divine. The meaning a religion places upon a particular revelation depends on the beliefs of that religion.

Alternative explanations for the experiences

Atheists might argue that revelations may be wishful thinking, caused by drugs or alcohol, or the result of a physical or mental illness. A person might have made a genuine error or they might be deliberately lying for fame or money.

APPLY

A Give **three** alternative explanations for revelations and develop each one.

B 'Revelation proves that God exists.'

Write a reasoned answer to express a non-theist response to this statement.

7 Exam practice

Test the 1 mark question

1 Which **one** of the following gives the meaning of the term 'transcendent'?

A Immanent
B Omnipotent
C Outside space and time
D All-knowing

[1 mark]

2 Which **one** of the following is an example of special revelation?

A God indirectly revealed through nature
B God directly revealed through a vision
C Reading scripture
D Meditation

[1 mark]

Test the 2 mark question

3 Give **two** weaknesses of the First Cause argument. **[2 marks]**

1) ______________________________

2) ______________________________

4 Give **two** reasons why religious believers would not accept suffering as an argument against the existence of God. **[2 marks]**

1) ______________________________

2) ______________________________

Test the 4 mark question

5 Explain **two** contrasting beliefs about the Design argument for God's existence.
In your answer you must refer to one or more religious traditions. You may refer to a non-religious belief. **[4 marks]**

• **Explain one belief.**	*Christians believe that the beauty and intricacy of nature proves that God created the world.*
• Develop your explanation with more detail/an example/reference to a religious teaching or quotation.	*William Paley said that just as a watch's intricate workings show evidence of design, so does the universe, which is more complex than a watch.*
• **Explain a second contrasting belief.**	*Atheists disagree with the Design argument because they do not believe there is a God.*
• Develop your explanation with more detail/an example/reference to a religious teaching or quotation.	*They think that the natural world evolved after the Big Bang, a random event, and through natural selection creatures designed themselves without a need for God.*

TIP
Remember, 'contrasting' means different. Here the answer refers to Christianity and contrasts it with an atheist view.

6 Explain **two** contrasting beliefs about miracles.
In your answer you must refer to one or more religious traditions. You may refer to a non-religious belief. **[4 marks]**

• **Explain one belief.**	
• Develop your explanation with more detail/an example/reference to a religious teaching or quotation.	
• **Explain a second contrasting belief.**	
• Develop your explanation with more detail/an example/reference to a religious teaching or quotation.	

7 Explain **two** similar beliefs about general revelation.
In your answer you must refer to one or more religious traditions. You may refer to a non-religious belief.

Test the 5 mark question

8 Explain **two** religious beliefs about visions.
Refer to sacred writings or another source of religious belief and teaching in your answer. **[5 marks]**

• **Explain one belief.**	*Christians believe that God can be revealed to people in a special, direct way through visions.*
• Develop your explanation with more detail/an example.	*Some people who have had visions may as a result have a dramatic conversion from one way of life or faith to another.*
• **Explain a second belief.**	*A vision can teach someone what God wants them to do.*
• Develop your explanation with more detail/an example.	*For example, Guru Nanak saw a vision of God in which God told him to repeat his name and teach others to do the same.*
• Add a reference to sacred writings or another source of religious belief and teaching. If you prefer, you can add this reference to your first belief instead.	*An example of a vision in the Bible is in Acts 9:1–19, where it says Saul (who later became Paul) received a vision of Jesus on the Damascus Road. Saul was temporarily blinded and when he regained his sight he changed from persecuting Christians to preaching the gospel of Jesus to everyone.*

TIP
You don't have to quote directly from scripture or sacred writing – it is acceptable to give a summary in your own words instead, as the student has done here.

9 Explain **two** religious beliefs about special revelation.
Refer to sacred writings or another source of religious belief and teaching in your answer. **[5 marks]**

• **Explain one belief.**	
• Develop your explanation with more detail/an example.	
• **Explain a second belief.**	
• Develop your explanation with more detail/an example.	
• Add a reference to sacred writings or another source of religious belief and teaching. If you prefer, you can add this reference to your first belief instead.	

TIP
This question is not an evaluation question, so do not give your opinion or write arguments against special revelation. Don't forget to include a source of religious teaching in the answer.

10 Explain **two** religious ideas about God.
Refer to sacred writings or another source of religious belief and teaching in your answer. **[5 marks]**

Test the 12 mark question

11 'The First Cause argument proves that God exists.'

Evaluate this statement. In your answer you:

- should give reasoned arguments in support of this statement
- should give reasoned arguments to support a different point of view
- should refer to religious arguments
- may refer to non-religious arguments
- should reach a justified conclusion.

[12 marks]
[+3 SPaG ma

REASONED ARGUMENTS IN SUPPORT OF THE STATEMENT ● **Explain why some people would agree with the statement.** ● Develop your explanation with more detail and examples. ● Refer to religious teaching. Use a quote or paraphrase or a religious authority. ● **Evaluate the arguments.** Is this a good argument or not? Explain why you think this.	*The First Cause argument says that everything that exists has a cause. It is obvious to everyone that the universe exists because we live in it! Therefore the universe too must have a cause – something must have started it. But that something had to be eternal and not caused by something else, otherwise that other thing would be the cause, and so on. Christians and Sikhs believe that God is the eternal, almighty cause that began the process of creation of everything we know. The Bible says that God merely said, 'Let there be light' and it was created. So God was the eternal being that set off the Big Bang which led to evolution and the world as we know it today.*
REASONED ARGUMENTS SUPPORTING A DIFFERENT VIEW ● **Explain why some people would support a different view.** ● Develop your explanation with more detail and examples. ● Refer to religious teaching. Use a quote or paraphrase or a religious authority. ● **Evaluate the arguments.** Is this a good argument or not? Explain why you think this.	*Atheists are people who do not believe there is a God. They would argue that the First Cause argument does not prove there is a God because there are flaws in the logic – the argument contradicts itself. For example, if everything has a cause, what caused God?* *Another argument against the First Cause argument is that although events have causes, it does not necessarily follow that the universe has to have a cause.*
CONCLUSION ● **Give a justified conclusion.** ● Include your own opinion together with your own reasoning. ● **Include evaluation.** Explain why you think one viewpoint is stronger than the other or why they are equally strong. ● Do not just repeat arguments you have already used without explaining how they apply to your reasoned opinion/conclusion.	*In conclusion, I think that although the First Cause argument may seem convincing because it depends on something everyone can observe – that everything that happens has a cause – in the end it fails to convince me that God is the First Cause of the universe. The argument relies on the universe having a beginning and a cause, but just because things in our world have causes does not necessarily mean the universe itself had one. Christians may use the Bible's creation stories to support their arguments in favour of the statement, but as I am an atheist, I am not persuaded by myths.*

TIP

This conclusion is good because it doesn't just repeat points already made to justify the opinion. It is also clearly linked to the statement in the question.

12 'The existence of miracles proves that God exists.'

Evaluate this statement. In your answer you:

- should give reasoned arguments in support of this statement
- should give reasoned arguments to support a different point of view
- should refer to religious arguments
- may refer to non-religious arguments
- should reach a justified conclusion.

[12 marks]
[+3 SPaG marks]

REASONED ARGUMENTS IN SUPPORT OF THE STATEMENT • **Explain why some people would agree with the statement.** • Develop your explanation with more detail and examples. • Refer to religious teaching. Use a quote or paraphrase or a religious authority. • **Evaluate the arguments.** Is this a good argument or not? Explain why you think this.	
REASONED ARGUMENTS SUPPORTING A DIFFERENT VIEW • **Explain why some people would support a different view.** • Develop your explanation with more detail and examples. • Refer to religious teaching. Use a quote or paraphrase or a religious authority. • **Evaluate the arguments.** Is this a good argument or not? Explain why you think this.	
CONCLUSION • **Give a justified conclusion.** • Include your own opinion together with your own reasoning. • **Include evaluation.** Explain why you think one viewpoint is stronger than the other or why they are equally strong. • Do not just repeat arguments you have already used without explaining how they apply to your reasoned opinion/ conclusion.	

13 'The existence of evil and suffering proves that God does not exist.'

Evaluate this statement. In your answer you:

- should give reasoned arguments in support of this statement
- should give reasoned arguments to support a different point of view
- should refer to religious arguments
- may refer to non-religious arguments
- should reach a justified conclusion.

[12 marks]
[+3 SPaG marks]

Check your answers using the mark scheme on page 161. How did you do?
To feel more secure in the content you need to remember, re-read pages 104–111.
To remind yourself of what the examiner is looking for, go to pages 7–13.

8 Religion, peace and conflict

8.1 Introduction to religion, peace and conflict

RECAP

Essential information:

- [ ] Some Christians (such as Quaker Christians) believe war is always wrong, because they believe 'there is that of God in every one'. Other Christians believe war is acceptable under certain conditions.
- [ ] Many Sikhs have been prepared to fight for their country and their faith.
- [ ] The concepts of peace, justice, forgiveness and reconciliation are important both in the aftermath of conflict and as tools to prevent war from happening in the first place.

Key concepts of peace, justice, forgiveness and reconciliation

Peace

- **Peace** is the absence of conflict and war, which leads to happiness and harmony.
- The aim of war may be to create peace, but this can be hard to achieve because of the instability and resentment left after a war ends.
- Peace is also a feeling of happiness and tranquillity that can come through prayer and meditation, which helps people to avoid conflict.
- **Christians** believe God will bring peace to the world at some time in the future (Isaiah 2:4).
- **Sikhs** believe that peace is not just an absence of war, but also the harmony that results from respect and forgiveness.

Justice

- **Justice** is bringing about what is right and fair, according to the law, or making up for a wrong that has been committed.
- Justice is linked to equality, and the idea that it is just to give everyone the same opportunities.
- If certain governments or parts of the world are seen to be the cause of inequality and injustice, conflict may result.
- **Christians** believe that God, as the ultimate judge, will establish justice at some point in the future (Isaiah 2:4).
- **Sikhs** believe in the equality of humanity and have worked hard to address injustice.

Forgiveness

- **Forgiveness** is showing compassion and mercy, and pardoning someone for what they have done wrong.
- Forgiveness does not necessarily mean no action should be taken to right a wrong, but when conflict is over forgiveness should follow.
- **Christians** are taught to forgive others if they wish to be forgiven (the Lord's Prayer). They believe God sets the example by offering forgiveness to all who ask for it in faith.
- For **Sikhs**, forgiveness is very important. Guru Granth Sahib 1372 says 'Where there is forgiveness, there is God himself.'

Reconciliation

- **Reconciliation** means restoring friendly relationships after conflict.
- It requires a conscious effort (and sometimes much work) to rebuild the relationship.
- Reconciliation doesn't mean ignoring the past but building a constructive relationship for the future.
- For **Sikhs**, actions to establish peace, justice and reconciliation should come after forgiveness, otherwise it is likely that problems will occur.

APPLY

A Give **two** religious beliefs about forgiveness. **Develop** each belief by explaining in more detail, adding an example, or referring to a relevant quotation from sacred writings or another source of religious belief and teaching.

B Decide whether the arguments below are reasons to agree or disagree with the statement, 'Religious believers should not take part in wars.' **Write a paragraph** to explain your views having evaluated the arguments.

1. Christians are taught to forgive others, but this does not mean actions to right wrongs should be avoided.	2. Religious believers may believe 'there is that of God in everyone' and so think all killing is wrong.
3. If there is injustice or inequality, religious believers such as Sikhs may see it as a duty to put this right.	4. The aim of war may be to create peace, but often leads to more instability, resentment and injustice.

8.2 Violent protest and terrorism

RECAP

Essential information:

- [ ] In the UK the right to **protest** (express disapproval, often in a public group) is a fundamental democratic freedom, but it is illegal to protest violently.
- [ ] **Terrorism** (the unlawful use of violence, usually against innocent civilians, to achieve a political goal) is a much more serious form of violent protest.
- [ ] Christianity and Sikhism are against violent protest and terrorism.

Violence and protest

- All religions generally agree that conflict should be avoided if possible, but they have different views about when violence may be justified.
- Protests allow people to express their objection to something in public, but protests can sometimes turn violent.
- Many Christians and Sikhs believe that protesting to achieve what is right is acceptable as long as violence is not used.

You might be asked to compare beliefs on violence between Christianity (the main religious tradition in Great Britain) and another religious tradition.

Here are two examples of peaceful protests organised by religious believers:

- In the 1950s and 1960s, the Christian pastor Dr Martin Luther King Jr organised peaceful protests against unjust racist laws in the USA.
- These succeeded in changing US law and bringing civil rights to all its citizens of any race.

- In 1972, Sikhs protested against the Road Traffic Act which made it compulsory to wear motorcycle helmets, as this was a problem for turban-wearing Sikhs.
- Persistent protesting led to a change in the law in 1976, which allowed motorbike riders to not wear helmets for religious reasons.

Terrorism

- Some individuals or groups use terrorism to further their cause by killing innocent people.
- Suicide bombers, gunmen shooting into crowds, and using vehicles to injure pedestrians are examples of terrorism.
- Terrorists aim to make society aware of their cause, frighten people and push authorities into giving way to their demands.
- Terrorists may link their cause with a religion but **no religion promotes terrorism.**
- Most **Christians** are against terrorism and prefer more peaceful ways of resolving issues.
- Most **Sikhs** condemn terrorism as they believe in the equality and freedom of all.
- Since India became independent in 1947, some Sikh groups have campaigned for equal allocation of resources such as water. This has led to some violent incidents.

TIP

Learning specific examples such as these can help you to develop your answers and gain more marks.

> “The purpose of terrorism lies not just in the violent act itself. It is in producing terror. It sets out to inflame, to divide, to produce consequences which [terrorists] then use to justify terror.”
>
> *Former UK Prime Minister Tony Blair*

APPLY

A Give **two** reasons why religious believers may wish to protest.

B ‘Terrorism is never justified.’

Develop this argument to support the statement by explaining in more detail, adding an example, or referring to a relevant religious teaching or quotation.

"Terrorism kills innocent people. It uses violence to frighten and intimidate ordinary citizens who are just going about their daily lives. It can never be justified no matter what the cause."

RECAP

Essential information:

- [ ] Some reasons for war include **greed** (selfish desire for something), **self-defence** (acting to prevent harm to yourself or others), and **retaliation** (deliberately harming someone as a response to them harming you).
- [ ] Christianity and Sikhism teach that war should never be motivated by greed or retaliation.
- [ ] Many Christians believe fighting in self-defence is morally acceptable. Sikhs are forbidden to fight for anything other than religious or social equality.

Greed, self-defence and retaliation as reasons for war

Greed

- Wars may be fought out of greed to gain more land or control of important resources (such as oil).
- **Christianity** teaches that greed is wrong.

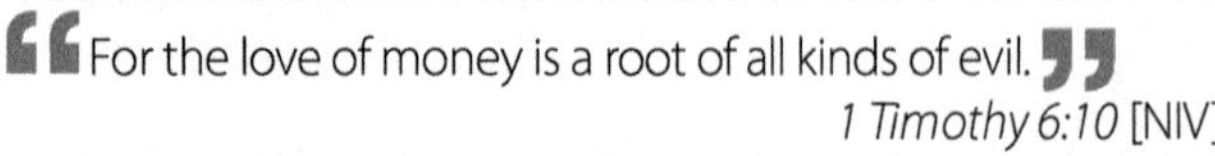

"For the love of money is a root of all kinds of evil."
1 Timothy 6:10 [NIV]

- Two of the moral evils in **Sikhism** are connected to greed: lobh, which means a strong desire to have more than one needs or deserves, and moh, which refers to the attachment to worldly possessions.
- Using greed as a reason for war would promote these moral evils and be unacceptable.

Retaliation

- Wars are sometimes fought in retaliation against a country that has done something very wrong.
- **Christians** try to follow the advice of Jesus, who taught that retaliation is wrong.

"But I tell you, do not resist an evil person. If anyone slaps you on the right cheek, turn to them the other cheek also."
Matthew 5:39 [NIV]

- Most **Sikhs** believe retaliation is wrong.

Reasons for war

Self-defence

- People might fight in self-defence when their country is under attack, or to help defend other nations who are under threat.
- E.g. during the Second World War the UK fought to defend itself against Nazi invasion, and also to defeat what it saw as an evil threat to the whole of Europe.
- Many **Christians** believe fighting in self-defence is morally acceptable, providing all peaceful ways of solving the conflict have been tried first.
- **Sikhs** believe that defending themselves and others from oppression and persecution is a religious duty, including using force if required.
- This duty was strengthened by the tenth Guru, Guru Gobind Singh, when he set up the Khalsa and made carrying the kirpan compulsory for Sikhs as a symbol of standing up to injustice.

TIP
Remember that the reasons for a war are complex and usually cannot be simplified to one motive.

APPLY

A Which **one** of the following is **not** a reason for war?

A) Self-defence B) Greed C) Retaliation D) Forgiveness

B Use the table below with arguments for and against the statement, 'Retaliation is a justifiable reason for war.' **Write a paragraph** to explain whether you agree or disagree with the statement, having evaluated both sides of the argument.

For	Against
If a country has attacked you for no reason, you have every right to get back at them by harming them. They started the conflict so should expect a response.	*Retaliation is wrong because it simply continues the cycle of violence and is not the way to lasting peace.*
The Bible teaches, 'An eye for an eye, a tooth for a tooth', so you should be able to retaliate when an enemy causes you harm. It's a matter of justice which is an important principle.	*Retaliation is different from self-defence. It may sometimes be justifiable to defend your country to protect others from harm, but retaliation is a kind of spiteful action, taken to punish the enemy for something they've done.*

8.4 Nuclear war and weapons of mass destruction

RECAP

Essential information:

- ☐ **Nuclear weapons** are weapons that work by a nuclear reaction. They devastate huge areas and kill large numbers of people.
- ☐ Other types of **weapons of mass destruction** (weapons that kill large numbers of people and/or cause great damage) include chemical weapons and biological weapons.
- ☐ No religion supports the use of these weapons, although some religious believers do support nuclear deterrence (stockpiling nuclear weapons to deter or prevent an enemy attack).

You might be asked to compare beliefs on weapons of mass destruction between Christianity (the main religious tradition in Great Britain) and another religious tradition.

The use of nuclear weapons

- US forces used atom (nuclear) bombs on the Japanese cities of Hiroshima and Nagasaki during the Second World War. In response Japan surrendered, ending the war.
- Some people say that as the atom bombs ended the war, their use was justified.
- Since then, many countries have developed powerful nuclear weapons as a deterrent.

Weapons of mass destruction

- In addition to nuclear weapons, other weapons of mass destruction are **biological weapons** (using living organisms to cause disease or death) and **chemical weapons** (using chemicals to harm humans and destroy the natural environment).
- The production, stockpiling and use of these weapons is illegal worldwide.
- Despite this, many countries still possess them.

Religious views

Christian views	Sikh views
• Only God has the right to end life. • One of the Ten Commandments is, 'You shall not murder' (Exodus 20:13). • Weapons of mass destruction kill huge numbers of innocent civilians, so their use can never be justified. • Their use goes against the teachings of Jesus. "any use of nuclear weapons would violate the sanctity of life and the principle of dignity core to our faith traditions" *Steve Hucklesby* • Some Christians see the stockpiling of nuclear weapons as a useful deterrent to maintain peace and prevent attack.	• Sikhs believe that everyone has a right to life so using weapons of mass destruction is unacceptable. • Sikhs aim to follow the example of Guru Arjan, who said: "No one is my enemy, and no one is a stranger. I get along with everyone." *Guru Granth Sahib 1299* • Sikhs believe weapons of mass destruction damage the world God made for humanity. • Some Sikhs believe that possessing weapons of mass destruction can be a deterrent against attack.

APPLY

A Explain **two** contrasting beliefs in contemporary British society about weapons of mass destruction.

B 'There are no good reasons for countries to possess nuclear weapons.'

Develop an argument to support this statement. **Refer to a relevant religious teaching or quotation** in your answer.

TIP

Make sure you choose contrasting viewpoints when answering this question.

8.5 The just war

RECAP

Essential information:

- ☐ A **just war** is a war that meets internationally accepted criteria for fairness.
- ☐ The just war theory gives the conditions that must apply to make a war justifiable, and the rules on how the war must be fought to make sure it is ethical.
- ☐ The just war theory was developed by Christians and is accepted by many Christians today, although most think it is much better to prevent war from happening at all.
- ☐ Sikhs have developed their own just war theory called **dharam yudh** ('war in defence of righteousness').

TIP

Learning about different wars might help to support your opinion about whether war can be justified according to the just war theory.

Christian views

The just war theory was developed by Christian thinkers including Augustine (in the fourth century) and Thomas Aquinas (in the thirteenth century).

Conditions for a just war		
• Must be fought for a just cause – not in retaliation or greed. • Must be declared by the correct authority (e.g. the government or lawful rulers of a country). • Must have a just intention (e.g. to promote good or prevent wrongdoing). • Must be a last resort – all other ways of solving the problem should be tried first. • Must have a reasonable chance of success – it is unjust to ask people to fight if the war is likely to be lost and they will die. • Must be proportional – fighters must not use excessive force or kill civilians.		
Rules on how war should be fought		
Must be fought by just means – avoiding harming civilians.	Only appropriate force should be used.	Internationally agreed conventions should be obeyed (e.g. the Geneva Convention).

Sikh views

Conditions for a just war		
• Wars must be fought for the right reason. • The person fighting the war must have their mind totally focused on what they believe God wants them to do. • There must be no thought of personal reward such as gaining land, wealth or power. • Reasons for fighting must be selfless (e.g. to defend those unable to defend themselves). • Only those selflessly committed to the fighting are allowed to take part – those who fight for money (mercenaries) must not be part of the fighting		
Rules on how the war should be fought		
1. Those who are attacked must be carrying weapons and be a threat to life.	2. Enemy fighters must be given a chance to lay down their weapons before fighting.	3. No private property should be stolen or destroyed.
4. No women should be abused or raped.	5. Attempts must be made to help enemy fighters if they do not pose a threat.	6. Any agreements made between the two nations or groups must be respected.
7. Ceasefires must not be broken.	8. Any killing that is not necessary to win the war must not happen.	9. Places of worship of any faith must not be damaged.
10. People who have surrendered must not be harmed.	11. Lying to the enemy is forbidden.	

> "When matters pass all other means, it is permitted to take up arms."
> *Guru Gobind Singh*

APPLY

Give **two** conditions of a just war.

'The just war theory is the best religious response to whether it is right to fight.'

Develop each of these arguments for and against this statement.

8.6 Holy war and religion as a cause of violence

RECAP

Essential information:

- [ ] A **holy war** is a war fought for a religious cause or God, controlled by a religious leader.
- [ ] Most Christians today believe that violence should not be used to defend the faith.
- [ ] Sikhism was founded as a religion of peace, but Sikhs believe that the use of force for the good of society (including being free to practise one's faith) is sometimes necessary.
- [ ] Although all religions generally promote peace and harmony, religion is sometimes seen as a cause of violence in the contemporary world.

What is a holy war?

- A holy war is **fought for a religious cause**, such as to defend the faith from attack.
- It must be **authorised by a religious leader**.
- It is believed those who take part **gain spiritual rewards**.
- **The Crusades** are examples of holy war. These were battles between Christians and Muslims in the eleventh to fourteenth centuries. Both believed God was on their side.
- Most **Christians** today believe it is better to defend the faith through words rather than violence.
- **Sikhs** believe it is better to defend the faith through words, but war may be necessary as a last resort to stand up against oppression.

Religion as a cause of violence

Christian views	Sikh views
• Most Christians today do not respond violently to an attack on their faith. • Most Christians accept Jesus' teaching that not only violence, but the anger that leads to violence, is wrong (Matthew 5:21–22). • Jesus said, 'Put your sword back in its place, for all who draw the sword die by the sword' (Matthew 26:52).	• Sikhs believe that all people should be able to live in peace and harmony and be tolerant of the beliefs of others. • Guru Har Gobind, the sixth Guru, believed military action was sometimes necessary to promote justice and defend the weak and innocent. "It is sinful to submit to the oppressor and the miscreants." *Guru Gobind Singh*

Although all religions generally promote peace and harmony, there are examples of conflicts that have had a religious aspect to them, or examples of violence that have been justified as helping to defend the faith. For example:

During 'the Troubles' in Northern Ireland (1968–1998), conflict between Catholics and Protestants led to acts of discrimination and violence. However, many consider this to have been a political conflict rather than a religious one.

- Guru Arjan, the fifth Sikh Guru, was killed for his faith.
- Guru Hargobind, the sixth Guru, started to strengthen the Sikh community so it could resist oppression with military power.
- Guru Gobind Singh created the Khalsa and intended that Sikhs would be able to defend their faith.

APPLY

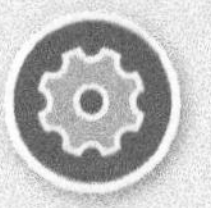

A Give **two** features of holy wars.

B **Evaluate** this argument to support the statement, 'There is no place for a holy war in contemporary Britain.'

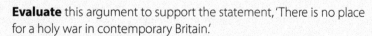

"There is no place for a holy war in Britain today. People have religious freedom. No one has to fight for the right to worship God in the way they wish. Jesus taught people to 'turn the other cheek' and not retaliate against someone who is being nasty to you. So even though the Christian religion seems under attack at times, it is not right to use violence against those who insult Christian beliefs."

TIP
Do not use the conflict in Northern Ireland as an example of a holy war.

8.7 Pacifism and peacemaking

RECAP

Essential information:

- ☐ **Pacifism** is the belief of people who refuse to take part in war and any other form of violence.
- ☐ Many Christians are not pacifists because they believe war is sometimes necessary in self-defence. Most Sikhs also accept war is justified to defend their faith or to combat oppression.
- ☐ **Peacemaking** is the action of trying to establish peace, and a **peacemaker** is someone who works to establish peace in the world or in a certain part of it.

You might be asked to compare beliefs on pacifism between Christianity (the main religious tradition in Great Britain) and another religious tradition.

What is pacifism?

Pacifists believe that:

- war and violence can rarely or never be justified
- it is best to prevent war from becoming a possibility by promoting justice and peace
- prayer and meditation can help people to be at peace with themselves and others.

Christian views	Sikh views
• The Religious Society of Friends (Quakers) is a Christian denomination that strongly supports pacifism. • Christian pacifists follow Jesus' example and teaching: "Blessed are the peacemakers, for they shall be called children of God." *Matthew 5:9* [NIV] • Many Christians are not pacifists because they believe war can be justified under certain criteria (see page 120).	• Sikhs believe it is best to work to prevent war from becoming a possibility. • Promoting justice and human rights is an important part of this. • Sikhism requires each Sikh to be a saint-soldier – praying and working for peace like a saint, but with the courage to fight for justice if needed.

Examples of peacemaking

Many pacifists and peacemakers believe it is important to resist oppression and injustice in non-violent ways, to help create a just and equal world where conflict is not necessary.

Three examples of modern-day peacemakers or peacemaking organisations are Mairead Corrigan, Betty Williams and Religions for Peace.

TIP

You need to be able to talk about individuals and organisations involved in peacemaking and the work they have done.

Mairead Corrigan and Betty Williams

- A Catholic and Protestant from Northern Ireland who formed the 'Peace People' organisation in 1976.
- Organised peace marches and other events throughout the UK to bring Catholics and Protestants together, and to call for peace between the two sides in Northern Ireland.
- Awarded the 1976 Nobel Peace Prize.

Religions for Peace

- A worldwide organisation with thriving groups in Britain. Members come from all faiths including Sikhism.
- The charity aims to provide a multifaith response to global challenges, to promote peace and prosperity for all.
- In February 2016, it issued a call for young people to get involved in peace activities.

APPLY

A Explain **two** contrasting beliefs in contemporary British society about pacifism.

B **Write down two arguments** in support of the statement, 'Promoting justice and human rights is the best way of preventing conflict'. Now **develop** each argument by explaining in more detail or by giving examples.

8.8 Religious responses to victims of war

RECAP

Essential information:

- [ ] Victims of war may include those directly involved in the fighting, their families and dependents, and refugees whose homes and societies have been destroyed.
- [ ] There are many organisations that offer help and care for victims of war (such as Caritas and Khalsa Aid). Christians and Sikhs support organisations such as these.

Providing help to victims of war

There are many organisations that help the victims of war, from those providing shelter and supplies for refugees to those providing medical and psychological care for members of the military.

Christian views	Sikh views
• Christians support such organisations because Jesus taught people to 'love your neighbour as yourself' (Mark 12:31). • In the parable of the Good Samaritan (Luke 10:25–37), Jesus taught that everyone is everybody else's neighbour, regardless of race, age, gender, religion or political beliefs.	• Sikhs have a duty to serve others and follow the teaching of caring for all. "No one is my enemy, and no one is a stranger." *Guru Granth Sahib 1299*

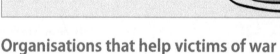

Organisations that help victims of war

Two examples of religious organisations that help victims of war are Caritas and Khalsa Aid.

Caritas

- A Catholic organisation that helps the poor and promotes justice worldwide.
- Inspired by the teachings of Jesus and the Catholic Church.
- Aims to provide practical help to those suffering through conflict.
- In 2015, provided food and shelter to refugees fleeing the civil war in Syria.
- Also provided translators and legal services so the refugees could make informed decisions about their futures.

Khalsa Aid

- A British Sikh charity helping people in need throughout the world, including in war zones.
- Founded on the Sikh principles of selfless service and universal love.
- In 2011, provided drinking water to the Choucha refugee camp in Libya.
- In 2014, set up a bakery in Iraq to provide fresh bread for Syrian refugees.
- In 2016, assisted many people who became refugees as a result of the invasion of their homeland by ISIS.

APPLY

(A) Give **two** ways in which religious believers help victims of war.

(B) 'The point of war is to kill the enemy, not help them to survive.'

Write one paragraph to support this view and another paragraph which gives a different point of view.

Test the 1 mark question

1 Which **one** of the following best expresses the religious ideal of bringing about what is right and fair?

A Peace B Forgiveness C Justice D Defence **[1 mark]**

2 Which **one** of the following are **not** weapons of mass destruction?

A Chemical weapons B Nuclear weapons

C Biological weapons D Conventional weapons **[1 mark]**

Test the 2 mark question

3 Give **two** conditions of a just war. **[2 marks]**

1) ______________________________

2) ______________________________

4 Give **two** reasons why many religious people do **not** support violent protest. **[2 marks]**

1) ______________________________

2) ______________________________

Test the 4 mark question

5 Explain **two** contrasting beliefs in contemporary British society about whether countries should possess weapons of mass destruction.

In your answer you should refer to the main religious tradition of Great Britain and one or more other religious traditions. **[4 marks]**

• **Explain one belief.**	*Some Christians and Sikhs approve of countries possessing some weapons of mass destruction as a deterrent.*
• Develop your explanation with more detail/an example/reference to a religious teaching or quotation.	*They believe that possessing them is necessary in order to prevent war and help to keep the peace.*
• **Explain a second contrasting belief.**	*No religion agrees with the use of weapons of mass destruction, but some Christians would also disagree with countries possessing them.*
• Develop your explanation with more detail/an example/reference to a religious teaching or quotation.	*These Christians might argue that possessing weapons of mass destruction would provide temptation to use them.*

TIP

Read the question carefully. It asks for beliefs about whether countries should 'possess' weapons of mass destruction, not whether they should 'use' them.

6 Explain **two** contrasting beliefs in contemporary British society about pacifism.

In your answer you should refer to the main religious tradition of Great Britain and one or more other religious traditions. **[4 marks]**

• **Explain one belief.**	
• Develop your explanation with more detail/an example/reference to a religious teaching or quotation.	
• **Explain a second contrasting belief.**	
• Develop your explanation with more detail/an example/reference to a religious teaching or quotation.	

7 Explain **two** similar religious beliefs about forgiveness.
In your answer you must refer to one or more religious traditions. **[4 marks]**

Test the 5 mark question

8 Explain **two** religious beliefs about helping victims of war.
Refer to sacred writings or another source of religious belief and teaching in your answer. **[5 marks]**

• **Explain one belief.**	*One Christian belief about helping victims of war is that Christians should treat everyone as if they were a neighbour to them.*
• Develop your explanation with more detail/an example.	*Victims of war may be suffering because they have lost everything including people they love, so even if Christians do not know them, they should not ignore their suffering but offer to help them in whatever way they can.*
• **Explain a second belief.**	*The Sikh just war theory gives guidance on helping victims of war, both civilians and those who fight.*
• Develop your explanation with more detail/an example.	*For example, attempts must be made to help enemy fighters if they do not pose a threat, and civilian property must be protected.*
• Add a reference to sacred writings or another source of religious belief and teaching. If you prefer, you can add this reference to your first belief instead.	*Guru Gobind Singh told Sikhs to treat others equally, whether enemies or not: 'all the human beings, as a species, are recognised as one and the same'.*

9 Explain **two** reasons why some religious people believe it is right to fight in a war.
Refer to sacred writings or another source of religious belief and teaching in your answer. **[5 marks]**

• **Explain one reason.**	
• Develop your explanation with more detail/an example.	
• **Explain a second reason.**	
• Develop your explanation with more detail/an example.	
• Add a reference to sacred writings or another source of religious belief and teaching. If you prefer, you can add this reference to your first reason instead.	

10 Explain **two** religious beliefs about reconciliation.
Refer to sacred writings or another source of religious belief and teaching in your answer. **[5 marks]**

Test the 12 mark question

11 'The just war theory is the best religious response to whether it is right to fight.'

Evaluate this statement. In your answer you:

- should give reasoned arguments in support of this statement
- should give reasoned arguments to support a different point of view
- should refer to religious arguments
- may refer to non-religious arguments
- should reach a justified conclusion.

[12 marks]
[+3 SPaG ma

REASONED ARGUMENTS IN SUPPORT OF THE STATEMENT ● **Explain why some people would agree with the statement.** ● Develop your explanation with more detail and examples. ● Refer to religious teaching. Use a quote or paraphrase or a religious authority. ● **Evaluate the arguments.** Is this a good argument or not? Explain why you think this.	*Although religious people think it is better to avoid war and violence, if faced with a decision about whether or not it is right to fight, the just war theory can give them some guidance. The theory has several criteria including that the war must be declared by a leader of a state, it should be proportional in the amount of force that is used and civilians should be protected.* *The theory is a good response because it makes sure wars are not fought about something unimportant or in a way which breaks internationally agreed rules. This is important because God wants people to protect innocent people rather than killing them. The just war theory was invented by Thomas Aquinas so that is why Christians follow it. Also the Bible teaches 'You shall not murder'. If wars are not just wars, more people will die, and they may be fighting for a wrong reason.* *The Sikh just war theory, dharam yudh, is similar to the Christian version in stating that it is only right to fight a war that is morally justifiable.*
REASONED ARGUMENTS SUPPORTING A DIFFERENT VIEW ● **Explain why some people would support a different view.** ● Develop your explanation with more detail and examples. ● Refer to religious teaching. Use a quote or paraphrase or a religious authority. ● **Evaluate the arguments.** Is this a good argument or not? Explain why you think this.	*Some Christians, such as Quakers, think it is never justifiable to fight in a war. They are pacifists who take a literal interpretation of Jesus' teaching to 'turn the other cheek' and refuse to fight back even if personally attacked. Jesus said, 'Blessed are the peacemakers'. Quakers have followed this teaching, often at great personal cost. This demonstrates their view that the just war theory is not an acceptable response to the question of whether it is right to fight.*
CONCLUSION ● **Give a justified conclusion.** ● Include your own opinion together with your own reasoning. ● **Include evaluation.** Explain why you think one viewpoint is stronger than the other or why they are equally strong. ● Do not just repeat arguments you have already used without explaining how they apply to your reasoned opinion/conclusion.	*In conclusion, I would agree with the statement that the just war theory is the right religious response. I have sympathy with the views of pacifists, and ideally war should be avoided, but in the real world there are always countries that will bully other countries or try to take their land or resources, so war is sometimes necessary. It is better to have rules that limit the damage war can do, and the just war theory helps in that way.*

TIP
This opening shows an excellent chain of reasoning. It starts by giving strong support to the statement and then demonstrates detailed knowledge of what the just war theory says. In the second paragraph it goes back to the issue of whether it is a good religious response and includes Christian teaching.

TIP
This is a good example of a justified conclusion as the student gives reasons for their opinion.

12 'Religion is the main cause of wars.'

Evaluate this statement. In your answer you:

- should give reasoned arguments in support of this statement
- should give reasoned arguments to support a different point of view
- should refer to religious arguments
- may refer to non-religious arguments
- should reach a justified conclusion.

[12 marks]
[+3 SPaG marks]

TIP
When evaluation questions ask whether something is the 'main' cause or 'best' response, or whether a religious belief is the 'most important' belief, they are asking you to think about whether other causes/responses/beliefs are more significant or whether there can be many of equal merit.

REASONED ARGUMENTS IN SUPPORT OF THE STATEMENT ● **Explain why some people would agree with the statement.** ● Develop your explanation with more detail and examples. ● Refer to religious teaching. Use a quote or paraphrase or a religious authority. ● **Evaluate the arguments.** Is this a good argument or not? Explain why you think this.	
REASONED ARGUMENTS SUPPORTING A DIFFERENT VIEW ● **Explain why some people would support a different view.** ● Develop your explanation with more detail and examples. ● Refer to religious teaching. Use a quote or paraphrase or a religious authority. ● **Evaluate the arguments.** Is this a good argument or not? Explain why you think this.	
CONCLUSION ● **Give a justified conclusion.** ● Include your own opinion together with your own reasoning. ● **Include evaluation**. Explain why you think one viewpoint is stronger than the other or why they are equally strong. ● Do not just repeat arguments you have already used without explaining how they apply to your reasoned opinion/conclusion.	

13 'Religious people should be the main peacemakers in the world today.'

Evaluate this statement. In your answer you:

- should give reasoned arguments in support of this statement
- should give reasoned arguments to support a different point of view
- should refer to religious arguments
- may refer to non-religious arguments
- should reach a justified conclusion.

[12 marks]
[+3 SPaG marks]

Check your answers using the mark scheme on pages 161–162. How did you do?
To feel more secure in the content you need to remember, re-read pages 116–123.
To remind yourself of what the examiner is looking for, go to pages 7–13.

9 Religion, crime and punishment

9.1 Crime and punishment

RECAP

Essential information:

- [ ] Crime and punishment are both governed by the law.
- [ ] Not all good actions are required by law and not all evil actions break the law.

What are crime and punishment?

- A **crime** is an offence that breaks the law set by the government. People who commit crimes face legal consequences.
- In the UK, people who commit crimes are arrested and questioned by police.
- They then appear before a court where a judge or jury determines their **punishment** (something done legally to somebody as a result of being found guilty of breaking the law).
- In the UK, the most serious crimes are punished with a life sentence in prison, while less serious ones might result in a shorter time in prison, community service or a fine. No legal punishment is allowed to deliberately cause harm to the offender.

Good and evil intentions and actions

- Some people assume a **good action** is an action that does not break a law. However, there are also many good actions which exist outside the law (such as giving to charity or helping people in need).
- Likewise, there are some actions that are not against the law but might be considered evil by some people (such as adultery or abortion). Generally, **evil actions** are considered to cause suffering and harm to others.

Christian views	Sikh views
• Teachings in the Bible warn against having any evil or wrong thoughts and intentions. "You have heard that it was said, 'You shall not commit adultery.' But I tell you that anyone who looks at a woman lustfully has already committed adultery with her in his heart." *Matthew 5:27–28* [NIV] • Evil actions such as using violence are considered to be sinful and against God. • Many Christians would claim there is no such thing as an evil person, because God created people to be good. • However, because of original sin (see page 24), all humans have a tendency to do evil things even though they are not evil in themselves.	• Sikhs believe humans are born good but they make mistakes and some do evil things because they have not resisted temptation. • Sikhism teaches that the root cause of evil or suffering is the human ego, which has become distracted by the five vices of anger, lust, greed, worldly attachment and pride. • Sikhs believe in reincarnation, so they believe in punishment after death. They know they must face punishment in this life for their wrongdoings too. • Having good intentions, such as to obey the law and perform sewa, helps build good karma. "The self-willed manmukh receives only more punishment." *Guru Granth Sahib 361*

APPLY

A Give **two** ways in which a crime might be punished in the UK.

B 'Intentions are more important than actions.'

Write a developed argument for this statement and another developed argument against it. Elaborate your arguments with religious teaching.

TIP

When faced with a statement that you have a strong opinion on, you must also focus on an alternative opinion, even if you strongly disagree with it.

RECAP

Essential information:

- ☐ There are many different reasons why people commit crimes, from poverty and addiction to greed and hatred.
- ☐ Christians and Sikhs believe crime is rarely justified, although both faiths believe it is right to protest against unjust laws.

Reasons why some people commit crime

Reason	Explanation	Christian views	Sikh views
Poverty	There are millions of people in the UK who live in **poverty**, who cannot always afford to buy food. Some believe the only way out of this is to steal. However, stealing for any reason is against the law, and those who steal food or other essentials can be arrested and punished.	Stealing is wrong, but people should do what they can to help make sure nobody finds themselves in the position of having to steal because of poverty.	Sikhs work to create situations where there is no poverty, for example by providing food to those in need through the langar.
Upbringing	Some young people grow up in a household where crime is a part of life. A troubled upbringing (for example because of neglect or abuse) might also lead a person to turn to crime.	Parents should teach their children the right way to behave through their own words and actions.	Sikhism emphasises a strong family structure where the wisdom of elders is respected. This helps ensure children do not turn to crime.
Mental illness	Some forms of **mental illness** (a medical condition that affects a person's emotions or moods) may lead to crime. E.g. anger management problems may lead to violence.	Treating the causes of the illness is the most loving and compassionate way of dealing with people with mental illness.	Any difficulty that leads to stress can make mental illness worse, so supporting others so they can cope with their situation is important.
Addiction	Taking illegal drugs is in itself a criminal act. A person's **addiction** (physical or mental dependency) may make them commit further crimes to be able to buy drugs. Legal drugs such as alcohol can also cause crime such as violence, rape and drunk driving if taken to excess.	Christians are against taking illegal drugs and support rehabilitation as a way of defeating an addiction. Most Christians believe alcohol is acceptable in moderation.	People under the influence of drugs lose awareness and so are less sensitive to others. Sikh teachings forbid the taking of intoxicants.
Greed	Some people want personal possessions they do not need and cannot afford. Their **greed** may lead them to steal them.	The Ten Commandments forbid envy, and it is envy that often causes greed.	In Sikhism, greed is one of the five evils and is seen as unnecessary and destructive.
Hate	Hate, the opposite of love, can lead to violence or aggression.	Jesus taught Christians to love everybody, including their enemies.	Sikhs believe every person is created by God and has a divine spark, so hating anyone would be wrong and against God's will.
Opposition to an unjust law	Sometimes people break a law they believe to be unjust in order to protest against it. These could be laws based on inequality or that deny basic human rights.	Some Christians may agree with this but only if no violence is involved and nobody gets harmed.	Sikhs have protested against laws they felt were unjust or that prevented them from fulfilling their religious duties.

APPLY

A Give **two** religious responses to the reasons why people commit crimes.

B 'Addiction is the only good excuse for committing crimes.'

Write down your own thoughts about this and **develop them by adding religious views**.

TIP

Remember that while Christianity and Sikhism condemn crime, they do not condemn criminals. Most Christians and Sikhs believe criminals should be treated with compassion and forgiveness, even though the crimes they committed were wrong.

9.3 Attitudes to lawbreakers and different types of crime

RECAP

Essential information:

- [ ] Christians and Sikhs believe criminals should be punished according to the law but also treated compassionately.
- [ ] Christianity and Sikhism condemn hate crime, theft and murder.

Religious attitudes to lawbreakers

Many **Christians** may disapprove of the crime but don't hate the criminal who committed it. They believe that:

- Offenders **must be punished by the law** according to how serious their crime was.
- Offenders **have basic rights** so should not be given a punishment that is inhumane or harmful.
- Through their punishment offenders should be **helped to become responsible members of society** so they do not reoffend.
- The parable of the Sheep and the Goats teaches that helping prisoners is good.

Sikhs believe that God requires them to **promote justice and equality**, both of which are damaged by crime.

Sikhs believe that **serious offenders should be put in prison to protect others** in society. Offenders should not be mistreated. Instead they should be **helped and educated** to not offend again.

Sir Mota Singh, Britain's first Sikh judge

TIP

You could use Jesus' teaching 'love your neighbour' in your exam to show that Christians believe committing crimes which hurt others is wrong, but that as Christians they should also show love to those who commit crimes.

Religious attitudes towards three different types of crime

Type of crime	Christian views	Sikh views
Hate crime (usually targeted at a person because of their race, religion, sexuality, disability or gender)	• Christians condemn hate crimes because they believe God created all humans equal and no one should be singled out for inferior treatment. • When Jesus taught his followers to 'love your neighbour' (Mark 12:31), he meant showing compassion, care and respect to everybody.	• Hate crimes make the Sikh ideal of a society without prejudice or discrimination impossible to achieve. • The Mool Mantra describes God as being without hate, and Sikhs believe they too should be without hate.
Theft (less serious than some crimes but still results in the victim suffering a loss)	• Theft goes against the Ten Commandments (Exodus 20:15). • Christians do not agree with any theft, including theft caused by need rather than greed.	• Sikhs believe stealing is wrong, but they may be more sympathetic towards people committing theft out of need rather than greed (which is one of the five evils). • Sikhs believe they should help to provide for the community (e.g. through the langar), so people are less likely to steal out of need.
Murder (viewed by many as the most serious crime)	• Murder is wrong because only God has the right to take life. • It goes against the Ten Commandments (Exodus 20:13).	• Sikhs oppose murder because only God has the right to give and take life at a time of his choosing. • Murder is strictly forbidden in the Sikh Code of Conduct, the Rehat Maryada.

APPLY

A **Explain** the similarities and differences between a hate crime and murder.

B 'Religious believers should hate the crime but not the criminal who committed it.'

Explain your opinion and develop it with religious teachings.

9.4 Three aims of punishment

RECAP

Essential information:

- ☐ Three aims of punishment are **retribution** (to get your own back), **deterrence** (to put people off committing crimes) and **reformation** (to change someone's behaviour for the better).
- ☐ Christians and Sikhs generally support reformation as the best aim of punishment.

Retribution, deterrence and reformation

	Explanation	Christian views	Sikh views
Retribution – to get your own back	• Society, on behalf of the victim, is getting its own back on the offender. • Criminals should be made to suffer in proportion to how serious their crimes are. • E.g. in the case of murder, the murderer should be killed as a punishment.	• Paul teaches, 'Do not be overcome by evil, but overcome evil with good' (Romans 21:21). • Many Christians focus on other aims of punishment, which they believe are less harmful and more positive. • Some Christians support the death penalty by quoting, 'life for life, eye for eye, tooth for tooth' (Exodus 21:23–24). But most think this means, for example, that murderers should be punished severely but not killed.	• Retribution could be seen as society getting its own back on the offender, which may be seen as revenge. Taking revenge is regarded as a crime in itself in Sikhism because it comes from anger. • For Sikhs, revenge is not compassionate. "Do not be angry with anyone else; look within your own self instead." *Guru Granth Sahib 259*
Deterrence – to put people off committing crimes	• The idea of deterrence is to use punishment as an example and warning to others. • If the punishment is harsh, it may deter the offender from repeating the crime and others from copying it. • In some countries, punishments are carried out in public as a form of deterrence.	• Although most Christians have no real problem with the idea of deterrence, they do not support punishments that are excessively harsh. • They oppose carrying out punishments in public because these could humiliate offenders rather than treating them with respect.	• Some Sikhs favour deterrence because it teaches that bad actions bring bad consequences, which is the basis of the belief of karma.
Reformation – to change someone's behaviour for the better	• Reformation aims to use punishment that helps offenders to give up crime and realise their behaviour is harmful. • This may involve therapy and counselling, community service, and meeting the victims. • It is hoped offenders will change their attitude and become law-abiding members of society.	• Most Christians favour reformation over other aims of punishment. • This is because it is positive rather than negative, and works with individuals to improve their life chances. • It should not be a replacement for punishment but should happen alongside punishment.	• Sikhs believe reformation is the best aim of punishment. • Reformation recognises that offenders have the potential to change, including choosing to follow the word of God. • Reformation embodies Sikh principles of compassion, forgiveness and equality.

APPLY

A **Explain** what each of the three aims of punishment are.

B **Write a developed argument** to support your own opinion about whether offenders should be punished severely. Include some religious teachings in your answer.

TIP

Protection is another aim of punishment (where criminals are imprisoned to protect the rest of society).

9.5 Religious attitudes to suffering and causing suffering to others

RECAP

Essential information:

- ☐ Christians and Sikhs believe in not causing suffering to others.
- ☐ They also believe it is important to help those who are suffering.
- ☐ For Christians, some suffering is not caused by God but is a result of human free will. Sikhs believe God does not cause suffering, but permits it to happen as a test of faith and courage.

Christian attitudes towards suffering

- Whatever the cause, Christians believe they **have a duty to help those who are suffering**.
- Christians try to **follow the example of Jesus**. He helped many whom he saw were suffering and told his followers to do the same.
- Christians should also **try not to cause others to suffer**.
- When they do cause others to suffer, they should **apologise and try to repair the damage they have caused** in order to restore relationships.
- Where it is unavoidable, suffering may **strengthen a person's character and faith**.

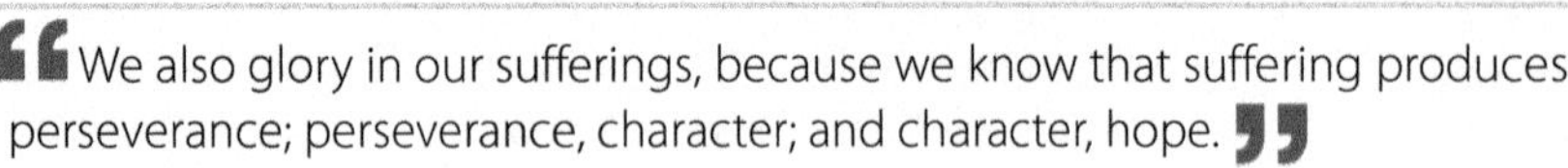

"We also glory in our sufferings, because we know that suffering produces perseverance; perseverance, character; and character, hope."

Romans 5:3–4 [NIV]

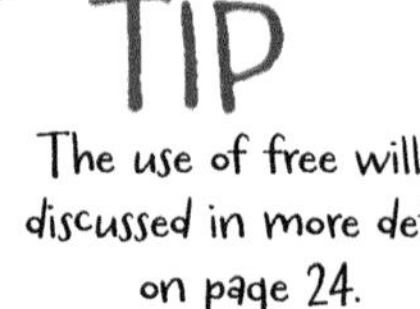

TIP
The use of free will is discussed in more detail on page 24.

How can a loving God allow people to suffer?

- Christians believe it is wrong to blame God for the suffering that results from human actions.
- This is because God gave humans **free will**: the ability to make decisions for themselves.
- God has also given plenty of guidance on how to use free will responsibly.
- The teachings and example of Jesus will reduce suffering if followed.
- The role of the law is to give more 'compulsory' guidance about the best way to use free will, together with punishments for those who cause suffering by committing crimes.

Sikh attitudes towards suffering

- When Sikhs become content with God's will, they **do not judge events as 'good' or 'bad'** but as part of the normal rollercoaster of life.
- Sikhs believe **bad actions have negative consequences** for spiritual development. They can lead to greater suffering and moving **further away from God**.
- If people **respond positively** to God by using their free will, there will be less suffering.

"Knowing their Lord and Master, people show compassion; then, they become immortal, and attain the state of eternal dignity."

Guru Granth Sahib 340

Sikhs believe their compassion and understanding of right and wrong means they should not cause suffering to others.

Sikhs believe that if they cause others to suffer, they themselves will suffer in this life or in the next one due to the law of karma.

Sikhs believe that evil and suffering are caused when a person's ego or sense of self is controlled by the five vices (anger, lust, greed, worldly attachment and pride).

APPLY

A Explain **two** contrasting religious beliefs about suffering.

B 'Suffering can lead to a positive outcome.'

Think carefully about this statement and **write a developed argument** to support your opinion on it.

9.6 Religious attitudes to the treatment of criminals

RECAP

Essential information:

- ☐ A **prison** is a secure building where offenders are kept for a period of time set by a judge. In the UK, people who commit more serious crimes are sent to prison.
- ☐ **Corporal punishment** is punishment that causes physical pain. It is illegal in the UK and not supported by Christianity or Sikhism.
- ☐ **Community service** is a way of punishing offenders by making them do unpaid work in the community. It is approved of by most Christians and Sikhs.

You might be asked to compare beliefs on corporal punishment between Christianity (the main religious tradition in Great Britain) and another religious tradition.

Prison

Features	Christian views	Sikh views
• The main punishment is a loss of liberty. • Prisoners are locked in cells for some of the day, and have to do manual work for little money. • Reserved for more serious crimes.	Many Christians support the use of prisons for more serious crimes. They also believe prisoners should be treated well, and involved in positive activities and education that help them to reform.	Sikhs agree with the use of prison if it is aimed at reforming the criminal. Prisons can also work as a deterrent and make society safer.

Corporal punishment

Features	Christian views	Sikh views
• Punishes offenders by inflicting physical pain. • Considered to be a breach of human rights laws. • Illegal in the UK and many other countries. • Muslim countries such as Iran and Saudi Arabia use corporal punishment (e.g. caning) for offences such as gambling and sexual promiscuity.	Christians do not support corporal punishment. It does not seek to reform an offender, so can be seen as a negative and harmful punishment. It does not show respect for the individual.	Corporal punishment goes against Sikh principles and teaching. Sikhs consider it to be harmful and lacking in compassion.

Community service

Features	Christian views	Sikh views
• Includes work in the community, such as cleaning graffiti, decorating or clearing wasteland. • Used for more minor offences, such as vandalism or benefit fraud. • May include treatment for addiction or medical conditions, counselling and education. • In some cases, a meeting may be set up so the victim can tell the offender the impact their crime had and the offender can apologise.	Most Christians approve of community service as it allows offenders to make up for what they have done wrong, deters them from committing future offences, and reforms them by making them realise the consequences of their actions. Another positive is that no harm is done to the offender.	The aim of community service reflects Sikh principles and reinforces sewa (the duty to serve the community). Community service earns good karma which can be set against the bad karma of the crime itself.

APPLY

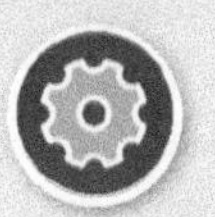

A Explain **two** similar religious beliefs about corporal punishment.

B 'Criminals should not be treated well.'

Make a list of the religious arguments you would use when evaluating this statement. Sort them into arguments in support of the statement and arguments against the statement.

TIP

Here you could explain one Christian belief against corporal punishment, and a similar Sikh belief against corporal punishment.

9.7 Religious attitudes to forgiveness

RECAP

Essential information:

- [ ] Christians and Sikhs emphasise the importance of **forgiveness** (showing mercy and pardoning someone for what they have done wrong).
- [ ] Most Christians and Sikhs believe forgiveness is not a replacement for punishment.

You might be asked to compare beliefs on forgiveness between Christianity (the main religious tradition in Great Britain) and another religious tradition.

Christian attitudes towards forgiveness

Forgiveness is a **key belief in Christianity**. Jesus taught forgiveness and showed it in his actions:

- When he was dying on the cross, **Jesus forgave those who crucified him**: 'Father forgive them, for they do not know what they are doing' (Luke 23:24).
- When asked how many times a person should be forgiven, Jesus said 'not seven times, but seventy-seven times' (Matthew 18:21–22). Christians interpret this to mean there should be **no limit to the amount of forgiveness they show to someone**.

The Lord's Prayer shows that Christians believe **God expects them to show forgiveness** to others. In turn, **God will forgive them** for the sins they commit ('Forgive us our sins as we forgive those who sin against us').

Many Christians argue that **forgiveness should not be a replacement for punishment**. They believe the offender should be forgiven as far as possible, but should also be punished to ensure justice is done (and to help the offender reform themselves).

TIP

Remember that forgiving a crime is not the same as forgetting a crime. It means acknowledging the crime happened while letting go of any anger or resentment towards the criminal.

Sikh attitudes towards forgiveness

- Forgiveness is a **fundamental principle** in Sikhism, closely linked to belief in **equality**. Sikhs should follow the example of the Gurus and show compassion for others, understanding that wrong actions are the result of weaknesses shared by all humans.
- Forgiveness is **not a replacement for punishment**, as humane punishment helps to reform a criminal and prevent further harm occurring.

> "Where there is forgiveness, there is God himself."
> *Guru Granth Sahib 1372*

> "Those who have... forgiveness as their chanting beads – they are the most excellent people."
> *Guru Granth Sahib 245*

The example of Pardeep Kaleka

Pardeep Kaleka's father was shot at a mass shooting at a gurdwara in Oak Creek, USA in 2012. He chose to respond with compassion and forgiveness, which he saw as a long process that he sometimes found difficult. As a result of the shooting, he helped to found Serve 2 Unite – an organisation bringing together children of all ethnicities and backgrounds.

TIP

A logical chain of reasoning could include four things:

- an opinion
- a reason for the opinion
- development of the reason
- the addition of religious teaching and examples.

APPLY

A Give **two** similar views on forgiveness in Christianity and Sikhism.

B 'Nobody should expect to be forgiven more than once.'

Write a logical chain of reasoning that agrees with this statement, and another one that gives a different point of view.

9.8 Religious attitudes to the death penalty

RECAP

Essential information:

- ☐ The **death penalty** (when a criminal is put to death for their crime) is illegal in the UK but still exists in some other countries.
- ☐ Many Christians and Sikhs oppose the death penalty.

You might be asked to compare beliefs on the death penalty between Christianity (the main religious tradition in Great Britain) and another religious tradition.

Arguments for and against the death penalty

The death penalty was abolished in the UK in 1969. It is also illegal in most of Europe, but still exists in some states in the USA, in China and in many Muslim countries, such as Saudi Arabia.

Arguments for and against the death penalty include the following:

For or against	Explanation
Against	• There is a chance of **killing an innocent person**. • E.g. three people executed in the UK in the 1950s have since been pardoned, because new evidence has cast serious doubt over their guilt.
	• There is **little evidence the death penalty is an effective deterrent**. • E.g. the UK murder rate is no higher than in countries that have the death penalty. • Often the threat of punishment does not enter into the murderer's thinking.
	• It is **not right to take another person's life**. This does not show forgiveness or compassion.
	• Society can still be protected by **imprisoning criminals** instead of executing them.
For	• The **principle of utility** states an action is right if it produces the maximum happiness for the greatest number of people affected by it. • If the use of the death penalty is proven to protect society – therefore creating happiness for a greater number of people – it can be justified.
	• It is **justified retribution** for people who commit the worst possible crimes.
	• It **protects society** by removing the worst criminals so they cannot cause harm again.

Religious attitudes to the death penalty

Most Christians and Sikhs do not support the death penalty, although some do. Their views may be based partly on the arguments given above, and partly on the religious teachings given below.

Christian views	Sikh views
• The **sanctity of life** is the idea that all life is holy as it is created by God, and only God can take it away. This teaching is used to oppose the death penalty. • Ezekiel 33:11 teaches that wrongdoers should be reformed (not executed). • Some Christians agree with the death penalty and use teachings from the Old Testament to support their views. "Whoever sheds human blood, by humans shall their blood be shed." *Genesis 9:6* [NIV]	• Sikh teaching is against the death penalty as only God has the right to take a life. • Sikhs believe the death penalty is based on retribution and revenge, which cannot be justified. • Imprisonment gives the opportunity for reformation and compassion, which the death penalty does not. "He alone has the Power in His Hands. He watches over all." *Guru Granth Sahib 7*

APPLY

(A) Give **two** religious teachings about the death penalty.

(B) **Write a paragraph** to support the statement, 'Religious believers should not support the death penalty.'

REVIEW

9 Exam practice

Test the 1 mark question

1 Which **one** of the following is a form of punishment in which physical pain is inflicted on the criminal?

A Corporal punishment B Prison C Forgiveness D Community service **[1 mark]**

2 Which **one** of the following suggests an action is right if it follows the principle of utility and promotes the maximum…?

A Pain B Sadness C Happiness D Profit **[1 mark]**

Test the 2 mark question

3 Give **two** aims of punishment. **[2 marks]**

1) ______________________________

2) ______________________________

4 Give **two** reasons why some people commit crimes. **[2 marks]**

1) ______________________________

2) ______________________________

Test the 4 mark question

5 Explain **two** contrasting beliefs in contemporary British society about whether the death penalty should exist in the UK.
In your answer you should refer to the main religious tradition of Great Britain and one or more other religious traditions. **[4 marks]**

• **Explain one belief.**	*Some Christians believe the death penalty is correct because it follows the Old Testament teaching of an 'eye for eye, tooth for tooth'.*
• Develop your explanation with more detail/an example/reference to a religious teaching or quotation.	*An eye for an eye and a tooth for a tooth means that an offender should receive back the same as he has done, so if he has murdered someone, he should be killed.*
• **Explain a second contrasting belief.**	*Sikhs are against the death penalty as they believe only God has the right to take a life.*
• Develop your explanation with more detail/an example/reference to a religious teaching or quotation.	*This is supported by Guru Granth Sahib 7, which says 'He alone has the Power in His Hands'.*

TIP
Both of the explanatior of beliefs in this answe have been clearly develop with religious teaching

6 Explain **two** contrasting beliefs about community service.
In your answer you should refer to the main religious tradition of Great Britain and one or more other religious traditions. **[4 marks]**

• **Explain one belief.**	
• Develop your explanation with more detail/an example/reference to a religious teaching or quotation.	
• **Explain a second contrasting belief.**	
• Develop your explanation with more detail/an example/reference to a religious teaching or quotation.	

TIP
The 'contrasting' beliefs here could be about the value of community service and whether it is the best method of punishment.

7 Explain **two** similar beliefs that oppose retribution as an aim of punishment.

In your answer you should refer to the main religious tradition of Great Britain and one or more other religious traditions. **[4 marks]**

Test the 5 mark question

8 Explain **two** religious beliefs about reformation as an aim of punishment.
Refer to sacred writings or another source of religious belief and teaching in your answer. **[5 marks]**

• **Explain one belief.**	*A Christian belief is that reformation is a preferable aim of punishment because it seeks to help offenders change their behaviour.*
• Develop your explanation with more detail/an example.	*This means they are less likely to commit any further offences, so they won't hurt anybody else or need to be punished again.*
• **Explain a second belief.**	*Sikhs believe reformation is the best aim of punishment as it recognises that offenders have the potential to change.*
• Develop your explanation with more detail/an example.	*This may include the desire to listen to and follow the word of God.*
• Add a reference to sacred writings or another source of religious belief and teaching. If you prefer, you can add this reference to your first belief instead.	*The Rehat Maryada explains what should happen when a person breaks their religious vows and this could apply to other people who need to reform their ways. The advice includes repentance and doing community service.*

9 Explain **two** religious beliefs about forgiveness.

Refer to sacred writings or another source of religious belief and teaching in your answer. **[5 marks]**

• **Explain one belief.**	
• Develop your explanation with more detail/an example.	
• **Explain a second belief.**	
• Develop your explanation with more detail/an example.	
• Add a reference to sacred writings or another source of religious belief and teaching. If you prefer, you can add this reference to your first belief instead.	

10 Explain **two** religious beliefs about hate crimes.

Refer to sacred writings or another source of religious belief and teaching in your answer. **[5 marks]**

Test the 12 mark question

11 'It is right to forgive all offenders whoever they are and whatever they have done.'

Evaluate this statement. In your answer you:

- should give reasoned arguments in support of this statement
- should give reasoned arguments to support a different point of view
- should refer to religious arguments
- may refer to non-religious arguments
- should reach a justified conclusion.

[12 marks]
[+3 SPaG ma

REASONED ARGUMENTS IN SUPPORT OF THE STATEMENT ● **Explain why some people would agree with the statement.** ● Develop your explanation with more detail and examples. ● Refer to religious teaching. Use a quote or paraphrase or a religious authority. ● **Evaluate the arguments.** Is this a good argument or not? Explain why you think this.	*Christians should always forgive anybody who wants to be forgiven. When the disciples asked Jesus how many times they should forgive, suggesting that seven was a fair number, Jesus told them it should be seventy-seven times. In other words, there should be no maximum. Jesus even asked God to forgive the people who crucified him because they didn't know what they were doing. So it should not matter how many times, who is asking to be forgiven or what they have done to be forgiven for.* *Sikhs believe in forgiveness as it follows the example of the Gurus and shows compassion for others. It also acknowledges that bad actions are the result of weaknesses which all humans share. Guru Granth Sahib 1372 shows how important forgiveness is when it says, 'Where there is forgiveness there is God himself.'*
REASONED ARGUMENTS SUPPORTING A DIFFERENT VIEW ● **Explain why some people would support a different view.** ● Develop your explanation with more detail and examples. ● Refer to religious teaching. Use a quote or paraphrase or a religious authority. ● **Evaluate the arguments.** Is this a good argument or not? Explain why you think this.	*Some people who are victims of serious crimes find it very difficult to forgive. They cannot imagine how they can ever feel anything but hatred for someone who has wronged them so horribly. A victim of rape may find it hard to forgive their attacker and they are highly unlikely to ever forget it. But time is a great healer and maybe forgiveness is more easily given some years later.* *The line in the Lord's Prayer that says: 'Forgive us our sins, as we forgive those who sin against us' is unrealistic because there are some awful things that should never be forgiven unless the offender shows they are truly sorry and remorseful, and even then, it is almost impossible. Many Sikhs might have found it difficult to forgive Wade Michael Page for the mass shooting at the gurdwara at Oak Tree, Wisconsin. I do not think they should be expected to.*
CONCLUSION ● **Give a justified conclusion.** ● Include your own opinion together with your own reasoning. ● **Include evaluation.** Explain why you think one viewpoint is stronger than the other or why they are equally strong. ● Do not just repeat arguments you have already used without explaining how they apply to your reasoned opinion/ conclusion.	*In my opinion, forgiveness is an ideal that religions want people to work towards. I think if they become the victims themselves, they may change their mind. We are only human.*

TIP
The first paragraph not only shows good knowledge of the Bible's teaching on forgiveness but also makes its meaning clear.

TIP
This student could improve their conclusion by going into more detail about their views on the statement. For example, they could explain why they think one viewpoint is stronger than the other, or express an opinion about the strength of the religious arguments given in the answer.

12 'The use of the death penalty is always wrong.'

Evaluate this statement. In your answer you:

- should give reasoned arguments in support of this statement
- should give reasoned arguments to support a different point of view
- should refer to religious arguments
- may refer to non-religious arguments
- should reach a justified conclusion.

[12 marks]
[+3 SPaG marks]

REASONED ARGUMENTS IN SUPPORT OF THE STATEMENT ● **Explain why some people would agree with the statement.** ● Develop your explanation with more detail and examples. ● Refer to religious teaching. Use a quote or paraphrase or a religious authority. ● **Evaluate the arguments.** Is this a good argument or not? Explain why you think this.	
REASONED ARGUMENTS SUPPORTING A DIFFERENT VIEW ● **Explain why some people would support a different view.** ● Develop your explanation with more detail and examples. ● Refer to religious teaching. Use a quote or paraphrase or a religious authority. ● **Evaluate the arguments.** Is this a good argument or not? Explain why you think this.	
CONCLUSION ● **Give a justified conclusion.** ● Include your own opinion together with your own reasoning. ● **Include evaluation.** Explain why you think one viewpoint is stronger than the other or why they are equally strong. ● Do not just repeat arguments you have already used without explaining how they apply to your reasoned opinion/conclusion.	

13 'There is no good reason why anyone should commit a crime.'

Evaluate this statement. In your answer you:

- should give reasoned arguments in support of this statement
- should give reasoned arguments to support a different point of view
- should refer to religious arguments
- may refer to non-religious arguments
- should reach a justified conclusion.

[12 marks]
[+3 SPaG marks]

Check your answers using the mark scheme on pages 162–163. How did you do?
To feel more secure in the content you need to remember, re-read pages 128–135.
To remind yourself of what the examiner is looking for, go to pages 7–13.

10 Religion, human rights and social justice

10.1 Social justice and human rights

RECAP

Essential information:

- [ ] **Human rights** are the basic rights and freedoms to which all human beings should be entitled. It is only possible for all people to have these rights if they acknowledge the responsibility to respect and help provide for the rights of others.
- [ ] **Social justice** means ensuring society treats people fairly whether they are poor or wealthy. It involves protecting everyone's human rights.

Human rights and responsibilities

- In 1948, the United Nations adopted the **Universal Declaration of Human Rights** (UDHR).
- This sets out the rights to which every person should be entitled.
- The UK government is obliged to provide these rights to people living in the UK.

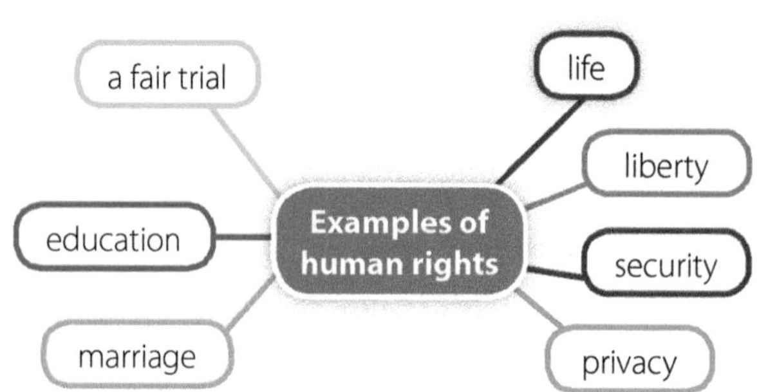

People can only have human rights if they acknowledge the responsibility to make sure these rights are available. This includes the responsibility to **respect other people's rights**, and the responsibility to **help create access to those rights**. For example:

- Humans have the right to freedom of speech, but the responsibility not to say something that causes offence.
- Children have the right to protection from cruelty, but the responsibility not to bully or harm each other.

Social justice

Social justice is about trying to protect people's rights and opportunities so the least advantaged members of society are treated with the same justice and compassion as more advantaged people.

Christian views	Sikh views
• There are many teachings in the Bible about the importance of social justice and caring for others. • Some of the Old Testament prophets were quick to condemn injustice and looked forward to a fairer society. For example, the prophet Amos said, 'Let justice roll on like a river and righteousness like a never-failing stream' (Amos 5:24). • Jesus stressed the need to help others, for example in his teaching 'love your neighbour as yourself' (Mark 12:31).	• Sikhism is founded on the principle of working together for the common good of all. • Guru Tegh Bahadur set an example of protecting the rights of all (regardless of faith) when he supported the Kashmiri Hindus to protect their way of life. • Lord Indarjit Singh of Wimbledon, in response to an attack on Sikhs, said, 'Human rights abuses against anyone are the responsibility of us all.'

APPLY

A Give **two** examples of human rights.

B 'Everybody's human rights should be protected.'

Write a detailed argument agreeing with this statement and a contrasting argument to support a different opinion.

10.2 Prejudice and discrimination

RECAP

Essential information:

- [ ] **Equality** means having equal rights, status and opportunities.
- [ ] Christianity teaches that all people are equal because they have all been made in God's image. Sikhs believe all people are created by God and are of equal value.

In 2014, Libby Lane became the first female bishop in the Church of England.

Gender prejudice and discrimination

- **Prejudice** means holding biased (usually negative) opinions about an individual or a group of people. These opinions are usually based on ignorance and stereotypical ideas about race, religion, gender, sexuality, disability, etc.
- Actions or behaviour arising from holding prejudiced views are called **discrimination**.

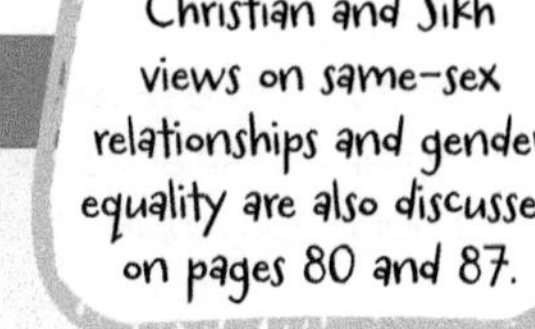

TIP

Christian and Sikh views on same-sex relationships and gender equality are also discussed on pages 80 and 87.

Christian views	Sikh views
• In early Christianity, women were not allowed to be leaders of the Church. "Women should remain silent in the churches [...] for it is disgraceful for a woman to speak in the church." *1 Corinthians 14:34–35* [NIV] • The Catholic and Orthodox Churches still do not allow women to be priests. They argue that men and women are equal but have different roles. • Other Christian denominations are happy to ordain women. They argue the Church should adapt to reflect the importance of equality in today's society.	• The Gurus taught that God is in every person: 'The Beloved Himself enjoys every heart; He is contained within every woman and man.' (Guru Granth Sahib 605) • The Guru Granth Sahib stresses the importance of women in bringing about the existence of the whole human race. • Sikh men and women play an equally important role in the rituals of worship and performing sewa (service).

Sexuality

Christian views	Sikh views
• Some Christians think heterosexual relationships that lead to procreation are what God intended (see Genesis 1:28 and 2:24). • They believe same-sex relationships are sinful. • Others think same-sex relationships are morally acceptable, and it is not loving to condemn people for their sexual orientation.	• The Guru Granth Sahib and the Sikh Gurus did not mention homosexuality, but did encourage heterosexual marriage and the life of a householder (family life). • Some Sikhs argue that as the soul does not have a gender, same-sex relationships should be permitted, although most would say they are not acceptable. • Sikhs welcome people to the langar and to worship with them whatever their sexuality, as attaining enlightenment and becoming one with God are considered much more important than sexuality.

APPLY

A Explain **one** similarity and **one** difference between Christianity and Sikhism over the roles women have in religion.

B 'Women should not be allowed to take on leadership positions in a religion.'

Write a developed argument to agree with this statement, and another argument to support a different opinion.

You might be asked to compare beliefs on the status of women in religion between Christianity (the main religious tradition in Great Britain) and another religious tradition.

10.3 Religious freedom

RECAP

Essential information:

- ☐ Christians and Sikhs generally believe people should have **freedom of religion** (the right to practise whatever religion one chooses), including **freedom of religious expression** (the right to worship, preach and practise one's faith in whatever way one chooses).
- ☐ These rights are protected by the UK government, and included in the Universal Declaration of Human Rights.

Freedom of religion

In Britain today:

- Christianity is the main religious tradition.
- But nobody is forced to be a Christian because the government protects the freedom of religious expression.
- This gives all individuals the right to follow whichever faith they choose or none.
- Laws forbid the persecution of members of any faith.
- Any person can encourage anybody else to follow their faith, provided they do not preach hatred and intolerance.

> "Everyone has the right to freedom of thought, conscience and religion; this right includes freedom to [...] manifest his religion or belief in teaching, practice, worship and observance."
> *Universal Declaration of Human Rights*

Religious teachings on freedom of religion

Christian views	Sikh views
• Christian teaching encourages tolerance and harmony. • Different Christian denominations fighting each other or other religions are not following teachings in the Bible. "If it is possible [...] live at peace with everyone." *Romans 12:18* [NIV] "Be completely humble and gentle; be patient, bearing with one another in love." *Ephesians 4:2* [NIV]	• Most Sikhs are not just tolerant of other faiths, but genuinely respect the devotion of those faiths. "Do not say that the Vedas, the Bible and the Koran are false. Those who do not contemplate them are false." *Guru Granth Sahib 1350* • The Adi Granth contains hymns from Hindu and Muslim writers as well as the Sikh Gurus. • The Gurus taught that the faith into which someone is born is the faith they should try to excel in.

Despite the fact that Christianity encourages religious tolerance, there have been examples where Christians have not been able to live in harmony with other denominations or religions. For example, in Northern Ireland, different political and religious views have caused problems between Catholics and Protestants.

APPLY

A **Explain** the attitudes to freedom of religion from the main religious tradition of Great Britain and one or more other religious traditions.

B **Explain** whether you think people should be free to follow any religion they choose without any interference from anyone else. **Refer to religious teachings** in your argument.

You might be asked to compare beliefs on freedom of religious expression between Christianity (the main religious tradition in Great Britain) and another religious tradition.

10.4 Prejudice and discrimination – disability and race

RECAP

Essential information:

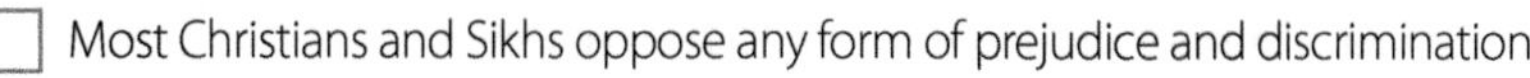

- [ ] Prejudice and discrimination based on **disability** (physical or mental impairments that affect day-to-day activities) or race is illegal in the UK, but still occurs regularly.

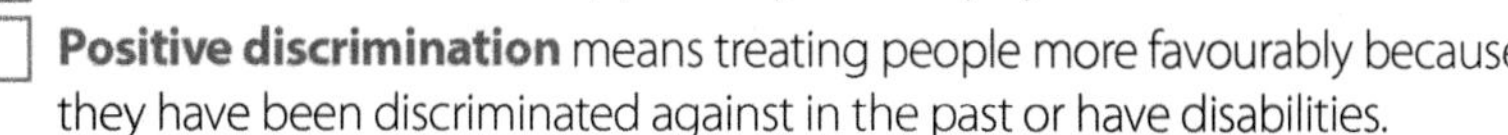

- [ ] Most Christians and Sikhs oppose any form of prejudice and discrimination.
- [ ] **Positive discrimination** means treating people more favourably because they have been discriminated against in the past or have disabilities.

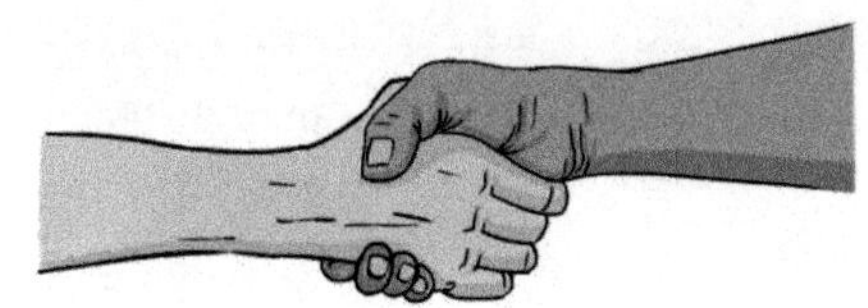

Disability

- There are over 500 million disabled people in the world today.
- Some people show prejudice or discrimination towards those with disabilities.
- Sometimes positive discrimination is used to give disabled people opportunities they would not otherwise have, such as giving wheelchair users front-row positions at a football ground so they can see the match.

Christian views	Sikh views
• Christians oppose discrimination against disabled people because it does not demonstrate equality or love. • In the Bible, Jesus helped the disabled by healing them, and he taught his followers to 'love your neighbour as yourself' (Mark 12:31).	• Sikhism teaches that as God created and is in every person, Sikhs should not show prejudice to anyone – including those who are disabled.

Racism

- Racism means to consider people of different races as inferior and to treat them badly as a result. Racism is often triggered by skin colour.
- Since 1976, various Acts have been passed that make racism illegal in the UK. Despite this, it still occurs regularly.
- 'Show Racism the Red Card' is one example of a campaign against racism. It is designed to educate football fans and remove racist abuse from football.
- Positive discrimination can be applied to race, e.g. a business might employ someone from an ethnic minority partly to help make the workplace more ethnically diverse.

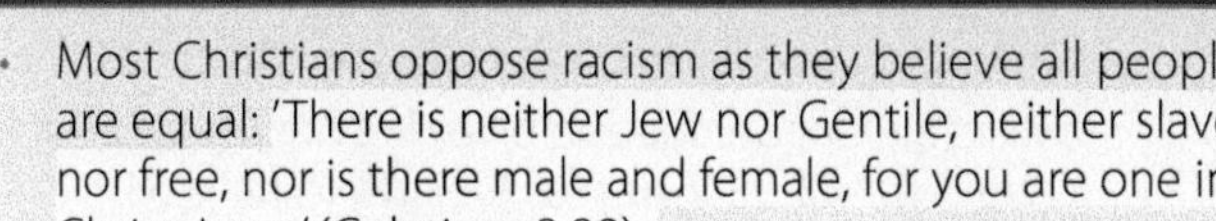

Christian views	Sikh views
• Most Christians oppose racism as they believe all people are equal: 'There is neither Jew nor Gentile, neither slave nor free, nor is there male and female, for you are one in Christ Jesus' (Galatians 3:28). • In the twentieth century, races were kept apart with black people being discriminated against in countries such as South Africa and the USA. • The actions of Christians such as Archbishop Desmond Tutu (South Africa) and Dr Martin Luther King Junior (USA), with the help of others, persuaded their respective governments that racist policies were unfair and needed to be changed.	• The Sikh Gurus taught that racism is wrong. "The clay is the same, but the Fashioner has fashioned it in various ways. There is nothing wrong with the pot of clay – there is nothing wrong with the potter." *Guru Granth Sahib 1350* • An example of equal treatment in Sikhism is that people of all races are welcome to eat in the langar.

APPLY

A **Explain** why Christians and Sikhs oppose discrimination based on race.

B 'All discrimination is wrong.'

Write a developed argument in support of this statement and a developed argument to support a different point of view. You can include your own opinion, but make sure you also **refer to religious teaching**.

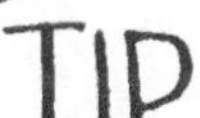

TIP

You might find a statement such as this difficult to argue against. But remember there are two forms of discrimination: negative and positive. Could you write an argument in favour of positive discrimination?

10.5 Religious teachings about wealth

RECAP

Essential information:

- [ ] Christianity and Sikhism do not teach it is wrong to be wealthy. But they do teach that focusing on wealth can lead to greed and selfishness, and the neglect of spiritual practice.
- [ ] Both religions also teach it is important to use wealth to help others in need.

Religious attitudes towards wealth

Christian views

- The Bible teaches that wealth is a blessing from God (1 Chronicles 29:12).
- The Bible also teaches that wealth is associated with dangers like greed and selfishness.

> "For the love of money is a root of all sorts of evil."
> *1 Timothy 6:10* [NIV]

TIP

If you use this quote in your exam, you must include the words 'For the love of' at the beginning, otherwise you change its meaning.

- Jesus did not teach it is wrong to be wealthy, but said that focusing on wealth brings the danger of ignoring God and neglecting the spiritual life.

> "You cannot serve both God and money."
> *Matthew 6:24* [NIV]

Sikh views

- The Gurus taught that people should earn an honest living while remembering God.
- The Guru Granth Sahib reminds people that wealth is not permanent.

> "No one has brought this wealth with him, and no one will take it with him when he goes."
> *Guru Granth Sahib 1251*

- Being poor is not seen as a virtue.
- Sikhs should avoid greed, which is one of the five evils.
- Guru Nanak said that the accumulation of wealth is not possible without sins.
- Sikhs are taught that nothing should distract them from becoming God-centred (gurmukh) – including the pursuit of wealth.

Religious attitudes towards using wealth

Christian views

- While everyone needs money to live, Christians believe those with excess money should give it to the Church for its upkeep and mission, including providing for the poor.
- Wealth should be used to help people in need.
- In the Bible, the parable of the Rich Man and Lazarus ends with the rich man in hell for not sharing his wealth with the poor beggar (Luke 16:19–31).
- The parable of the Sheep and the Goats states that those who help the poor are rewarded with a place in heaven (Matthew 25:31–46).

Sikh views

- Sikhs believe everyone in the world should have the right to enjoy the wealth God has provided.
- Sikhs are encouraged to give **dasvandh** (at least one tenth of their surplus wealth) to help with community projects.
- Wealth is a blessing that should be used to help others and increase equality in the world.

APPLY

A Explain **two** religious teachings about wealth.

B **Write a developed argument** to support the idea that giving to charity should be compulsory.

You might be asked to compare beliefs on the uses of wealth between Christianity (the main religious tradition in Great Britain) and another religious tradition.

RECAP

Essential information:

- [ ] Many people throughout the world live in **poverty**, without money, food or basic necessities.
- [ ] Some of the causes of poverty include debt, unemployment, exploitation and natural disasters.
- [ ] While many Christians and Sikhs believe it is important to help those living in poverty, they also think the poor have a responsibility to help themselves out of poverty if they are able to do so.

The causes of poverty

- Every person has basic needs in order to live (such as food, shelter and health care), but those living in poverty are not able to meet these needs.
- Poverty is a complex global problem that has many causes. A few of these include the following:

Debt	• Many of the poorest countries owe money to wealthier countries, which they have borrowed for such things as health care and education. • Debt is also a reason why individual people go into poverty in the UK, e.g. if they can't pay back money they owe to a bank.
Unemployment	• Unemployment is one of the main causes of poverty in the UK, as not everyone is able to find work or is fit to work.
Natural disasters	• Flooding, drought and other natural disasters are common throughout the world. They can destroy crops and properties, leaving people with no food or shelter.

Responsibilities of those living in poverty

- Even though the Bible says 'the one who is unwilling to work shall not eat' (2 Thessalonians 3:10), **Christians** believe it is important to help those who need assistance.
- Christians also encourage the poor to help themselves by finding work, but realise some are unable to do so.
- **Sikhism** teaches that those who are poor have a responsibility to try to get themselves out of poverty. Not working is regarded as being lazy and selfish if jobs are available.
- However, Sikhs also show compassion to those in poverty and try to help them where possible (for example by providing food in the langar).

TIP

People have different views on who is responsible for helping those in poverty. Some think it is society's responsibility, especially if people are in poverty through bad luck as a result of how society works. Others think more responsibility should be placed on people to make an effort to get out of poverty or to not get into poverty in the first place.

Christians Against Poverty (CAP)

Christians Against Poverty is a charity that helps those who are living in debt to find their way out of poverty. The charity works with people to help them create and stick to realistic budgets. It also negotiates fair payments with creditors so people can pay off their debts gradually. The charity is inspired by Christian beliefs to help thousands of people each year to get themselves out of poverty.

APPLY

A Give **two** causes of poverty in Britain.

B 'Those living in poverty should help themselves to get out of it rather than relying on the help of others.'

Write a paragraph that gives your opinion on this statement and explains your reasoning. **Refer to religious teachings** as part of your answer.

TIP

Don't forget, you are assessed on your reasoning, not your opinion. This means it doesn't matter what your opinion is as long as you have explained it well.

10.7 Exploitation of the poor

RECAP

Essential information:

- [ ] **Exploitation** is the misuse of power or money to get other people to do things for little or unfair reward.
- [ ] The poor are exploited worldwide in various ways, including by being paid unfairly, being charged excessive interest on loans, and being involved in people-trafficking.
- [ ] All of these practices go against the teachings of Christianity and Sikhism.

Fair pay

- An important way to stop exploitation of the poor is to make sure they receive **fair pay** for the work they do.
- In the UK, the National Minimum Wage sets the lowest amount an employer can pay a worker per hour.
- In many developing countries, large companies pay their workers very low wages in order to increase their profits.
- For example, in West Bengal in India, hundreds of thousands of people work on tea plantations for around £1 per day, which is about half of what they are legally entitled to.

Religious responses

- Most Christians support fair pay for everyone as this contributes to an equal and just society.

> "Do not exploit the poor because they are poor."
> *Proverbs 22:22* [NIV]

- Sikh employers have a duty to give employees good working conditions and fair wages.

Excessive interest on loans

- Poor people sometimes have little choice but to borrow money from loan companies that charge very high rates of interest (**excessive interest on loans**).
- If they cannot repay the loans fast enough, the huge interest rates mean they can quickly end up in debt, as they end up owing much more than the amount they borrowed.

Religious responses

- Christians believe it is hypocritical to claim to follow Jesus and treat others badly.
- Sikhs believe greed must be avoided.

> "The greedy mind is enticed by greed. Forgetting the Lord, it regrets and repents in the end."
> *Guru Granth Sahib 1172*

People-trafficking

- **People-trafficking** is the illegal movement of people, typically for the purposes of forced labour or commercial sexual exploitation.
- People who are desperate for a better way of life may pay smugglers to get them into a more prosperous country.
- Once in the new country, they have few rights and may be forced by the smugglers to work in poor conditions for little pay.
- Some are kidnapped and forced to work against their will.

Religious responses

- People-trafficking goes against Jesus' teaching to 'love your neighbour as yourself', and it is against Sikh teaching.

APPLY

A Explain **two** ways in which poor people might be exploited.

B 'Developed countries requiring cheap goods are to blame for exploitation.'

Write two developed arguments, one supporting the statement and one supporting a different opinion. **Refer to religious teaching** in your writings.

Remember that if you refer to religious teachings in your answer, they need to be relevant to the point you are making.

10.8 Giving money to the poor

RECAP

Essential information:

- [ ] There are two main ways to help the poor – by giving **short-term aid** (immediate help that focuses on short-term survival) or **long-term aid** (help over a longer period of time that has a more lasting effect).
- [ ] Many Christians and Sikhs try to help provide both types of aid, by supporting charities and campaigns that help those living in poverty.

Giving aid

There are two main types of help that can be given to the poor – short-term aid and long-term aid.

	Short-term aid	Long-term aid
Definition	• Help given to communities in a time of disaster or crisis. • Help given directly to the poor to relieve their immediate needs. • Also called emergency aid.	• Help given to communities over a longer period of time, which has a more lasting effect.
Examples	• Providing supplies of food and water after an earthquake. • Giving money directly to homeless people on the streets.	• Providing education to help people find better-paid work. • Providing farmers with tools to improve their efficiency.
Pros	• Important for survival in the short term. • Displays compassion and kindness.	• Helps people to become more self-reliant. • Helps to solve the root causes of poverty.
Cons	• Does not tackle the underlying causes of poverty. • Can make people reliant on whoever is giving out the aid.	• May take time to have an effect. • Does not help with short-term survival.

Christian and Sikh responses

- **Christians** believe they have been given a responsibility by God to look after the world and the poor.
- Jesus' teachings mean they have a duty to show compassion and to 'love your neighbour as yourself'.
- Many Christians try to balance providing immediate help to those in poverty (short-term aid) with helping people to use their own gifts and talents to get themselves out of poverty (long-term aid).
- Guru Amar Das started the practice among **Sikhs** of giving a tenth of their surplus wealth to the service of the community. This is known as dasvandh.
- This money is often used for projects to support long-term aid, such as building hospitals or maintaining the gurdwara (where the langar offers free food to all).
- Sikhs regard it as a privilege and a duty to share in the tasks of the langar.

Christians and Sikhs might donate to charities such as CAFOD or Khalsa Aid to help those living in poverty. Other ways they might help include:

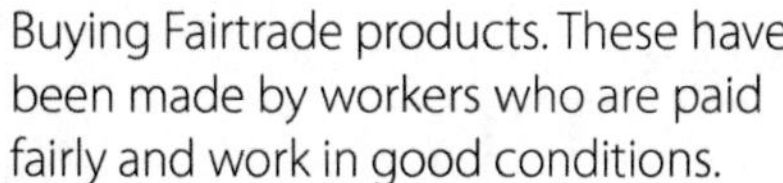

Buying Fairtrade products. These have been made by workers who are paid fairly and work in good conditions.

Supporting soup kitchens, food banks, and charities that provide help for those in poverty or assist them in finding work.

Supporting campaigns that promote greater equality and a just society, such as the Living Wage campaign.

APPLY

A Explain **two** ways in which long-term aid helps people to provide for themselves.

B 'Aid simply perpetuates poverty and dependence.'

Prepare one developed argument in favour and one developed argument against this statement.

10 Exam practice

Test the 1 mark question

1 Which **one** of the following best describes prejudice?

A Doing something to someone which is unfair

B Misusing power to get people to do things

C Negative thoughts, feelings or beliefs about a person based on a characteristic they have

D Using violent action to threaten or harm someone **[1 mark]**

2 Which **one** of the following is **not** an action which goes against human rights?

A Promoting tolerance B People-trafficking C Racial prejudice D Exploiting the poor **[1 mark]**

Test the 2 mark question

3 Give **two** ways in which the poor are exploited. **[2 marks]**

1) ____

2) ____

4 Give **two** ways in which a religious person should use their wealth. **[2 marks]**

1) ____

2) ____

Test the 4 mark question

5 Explain **two** contrasting beliefs in contemporary British society about what role women should be allowed in worship.
In your answer you should refer to the main religious tradition of Great Britain and one or more other religious traditions. **[4 marks]**

• **Explain one belief.**	*The main religious tradition of Great Britain is Christianity and in the denomination of Catholicism, women are not allowed to be ordained as priests.*
• Develop your explanation with more detail/an example/ reference to a religious teaching or quotation.	*Catholicism teaches that men and women are equal but have different roles to play within the Church.*
• **Explain a second contrasting belief.**	*In contrast, in Sikhism, men and women can both lead services in the gurdwara.*
• Develop your explanation with more detail/an example/ reference to a religious teaching or quotation.	*This follows the teaching of Guru Nanak, who believed that men and women are equal.*

TIP

This is a good start to the answer. It immediately identifies Christianity as the main religious tradition of Great Britain.

6 Explain **two** similar religious beliefs about prejudice based on sexuality.
In your answer, you should refer to one or more religious traditions. **[4 marks]**

• **Explain one belief.**	
• Develop your explanation with more detail/an example/ reference to a religious teaching or quotation.	
• **Explain a second similar belief.**	
• Develop your explanation with more detail/an example/ reference to a religious teaching or quotation.	

TIP

'Prejudice based on sexuality' usually means holding negative opinions about people who are not heterosexual. To answer this question, you could explain similar Christian and Sikh beliefs about same-sex relationships.

7 Explain two similar religious beliefs about human rights.
In your answer, you should refer to one or more religious traditions. **[4 marks]**

Test the 5 mark question

8 Explain **two** religious beliefs about social justice.
Refer to sacred writings or another source of religious belief and teaching in your answer **[5 marks]**

● **Explain one belief.**	*Sikhs believe all people are of equal value, so they should work to create social justice.*
● Develop your explanation with more detail/an example.	*Guru Granth Sahib 349 says, 'Recognise the Lord's light within all, and do not consider social class or status.'*
● **Explain a second belief.**	*Christians believe that working to promote social justice brings them closer to God.*
● Develop your explanation with more detail/an example.	*Many Christians have campaigned to improve human rights, for example Martin Luther King Jr, who led a peaceful movement to achieve social justice for black people who were discriminated against in America.*
● Add a reference to sacred writings or another source of religious belief and teaching. If you prefer, you can add this reference to your first belief instead.	*The parable of the Sheep and the Goats supports this Christian belief: 'Take your inheritance, the kingdom prepared for you since the salvation of the world. For I was hungry and you gave me something to drink, I was a stranger and you invited me in...' (Matthew 25:34–36)*

TIP
The parable of the Sheep and the Goats is a useful story to quote when dealing with issues of justice, poverty or helping those in need.

9 Explain **two** religious beliefs about the duty to tackle poverty.
Refer to sacred writings or another source of religious belief and teaching in your answer. **[5 marks]**

● **Explain one belief.**	
● Develop your explanation with more detail/an example.	
● **Explain a second belief.**	
● Develop your explanation with more detail/an example.	
● Add a reference to sacred writings or another source of religious belief and teaching. If you prefer, you can add this reference to your first belief instead.	

10 Explain **two** religious beliefs about the right attitude to wealth.
Refer to sacred writings or another source of religious belief and teaching in your answer. **[5 marks]**

Test the 12 mark question

11 'All religious believers must give to charities that help the poor.'

Evaluate this statement. In your answer you:

- should give reasoned arguments in support of this statement
- should give reasoned arguments to support a different point of view
- should refer to religious arguments
- may refer to non-religious arguments
- should reach a justified conclusion.

[12 marks]
[+3 SPaG mar

REASONED ARGUMENTS IN SUPPORT OF THE STATEMENT ● **Explain why some people would agree with the statement.** ● Develop your explanation with more detail and examples. ● Refer to religious teaching. Use a quote or paraphrase or a religious authority. ● **Evaluate the arguments.** Is this a good argument or not? Explain why you think this.	*If all religious believers gave to charities it would go a long way to ending a lot of poverty in the world. So many people are suffering because they do not have enough money to buy food, clothes and provide a home for themselves. While a lot of food is thrown away in rich countries other people struggle to have one meal a day. So if all religious believers were generous in their giving it would make life a lot more bearable for the poor. Some people are poor because of natural disasters or are refugees from war. They need emergency aid and religious believers should respond and it should be their duty to give to charities that are helping.*
REASONED ARGUMENTS SUPPORTING A DIFFERENT VIEW ● **Explain why some people would support a different view.** ● Develop your explanation with more detail and examples. ● Refer to religious teaching. Use a quote or paraphrase or a religious authority. ● **Evaluate the arguments.** Is this a good argument or not? Explain why you think this.	*However, some religious believers are poor themselves, so will not be able to afford to help others. They are struggling to survive and have no extra money to give to charity. So you can't expect those religious believers to starve in order to give to the poor. Some may prefer to do work to help the charities like distributing and collecting envelopes for Christian Aid. Not all religious believers have to give money; they can help in other ways.*
CONCLUSION ● **Give a justified conclusion.** ● Include your own opinion together with your own reasoning. ● **Include evaluation.** Explain why you think one viewpoint is stronger than the other or why they are equally strong. ● Do not just repeat arguments you have already used without explaining how they apply to your reasoned opinion/conclusion.	*It is true that charities do a lot of good in helping those who are poor. However, it is unfair just to expect religious believers to donate money to the charities. Everyone should try and help if they can whether they are religious or not. Not all religious believers are able to donate money but they can pray or give their time to help charities.*

TIP

This answer could be improved by referring to specific religious teachings. For example, in this section the student could refer to the Christian teaching to 'love your neighbour' and the parable of the Sheep and the Goats, or the Sikh practice of giving dasvandh.

TIP

A key word in the statement 'all'. It hints that some religiou believers might not have a du to give to charities, for examp if they are very poor themselv The student has rightly explai other ways people could help for example volunteering their time.

12 'Treating people equally is the most important teaching for religious believers.'

Evaluate this statement. In your answer you:

- should give reasoned arguments in support of this statement
- should give reasoned arguments to support a different point of view
- should refer to religious arguments
- may refer to non-religious arguments
- should reach a justified conclusion.

[12 marks]
[+3 SPaG marks]

REASONED ARGUMENTS IN SUPPORT OF THE STATEMENT ● **Explain why some people would agree with the statement.** ● Develop your explanation with more detail and examples. ● Refer to religious teaching. Use a quote or paraphrase or a religious authority. ● **Evaluate the arguments.** Is this a good argument or not? Explain why you think this.	
REASONED ARGUMENTS SUPPORTING A DIFFERENT VIEW ● **Explain why some people would support a different view.** ● Develop your explanation with more detail and examples. ● Refer to religious teaching. Use a quote or paraphrase or a religious authority. ● **Evaluate the arguments.** Is this a good argument or not? Explain why you think this.	
CONCLUSION ● **Give a justified conclusion.** ● Include your own opinion together with your own reasoning. ● **Include evaluation.** Explain why you think one viewpoint is stronger than the other or why they are equally strong. ● Do not just repeat arguments you have already used without explaining how they apply to your reasoned opinion/conclusion.	

TIP
Don't forget that your spelling, punctuation and grammar are assessed in the 12 mark questions.

13 'Everybody should have the freedom to follow whichever religion they wish to.'

Evaluate this statement. In your answer you:

- should give reasoned arguments in support of this statement
- should give reasoned arguments to support a different point of view
- should refer to religious arguments
- may refer to non-religious arguments
- should reach a justified conclusion.

[12 marks]
[+3 SPaG marks]

Check your answers using the mark scheme on page 163. How did you do?
To feel more secure in the content you need to remember, re-read pages 140–147.
To remind yourself of what the examiner is looking for, go to pages 7–13.

Apply answers

1 Christianity: Beliefs and teachings

Please note that these are suggested answers to the Apply questions, designed to give you guidance, rather than being definitive answers.

1.1 **A** 'We believe in one God' (the Nicene Creed)/ the first of the Ten Commandments. **B** *You might include*: Christians are inspired to follow the teaching of the Bible/ believe they have a relationship with God/ communicate with God through prayer/ find comfort in God in challenging times/ pray and worship/ try to follow Jesus' example.

1.2 **A** Creating humans/ caring for humans/ sending his son, Jesus, to live among humans/ requiring justice. **B** Suffering was brought into God's perfect world by Adam and Eve's disobedience/ the result of human free will/ a test of faith/ without suffering people can't show positive human qualities such as compassion/ by overcoming suffering humans learn to be strong and appreciative of good in the world. *Remember to develop each point with more detail.*

1.3 **A** 1: These persons are God the Father, the Son (Jesus) and the Holy Spirit/ these three persons are named in the Apostles Creed and the Nicene Creed. 2: God the Father is the creator of all life/ acts as a good father towards humankind, who are his children/ is omnipotent, omnibenevolent, omniscient and omnipresent. **B** *Arguments for:* 1, 2, 4, 6, 7. *Arguments against*: 3, 5, 8. *In your justified conclusion you should weigh up both sides of the argument and then say which side you personally find more convincing and why.*

1.4 **A** They value every human being as created by God/ they believe people should look after the natural world. **B** *You might conclude that this is a strong argument because it is true that Christians believe in God's omnipotence and the truth of the Bible. But you might think it is a weak argument because theories of evolution and the Big Bang are widely accepted by many Christians despite not being 'proved'. It doesn't matter whether you think the argument is weak or strong, the important thing is to carefully explain* why *you think it is weak or strong.*

1.5 **A** Jesus was God in human form/ 'The Word became flesh and made his dwelling among us' (John 1:14 [NIV])/ Jesus was born of a virgin, Mary. **B** *E.g. 'The belief that Jesus was conceived by the Holy Spirit is given in Matthew 1:18, which says, 'His mother Mary was pledged to be married to Joseph, but before they came together, she was found to be pregnant by the Holy Spirit."*

1.6 **A** 1: Jesus' death restored the relationship between people and God. 2: God understands human suffering because Jesus, who is God, experienced it. **B** When Jesus died he took the sins of everyone on himself (the atonement)/ if Jesus had not died he would not have risen from the dead. *The answer could be improved by developing reasons why the crucifixion is an important belief rather than merely describing what took place.*

1.7 **A** The women were told by angels that Jesus had risen/ Jesus appeared to the disciples. **B** Paul wrote, 'And if Christ has not been raised, our preaching is useless and so is your faith' (1 Corinthians 15:14 [NIV])/ 'He rose again according to the scriptures' (the Nicene Creed)/ the resurrection shows the power of good over evil and life over death/ Christians will be resurrected if they accept Jesus/ 'I look for the resurrection of the dead and the life of the world to come' (the Nicene Creed).

1.8 **A** Gives hope of life after death with Jesus/ inspires Christians to live in the way God wants. **B** *In your paragraph you should weigh up both sides of the argument and then say which side you personally find more convincing and why.*

1.9 **A** Christians believe that when they die God will judge them on their behaviour and actions during their lifetime/ as well as their faith in Jesus/ God will judge people based on how they serve others unselfishly. *Refer to the Parable of the Sheep and the Goats to support your points.* **B** *You might include*: the promise of heaven inspires people to be kind to others/ people want to be with Jesus when they die so they follow his teachings/ on the other hand, no one can be sure there is an afterlife, so it is not a good way to get people to behave/ an atheist would question how a loving God could punish people forever in hell. *In your justified conclusion you should weigh up both sides of the argument and then say which side you personally find more convincing.*

1.10 **A** A loving God would not condemn people to hell/ God is forgiving so would offer everyone a second chance to repent. **B** *Arguments in support might include*: the promise of heaven would encourage good behaviour/ the threat of hell would prevent bad behaviour/ belief in heaven takes away the fear of death/ gives hope that people will experience eternal happiness even if their life on earth has been hard. *Other views might include*: atheists don't believe in heaven or hell but still have moral principles/ most people do not consider belief in the afterlife when deciding how to behave/ morality is formed in childhood by parental teaching/ if heaven and hell were made up to encourage good behaviour, it hasn't worked.

1.11 **A** Salvation by grace of God freely given through faith in Jesus/ 'For it is by grace you have been saved' (Ephesians 2:8 [NIV])/ salvation by doing good works/ 'In the same way, faith by itself, if it is not accompanied by action, is dead' (James 2:17 [NIV]). **B** *In deciding whether you find this argument convincing, try to think of what others might say against it.*

1.12 **A** Jesus' death made up for the original sin of Adam and Eve/ Jesus' resurrection was proof that his sacrifice was accepted by God. **B** *There is no 'right' order, but suggested arguments in support*: 4, 5, 2, 8. *Arguments against*: 1, 6, 7, 3. *Missing from this evaluation is any reference to specific Christian teaching, for example a reference to sacred writing. A justified conclusion is also needed.*

2 Christianity: Practices

Please note that these are suggested answers to the Apply questions, designed to give you guidance, rather than being definitive answers.

2.1 **A** Private prayer/ singing hymns of praise in church. **B** *Arguments in support might include:* a set ritual is familiar to people/ provides a powerful emotional bond/ liturgical worship may be more formal, so more dramatic/ gives a powerful sense of tradition. *Arguments in support of other views might include:* spontaneous worship is more powerful as it comes from the heart/ charismatic worship involves speaking in tongues so is a powerful emotional experience/ the silence of a Quaker service may be more powerful than one that uses words and hymns/ it depends on an individual Christian's point of view whether one type of service is more powerful than another.

2.2 **A** It is the prayer Jesus taught his disciples/ it is a model of good prayer as it combines praise to God with asking for one's needs. **B** *You might include an example*: a Christian may wish to pray for something personal using their own words, such as the strength to overcome an illness. *Or add a religious teaching*: Jesus said to pray in your room with the door closed so that God who sees in secret will reward you (Matthew 6:6).

2.3 **A** 1: Believers' baptism: full immersion in a pool/ person is old enough to make a mature decision about their faith. 2: Infant baptism: blessed water is poured over the baby's head/ parents and godparents make promises of faith on behalf of the child. **B** *Arguments in support might include*: at baptism the parents promise to bring up the child as a Christian so they would be lying/ it is hypocritical/ the symbolic actions have no meaning for them. *Arguments against might include*: they may not be religious themselves but that doesn't mean they should not give their child a chance to be a member of the Church/ the child receives grace at baptism regardless of their parents' future actions/ the child is cleansed from sin.

2.4 **A** 1: Christians receive God's grace/ by joining in the sacrifice of Jesus/ their faith is strengthened/ they become closer to God. 2: Communion brings the community of believers together in unity by sharing the bread and wine/ this provides support and encouragement for those going through a difficult time/ encourages church members to love others in practical ways. **B** *In your paragraph you should weigh up both sides of the argument and then say which side you personally find more convincing and why.*

2.5 **A** 1: An Orthodox Holy Communion is mainly held behind the iconostasis/ the priest distributes the consecrated bread and wine on a spoon. 2: Holy Communion in the United Reformed Church has an 'open table' so anyone can receive communion/ bread is broken and passed around the congregation/ wine is distributed in small cups. **B** *Arguments for the statement might include:* the ministry of the Word is very important because it focuses on the life and teaching of Jesus/ reminds people of sacred writing in the Old Testament/ provides spiritual education for the congregation through the sermon given by the priest/ allows the community to pray for themselves and others. *Arguments against might include*: Holy Communion services should focus on the consecration and sharing of bread and wine because that is the most important part of the service/ people receive the body and blood of Jesus/ recall Jesus' death and resurrection which saved them from sin.

2.6 1: Lourdes: pilgrims go there to seek healing, both spiritual and physical/ to help the sick bathe in the waters/ to strengthen their faith/ to take part in services with people speaking many different languages from many countries/ it is a busy place with crowds of people, unlike Iona which is quieter and more remote. 2: Iona: pilgrims wish to spend time in quiet prayer, reading the Bible or meditating/ to enjoy the natural beauty of the place so they feel closer to God who created nature/ to worship with others who are like-minded/ some prefer to feel God's presence in silence and solitude rather than in a busy place like Lourdes. **B** On a pilgrimage there are many opportunities for prayer and meditation/ for reading the scriptures/ for reflecting on one's life/ whereas on a holiday people usually spend time enjoying themselves and reading novels rather than scriptures, etc. *A Christian teaching that supports pilgrimage might include*: Jesus withdrew to a lonely place when he wanted to pray/ Bernadette was told by Mary in a vision to build a church in Lourdes and pray for sinners, so Christians are following their traditional teaching by going there.

2.7 **A** By attending services which emphasise Jesus is risen/ by celebrating with family and friends/ giving Easter eggs to children to symbolise new life. **B** *Arguments for might include*: Christmas is very commercialised/ many people think about food, presents and seeing their relatives, not about Jesus/ not many people go to church on Christmas/ some think that in multicultural Britain, celebrating Christmas as a religious festival might offend others. *Arguments against might include*: Christmas is still a religious holiday in Britain/ the royal family go to church on Christmas Day and many Christians attend Midnight Mass/ carol services are held to prepare for the coming of Jesus into the world/ schools have nativity plays about Jesus' birth and often collect presents to give to children who are less fortunate.

2.8 **A** 1: The community of Christians/ holy people of God/ Body of Christ. 2: A building in which Christians worship. **B** The Church is the Body of Christ and as such has a duty to help the needy/ Christians are taught to love their neighbour/ the Parable of the Sheep and the Goats/ the parable of the Good Samaritan.

2.9 **A** Patrol streets in urban areas to support vulnerable people/ challenge gang and knife crime/ listen to people's problems/ help young people who have had too much to drink and may end up in trouble/ try to stop anti-social behaviour/ in this way they show love of neighbour/ 'Faith by itself, if it is not accompanied by action, is dead' (James 2:17 [NIV]). **B** *Two religious arguments might include*: Jesus taught that Christians should help others by showing agape love towards them/ this means being unselfish, caring and putting others' needs before your own, including praying for your neighbours' needs/ Jesus taught Christians should give practical help to others in the parable of the Sheep and the Goats/ he said to feed the hungry, clothe the naked, etc. *Two non-religious arguments against the statement might include*: praying is pointless/ not a practical action/ no one will know if prayer works to help them/ Christians should not have to be street pastors or social workers/ it is the police and social services' responsibility, not the Church's responsibility.

2.10 A By telling non-believers that Jesus Christ, the Son of God, came into the world as its saviour/ by spreading the Christian faith through evangelism. **B** *Arguments for*: 1, 3, 5. *Arguments against*: 2, 4, 6. *You should weigh up both sides of the argument and then say which side you personally find more convincing.*

2.11 A Through organisations that promote evangelism, such as Christ for all Nations/ through personal witness and example. **B** *You should weigh up the argument and suggest how it could be improved – e.g. by referring to the Great Commission (which suggests all Christians have a duty to spread the gospel), or by considering arguments for the statement.*

2.12 A 1: The Church works on a personal level to try to restore relationships between individuals/ between conflicting groups in the community. 2: The Church has sponsored different organisations that work for reconciliation/ e.g. the Irish Churches Peace Project. **B** Jesus taught, 'Love the Lord your God with all your heart and with all your soul and with all your mind. This is the great and first commandment.' (Matthew 22: 37–38 [NIV])/ therefore reconciliation to God is most important/ reconciliation to one's neighbour is second: 'Love your neighbour as yourself' (Matthew 22:39 [NIV]).

2.13 A Smuggling Bibles into the USSR to give comfort to persecuted Christians/ sending money to projects that support persecuted Christians. **B** *A religious argument might include*: it is possible for a Christian to be happy even in times of persecution because they believe they are sharing in the sufferings of Jesus/ their courage can inspire others to become Christians/ persecution strengthens their faith. *A non-religious argument might include*: no one can be happy while being persecuted/ they may be angry at the injustice of their treatment and turn to violence or stop believing in God.

2.14 A 1: Emergency relief includes food, shelter and water to people suffering from a natural disaster or sudden war/ parables such as the Rich Man and Lazarus and the Good Samaritan encourage Christians to help the needy. 2: Long-term aid may include education or new farming equipment that helps to make people independent of aid/ 'If anyone has material possessions and sees a brother or sister in need but has no pity on them, how can the love of God be in that person?' (1 John 3:17 [NIV]). **B** *Arguments for the statement might include*: religious charities can respond quickly to emergencies but it is not their role to provide long-term aid/ the countries themselves should be helping their own people/ long-term aid might make people dependent on religious charities. *Arguments against might include*: religious charities should provide long-term aid because people are still in need/ it will give independence eventually/ it is better to teach people how to make a living for themselves than merely to feed them for a short period of time/ the parable of the Sheep and the Goats teaches that God will judge people on whether they have helped their fellow humans because helping them is helping Jesus Christ.

3 Sikhism: Beliefs and teachings

Please note that these are suggested answers to the Apply questions, designed to give you guidance, rather than being definitive answers.

3.1 A Only one God/ God is beyond human description/ God is in everything (immanent)/ God is above and beyond everything (transcendent)/ creator and sustainer/ eternal/ made known by his word/ has no fear or hatred. **B** *E.g. 'The Mool Mantra summarises key Sikh beliefs about God such as being eternal truth and Creator. An example of this is 'Creative being personified', which demonstrates that God is seen as Creator.'*

3.2 A God created everything/ God wills the universe to exist/ God is separate from the universe but present in every human soul/ the creation of the universe can be described as God's 'pastime' or 'play'. **B** *Arguments supporting the statement*: God is beyond human understanding/ God is without qualities or form (known as 'nirgun')/ described in the Guru Granth Sahib as 'Transcendent Lord'/ God has never assumed a physical form. *Arguments in support of different views*: Sikh belief that every part of the universe reveals God/ Sikh belief that God's presence is within human beings/ God is with qualities or form (known as 'sargun')/ Guru Granth Sahib praises God as 'within all'.

3.3 A Truthful living/ compassion/ contentment/ humility/ love. **B** The virtues are interlinked and therefore equally important, e.g. one cannot show love without being truthful/ the virtues are similar as they respond to God's characteristics – one cannot choose which of God's characteristics is more important than the others/ all of the virtues need to be practised in order to make good spiritual progress during life/ Sikhs also need other virtues, e.g. courage to stay true to the faith even in difficult and dangerous situations.

3.4 A Freedom/ release/ liberation/ salvation. **B** Human beings can change their future karma as the Guru Granth Sahib states 'The body is the field of karma in this age; whatever you plant, you shall harvest'/ the story of the proud man and the blind man illustrates that how people think about and act towards others changes their future karma/ a person can change their future karma by doing good actions and being open to receiving God's grace/ bad karma can be removed by meditating on God's name, hearing his word and serving others.

3.5 A Piety/ knowledge/ effort/ grace/ truth. **B** The five evils can be seen to cause problems everywhere, e.g. greed causing ecological issues/ although non-religious people such as Humanists do not believe in God, they acknowledge the hurt and difficulties caused between people when anger, greed and pride are encouraged/ all religions have an equivalent teaching that these evils should be rejected, for example the Sermon on the Mount in Christianity teaches against adultery and lust.

3.6 A Mind centred on God/ living according to Sikh teaching/ seeking to be free from attachment, pride and ego/ doing good for its own sake. **B** Haumai is seen to produce confusion and suffering/ the only way to overcome it is to become gurmukh, by remembering God and forgetting self/ 'Egotism [haumai] is opposed to the Name of the Lord' (Guru Granth Sahib 560).

3.7 A Kesh/ kangha/ kara/ kachera/ kirpan. **B** Sikhs believe in the oneness of humanity which implies equality/ Sikhs believe there is a divine spark within each human and so they should be treated with equal respect/ Guru Ram Das taught, 'All are made of the same clay; the light within is all the same' (Guru Granth Sahib 96)/ Sikhs practise equality within their religious practice/ both men and women within Sikhism take part in worship, read the Guru Granth Sahib, play music and cook and serve in the langar.

3.8 A Men and women are equal/ all humans are created by God and are equal/ all should work and eat equally in the langar. **B** *Arguments in support of the statement: 1, 3, 4. Arguments in support of a different point of view: 2, 5, 6. You should weigh up both sides of the argument and then say which you personally find more convincing.*

3.9 A Established the Guru Granth Sahib as the final Guru/ established the Khalsa/ reinforced equality by establishing the use of the last names 'Kaur' and 'Singh'.
B *Arguments for the statement*: Guru Gobind Singh established the Guru Granth Sahib as the living Guru/ established the Khalsa/ encouraged equality between men and women in the Khalsa. *Arguments against the statement*: Guru Nanak had the original vision which led him to found Sikhism/ he established that there was to be equality between men and women and people from different castes and faiths/ he established the langar/ he taught that all humanity was equal.

3.10 A People of different races, faiths, gender and class are treated equally in the langar/ women take an equal role with men in leading worship and performing sewa/ Sikh men and women have equal roles and status at home. **B** *Statements that are true*: 3, 4, 5, 7.

3.11 A Tan (physical sewa)/ man (mental sewa)/ dhan (material sewa). **B** *Arguments in support of the statement: 1, 3, 4. Arguments in support of different views: 2, 5, 6. Your conclusion should reflect your arguments, but not simply restate them.*

3.12 A Chakra: a circle reminding Sikhs of the eternity of God/ khanda: a double-edged sword representing the balance of divine justice, and freedom and authority/ two kirpans: symbolising political power and spiritual authority and the need to balance these. **B** The sangat provides opportunities to meditate and worship/ allows Sikhs to learn more about the faith by listening to talks/ helps Sikhs to become gurmukh (God-centred)/ provides opportunities for sewa.

4 Sikhism: Practices

Please note that these are suggested answers to the Apply questions, designed to give you guidance, rather than being definitive answers.

4.1 A The Sikh flag (Nishan Sahib)/ the raised platform (takht)/palki (a canopy above the raised platform)/ the manji/ the chanani. **B** *Arguments supporting the statement: 1, 2, 6. Arguments supporting another point of view: 3, 4, 5 Your conclusion should evaluate which point of view is stronger and why.*

4.2 A Refer to it as Sahib/ keep the layout and wording identical to ensure accuracy/ sit on the floor at the gurdwara below the level of the Guru Granth Sahib/ avoid pointing their feet towards the Guru Granth Sahib when sitting/ a chauri is used as it would be for a human Guru. **B** The eleventh Guru/ contains the Gurus' teachings about God/ provides teaching and guidance on how to become gurmukh/ provides teaching and guidance on how to approach God/ daily prayers such as the Mool Mantra are found in the Guru Granth Sahib/ there can be no gurdwara unless the Guru Granth Sahib is present.

4.3 A Removing shoes/ covering their heads/ washing feet and hands/ bowing and touching the floor before the Guru Granth Sahib/ sitting below the Guru Granth Sahib.
B *Arguments to support the statement:* Prayers, hymns and readings from the Guru Granth Sahib encourage Sikhs to focus on God/ sermons or talks help Sikhs to learn more about God/ it is important for Sikhs to be part of a community and worshipping in the gurdwara rather than alone is one way of doing this. *Arguments to support a different point of view*: The most important part of worship is keeping God in mind – this can be done in gurdwara services or elsewhere/ Sikhs can worship God through performing sewa and this also helps other people in a practical way.

4.4 A Established by Guru Nanak/ continued by other Gurus/ Guru Gobind Singh emphasised it should be continued/ a way of offering sewa/ demonstrates the Sikh belief in equality and brotherhood/ prevents the very poorest from going without food. **B** Brings Sikhs together for shared meals and celebrations/ all are welcome to attend, regardless of faith, gender, age, race/ the langar ensures that no one in the community is left without food/ all Sikhs are invited to take part in preparing and serving langar/ demonstrates the equality of each person in the community.

4.5 A Recite the Japji, Jap and Swayyas prayers in the morning/ given by Guru Nanak and Guru Gobind Singh/ say prayers in a gurdwara service in the morning/ recite the Rahiras prayer at dusk/ recite the Sohila prayer before bed. **B** *Your answer should explain whether you think the statement is true or not, giving the reasons why. You should refer to specific knowledge of Sikhism, and consider arguments for and against the statement. Arguments in support of the statement might include*: Sikhs are expected to remember God at all times/ Sikhs will only become gurmukh if they focus on God/ the morning and evening prayers require Sikhs to focus on God at specific times every day. *Arguments in support of another point of view might include*: Sikhs are also required to do honest work/ every Sikh is expected to give to charity and be involved in sewa/ this implies that prayer cannot be the only focus for Sikhs.

4.6 A Reading the Guru Granth Sahib/ overseeing performances of the akhand path/ leading ceremonies such as weddings and funerals/ organising the ceremonies to take the Guru Granth Sahib to and from the rest room. **B** *Your answer should say whether you think the statement is true or not, giving the reasons why. You should refer to specific knowledge of Sikhism, and consider the arguments for and against the statement. Arguments in support of the statement might include:* The daily services always include reading of the Guru Granth Sahib, showing its importance/ the ceremonies around the Guru Granth Sahib (such as moving it to and from the rest room) show how important it is/ the main role of the granthi is to read the Guru Granth Sahib/ children learn the script of the Guru Granth Sahib so they can understand it better. *Arguments in support of another point of view might include:* The langar is focused on providing food to the Sikh and local community/ this is important to make sure no one goes without food/ education is an important role of the gurdwara/ without classes to learn Gurmukhi and a library of Sikh literature, it is harder to understand God and the Guru Granth Sahib.

4.7 **A** Holding an akhand path/ performing kirtan/ processions of the Guru Granth Sahib/ sending cards/ new clothes/ giving away free sweets and drinks/ community meals. **B** *Arguments in support of the statement: 1, 2, 5. Arguments in support of a different point of view: 3, 4, 6. In your paragraph you should weigh up both sides of the argument and explain which you find more convincing and why.*

4.8 **A** An akhand path is held/ there are street processions/ homes are spring cleaned, decorated and lit up with lights/ presents are given, especially to children/ bonfires and firework displays/ langars are often held, some in the open air/ many Sikhs travel to the Golden Temple in Amritsar to celebrate. **B** *You should decide whether it is a strong or weak argument and explain why you think this. E.g. you might decide the argument is good because it mentions Guru Hargobind and Bhai Mani Singh, but it could be improved by explaining how these two figures link to the important Sikh belief of freedom of religion.*

4.9 **A** Processions to carry the Guru Granth Sahib/ with five Sikhs representing the Panj Paire in front/ special langars/ an akhand path/ hymns, songs and talks connected to the Guru. **B** *Arguments to agree with the statement*: An akhand path is held before every gurpurb/ worship includes songs written by the Gurus/ there are talks about the Gurus/ the gurpurbs often remember serious events, such as the anniversary of a death or martyrdom. *Arguments to agree with other points of view:* There are celebrations and street processions/ cards and presents are exchanged/ competitions may be arranged/ there are firework displays and fairs in India.

4.10 **A** It houses the restroom for the Guru Granth Sahib, which is taken across from there to the Golden Temple/ it is where the spiritual leader of the Sikhs works/ it is the centre of religious government. **B** A Sikh's spiritual state of mind is most important/ pilgrimage rituals (such as bathing in the Golden Temple pool) will do nothing if people are not clean inside/ focusing on God's name is more important/ the Guru Granth Sahib states, 'There is no sacred shrine equal to the Guru.'

4.11 **A** Bowing before the Guru Granth Sahib/ offering food or money/ the parents take karah parshad or pay for it/ the Mool Mantra is said/ hymns of praise and thanksgiving are said or sung/ the baby is given amrit/ the granthi recites the first few verses of the Japji as they stir the amrit/ the parents choose the name based on the first letter of the first word on the left-hand page when the Guru Granth Sahib is opened at random. **B** The naming ceremony includes prayers of thanksgiving to God/ the child is named with the guidance of the Guru Granth Sahib/ at the beginning of the ceremony everyone bows to the Guru Granth Sahib and makes offerings of food or money/ the naming ceremony is often part of a service of worship to God.

4.12 **A** Prayers/ amrit sprinkled on the hair and eyes/ reading from the Guru Granth Sahib/ reciting the Mool Mantra/ eating karah parshad. **B** Becoming a member of the Khalsa is an important way for a Sikh to demonstrate their commitment to God/ becoming a member of the Khalsa is a significant commitment with an expectation to pray daily and follow rules about how to live/ the Rehat Maryada describes the event as being 'reborn in the true Guru's household'.

5 Relationships and families

Please note that these are suggested answers to the Apply questions, designed to give you guidance, rather than being definitive answers.

5.1 **A** *Beliefs must be contrasting.* 1: Many Sikhs oppose same-sex relationships/ the Guru Granth Sahib encourages heterosexual marriage/ '[same-sex marriage] is unnatural and ungodly, and the Sikh religion cannot support it' (Manjit Singh Kalkatta). 2: Some Christians accept same-sex relationships/ the Church of England welcomes committed, celibate same-sex couples. **B** *An example of a religious argument*: Christians believe sex expresses a deep, lifelong union and casual sex does not represent this. *An example of a non-religious argument*: the acceptance of contraception and legal abortion has made casual sex more common.

5.2 **A** 1: 'You shall not commit adultery' (Exodus 20:14 [NIV]). 2: 'The blind fool abandons the wife of his own home, and has an affair with another woman' (Guru Granth Sahib 1165). **B** *In support:* it can be a valid expression of love for each other/ some Christians think it is acceptable if the couple are in a committed relationship. *Against:* 'your bodies are temples of the Holy Spirit' (1 Corinthians 6:19 [NIV])/ Anglican and Catholic Churches teach that sex requires the commitment of marriage/ the Rehat Maryada says that anyone who has sex before marriage is not a true Sikh. *A development may be:* the Catholic Church teaches that sex should be open to the possibility of creating new life/ having sex before marriage risks pregnancy.

5.3 **A** Catholic and Orthodox Churches believe the use of contraception within marriage goes against the natural law/ other Christian churches accept its use e.g. to avoid harming the mother's health/ most Sikhs believe it is acceptable to use contraception as part of responsible family planning. **B** *The argument is strong as it explains why the Church is right to have a view on family planning by referring to specific Christian teachings. It could perhaps be expanded by mentioning relevant passages in the Bible, such as Genesis 1:28 and 2:24.*

5.4 **A** For Christians, it is a covenant before God/ it reflects the love of Christ for the Church/ for Sikhs, marriage is how God intended them to live/ it is a religious act and a union witnessed by God. **B** *Arguments for*: marriage is a legal contract/ society is more stable if the rights of all people are protected/ 'The Church sees marriage between a man and a woman, as central to the stability and health of human society' (House of Bishops of the General Synod of the Church of England). *Arguments against*: many marriages end in divorce/ relationships between cohabiting couples can be just as stable and loving.

5.5 **A** Adultery/ addiction/ people changing and growing apart, etc. **B** *For*: children are badly affected by divorce/ for Christians, marriage is a sacrament and reflects the love Christ has for his Church/ Jesus taught that anyone who divorced and remarried was committing adultery (Mark 10:11–12)/ Sikhs believe marriage should be for life/ the Rehat Maryada teaches that, in general, no Sikh should remarry while their spouse is still alive. *Against*: continual arguments or abuse can damage children more than divorce/ some Christians think the Church should reflect God's forgiveness and allow couples a second chance for happiness/ Sikhs reluctantly accept civil divorce for reasons such as adultery or desertion.

5.6 **A** For Christians, the nuclear family fulfils God's plan for a man and woman to be united together and increase in number/ some Christians and many Sikhs believe children should have male and female parents as role models/ Christianity teaches that a polygamous family can lead to sexual immorality (1 Corinthians 7:2). **B** *Arguments for the statement*: same-sex parents can be just as loving as other parents/ same-sex parents who adopt children are probably more committed to being good parents than other people/ same-sex parents can pass on religious beliefs and moral values to their children. *Arguments against the statement*: children of same-sex parents will not grow up with a male and female role model/ same-sex parents cannot pass on religious faith if their religion disapproves of their relationship/ children of same-sex parents may be teased at school.

5.7 **A** 1: Amritdhari Sikhs teach their children how to wear the five Ks/ the Rehat Maryada states that educating children in the Sikh faith is a duty. 2: Many Christian parents present their babies for baptism/ teach them to pray/ some send them to faith schools. **B** *E.g. 'This argument is good because it suggests why it is important for families to help their elderly relatives, gives specific examples of how families can do this, and includes religious teachings. It could be developed further by giving more reasons for why families should help their elderly relatives, for example because it shows love and compassion (important values in both Christianity and Sikhism).'*

5.8 **A** All people are created equal in the image of God/ the command to love one's neighbour as oneself shows that discrimination is wrong/ Guru Nanak described how without women 'there would be no one at all' (Guru Granth Sahib 473). **B** *E.g. 'For example, some traditional Christians think husbands should rule over their wives. Paul taught that this was wrong when he said, 'There is neither… male nor female, for you are all one in Christ Jesus' (Galatians 3:28 [NIV]).'*

6 Religion and life

Please note that these are suggested answers to the Apply questions, designed to give you guidance, rather than being definitive answers.

6.1 **A** 1: Some Fundamentalist Christians believe God made the universe and all life in it in six days/ many Sikhs believe God created the universe through the Big Bang, as the Guru Granth Sahib supports the idea of an expanding universe. **B** *For*: liberal Christians believe the Genesis creation stories are symbolic, with the main message being that God created the universe/ the Big Bang theory explains how God did this. *Against*: atheists might say that God is not responsible for the Big Bang, this is just something that happened by chance.

6.2 **A** Oil and other non-renewable resources are important sources of energy and will eventually run out/ without renewable energy sources to replace them, people will suffer. **B** For Christians and Sikhs, stewardship means looking after the environment for God/ not being stewards is letting God down/ stewardship means taking care of the planet rather than simply exploiting it/ dominion suggests ruling over the world with power and authority, whereas stewardship emphasises care and love.

6.3 **A** Pollution causes harm to living things including humans/ not good stewardship and therefore against God's wishes (Genesis 1:28)/ pollution damages God's creation. **B** *E.g. 'Even if individual actions don't make a huge difference, Christians and Sikhs would say people should try to pollute less anyway because it is damaging God's creation. For Christians, it also doesn't show love of neighbour.'*

6.4 **A** Most Sikhs do not eat meat because they believe animals have souls/ animals should be treated with compassion and respect/ the Guru Granth Sahib forbids killing living beings/ some Christians argue that if more people were vegetarian there would be more food to go round, which would please God. **B** Animals bred for experimentation have no freedom in their lives and will probably suffer before they die/ Sikhs believe animals should be treated with kindness and compassion/ experimenting on animals for nonessential reasons creates bad karma/ the Bible says humans should care for animals (e.g. Proverbs 12:10)/ Christians believe experimenting on animals is not good stewardship.

6.5 **A** 1: The theory of evolution says that life started with single-celled creatures in the sea/ evolved into creatures living on land/ creatures resembling humans evolved around 2.5 million years ago/ this happened because of the survival of the fittest. 2: The Bible teaches that human life was created last/ life was breathed into Adam by God/ Eve was created by God from Adam/ humans were created in God's image. **B** *One opinion is given, i.e. agreement with Genesis, science or a combination of both, and two reasons to support it which may be based on the answers for 6.5 A, perhaps with further content on the existence and/or role of God.*

6.6 **A** Christians believe life is a gift from God and abortion is taking life/ the sanctity of life means life should be valued and respected/ Sikhs believe abortion is taking life given by God and so is a sin/ 'The Lord infused His Light into you, and then you came into the world' (Guru Granth Sahib 921). **B** *For*: being brought up with a poor quality of life is not loving/ possibly not the child's preferred option had they been able to choose. *Against*: preventing life is never the best option/ the sanctity of life/ the family should be supported to improve the child's quality of life/ better a poor quality of life than no life.

6.7 **A** *For*: if someone is suffering unbearably and going to die anyway, it may be kinder to help them to die than to keep them alive to suffer more. *Against*: Christians believe euthanasia interferes with God's plan for a person's life/ only God has the right to take away life/ for Sikhs, escaping suffering in this life through euthanasia will mean suffering in the next life. **B** *Your opinion should be supported by arguments for or against the statement, with reference to religious teachings. Arguments for might include*: it is every person's right to decide what to do with their life/ if someone is suffering unbearably they should be able to end their life with dignity/ some Christians believe it is the most compassionate thing to do in some situations. *Arguments against might include*: it is murder ('do not kill')/ interferes with God's plan/ open to abuse/ disrespects the sanctity of life/ only God should take life.

6.8 **A** Sikhs believe that when people die they will be reborn according to their karma/ this process will continue until they reach union with God/ many Christians believe that after death they are judged by God/ they will either be eternally with God (heaven) or eternally without God (hell). **B** *For*: Sikhs believe they need to purify their souls in order to escape the cycle of samsara and achieve union with God/ this motivates them to act ethically/ some Christians believe if they follow Jesus' teachings to help others they are more likely to be judged favourably by God and spend the afterlife in heaven. *Against*: helping others brings its own rewards without needing to think about the afterlife/ religious believers should help others simply because it is a good thing to do.

7 The existence of God and revelation

Please note that these are suggested answers to the Apply questions, designed to give you guidance, rather than being definitive answers.

7.1 **A** The earth and humans were created for a purpose/ the intricacy and complexity of earth shows it cannot have appeared by chance/ the designer can only have been God/ the thumb is evidence of design because it allows precise delicate movement/ everything in the universe is in a regular order so must have been designed/ everything in the universe is perfect to sustain life. **B** *See the answers to 7.1 A for arguments to agree with the statement. Arguments against could include*: natural selection happens by chance/ species are developed by evolution, not a designer/ suffering proves there is no designer God/ order and structure in nature is imposed by humans, not God.

7.2 **A** Everything must have a cause/ including the universe/ something eternal must exist that has no cause/ the eternal first cause is God/ this means God exists. **B** *Points could include*: what caused God?/ the universe may be eternal, not God/ the universe may not need a cause/ the Big Bang was random chance.

7.3 **A** As science cannot explain miracles, they must be caused by something outside nature/ the only thing that exists outside nature is God/ therefore miracles must be the work of God. **B** *E.g. 'There is never enough evidence to prove that miracles are the work of God, instead of having a (perhaps unknown) scientific explanation. People who claim to have witnessed miracles are making them up or mistaken about what they have experienced. On the other hand, anyone who has witnessed a miracle is unlikely to remember it wrongly and there are 69 recorded miracles at Lourdes alone. They cannot all have been remembered wrongly. If Jesus had not performed miracles, they wouldn't have been written down in the Bible, and people who were there at the time would have spoken out if they thought the miracles were made up.'*

7.4 **A** *Reasons might include*: if God was loving, he would not allow suffering/ evil exists because God does not/ an all-knowing and all-powerful God would know about suffering and do something to prevent it. *Counter-arguments might include*: suffering is caused by wrong use of free will which God gifted to humans/ without evil, there would be no good/ suffering allows others to show love and compassion/ suffering is permitted by God to test people's faith and courage. **B** *E.g. 'Science challenges the existence of God because it gives explanations for things that used to be explained with God, which means God is no longer needed as the answer to these things. For example, some people would say the Big Bang theory removes the need to believe that God created the universe. However, others believe science can help to explain God's creation. For example, the Big Bang theory explains how God created the universe, and the theory of evolution explains how God brought life to earth and developed it to what it is like now.'*

7.5 **A** A specific experience of God such as a dream, vision, prophecy or miracle. *Any example from scripture, tradition, history or the present day can be given, e.g. God's self-revelation to Guru Nanak.* **B** *E.g. 'I don't think the statement can be true because visions can have a profound effect on people's lives, which would be unlikely to happen if they were not real. For example, Saul converted to Christianity after he saw a blinding light and heard Jesus' voice. The way he changed his life as a result of this vision means it probably did happen. Also, he certainly didn't expect to experience God in this way because he was very opposed to Christianity. However, at the same time we don't really know what Saul experienced. It is possible that the writers of the Bible dramatised a process of conversion and there was no vision.'*

7.6 **A** By gaining greater insight about God from events in nature/ e.g. the natural world reveals God to be creative, clever and powerful/ by learning about God's past actions through reading scripture/ by learning about God's relationship with people through reading scripture. **B** *Arguments for might include*: as the texts were written so long ago it is difficult to verify their accuracy/ ancient texts are not relevant to the modern world. *Arguments against might include*: ancient texts contain eternal truths/ can still help people today to learn about God/ can still inspire those in the modern world.

7.7 **A** Omniscient: all-knowing, aware of everything that has happened/ omnipotent: all-powerful, capable of doing anything/ transcendent: beyond and outside life on earth, etc. **B** *Arguments for might include:* Christians and Sikhs believe it is impossible to describe or understand God fully/ God is not limited by the world, time or space/ God has qualities no human does, e.g. God is omnipotent and omniscient/ this makes God's nature difficult to understand or put into words. *Arguments against might include:* there are certain words that can be used to give humans some idea of what God is like/ e.g. 'omnipotent', 'immanent', etc./ God is revealed in holy scriptures, such as the Bible or Guru Granth Sahib.

7.8 **A** Drugs or alcohol can make a person lose touch with reality/ wishful thinking means people can persuade themselves that something has happened purely because they want it to/ hallucinations can be symptoms of some illnesses/ some people might lie to become famous or rich, as it is hard to disprove their lies/ some may genuinely believe they have had a revelation but there may be a perfectly normal explanation that they do not know about. **B** *E.g. 'There is no way to prove that a revelation means God does exist. There are perfectly normal explanations for what people say are revelations, so they cannot be considered as evidence for God. For example, they might just be hallucinations caused by illness, or made up by someone to get attention. There is no way to know if a person's 'revelation' is genuine or not, so it cannot act as proof that God exists.'*

8 Religion, peace and conflict

Please note that these are suggested answers to the Apply questions, designed to give you guidance, rather than being definitive answers.

8.1 **A** Christians have a duty to forgive others if they wish to be forgiven/ the Lord's Prayer says, 'Forgive us our sins as we forgive those who sin against us'/ forgiveness is very important to Sikhs/ 'Where there is forgiveness, there is God himself' (Guru Granth Sahib 1372). **B** *Arguments for*: 2. Religious believers may believe that 'there is that of God in everyone' and so think all killing is wrong/ 4. The aim of war may be to create peace, but often leads to more instability, resentment and injustice. *Arguments against*: 1. Christians are taught to forgive others, but this does not mean actions to right wrongs should be avoided/ 3. If there is injustice or inequality, religious believers such as Sikhs may see it as a duty to put this right.

8.2 **A** There is an injustice/ they believe in loving their neighbours/ they believe in equality for all. **B** 'You shall not murder' (Exodus 20:13 [NIV])/ Christians and Sikhs believe it is important to condemn terrorism because it expresses hatred/ there are peaceful and democratic ways to express protest and draw attention to important issues.

8.3 **A** D) Forgiveness. **B** *Read the statements carefully. You should weigh up both sides of the argument and then say which side you personally find more convincing.*

8.4 **A** *Beliefs must be contrasting.* All religions are against the use of weapons of mass destruction/ Christians believe life is sacred (sanctity of life)/ only God has the right to end life/ nothing can justify the use of WMDs which target innocent people/ some people think all nuclear weapons should be abolished as there is always a risk they will be used/ some people agree with the possession of nuclear weapons as a deterrent/ to maintain peace and prevent attack/ some people think the use of nuclear weapons in war can be justified/ e.g. they ended the Second World War. **B** If nuclear weapons were used, they could kill huge numbers of people and destroy much of the earth/ 'You shall not murder' (Exodus 20:13 [NIV])/ 'No one is my enemy, and no one is a stranger. I get along with everyone.' (Guru Granth Sahib 1299)/ there are less threatening ways to maintain peace.

8.5 **A** Just cause/ proper legal authority/ just intention/ last resort/ chance of success/ proportional/ totally focused on what God wants/ no personal reward/ selfless reasons for fighting. **B** *For*: the just war theory says war should be a last resort/ all other means of settling disputes should be tried first/ limited retaliation is accepted by some Christians based on the teaching 'eye for eye, tooth for tooth' (Exodus 21:24 [NIV]). *Against*: Quakers believe war is never justified/ Jesus said to love your enemies and pray for those who persecute you/ responding to violence with more violence solves nothing.

8.6 **A** Fighting for God or a religious cause/ authorised by a high religious authority. **B** *E.g. 'This is a good argument because it gives reasons why there is no place for a holy war today (e.g. 'no one has to fight for the right to worship God'), and includes reference to religious teachings (e.g. 'turn the other cheek'). It finishes with a sentence that sums up why holy war is not the right response to an attack on the Christian faith in Britain today. It could perhaps be developed further by including reference to other religions in contemporary Britain.'*

8.7 **A** *Beliefs must be contrasting.* Many Christians and Sikhs are not pacifists because they believe war can be justified under certain circumstances/ as explained by the just war theory/ some Christians are pacifists who refuse to take part in war or violence of any kind/ 'Blessed are the peacemakers' (Matthew 5:9 [NIV]). **B** One of the causes for war is when people feel an injustice has been done/ e.g. if a group of people in a country feel they are being treated unfairly by the government they could retaliate, leading to a civil war/ if everyone has access to basic human rights, this might prevent conflict that tries to gain these rights by force/ e.g. if everyone had access to food this might prevent conflict in regions where food is very scarce.

8.8 **A** By raising money to help refugees through organisations such as Caritas and Khalsa Aid/ by going to war-torn areas to deliver emergency supplies to victims. **B** *E.g. for the statement: 'To win a war there should be a strong, decisive victory against the enemy. Killing the enemy demonstrates strength and resolve. War should also be ended as quickly as possible, and this means casualties are sometimes unavoidable. For example, many Japanese died as a result of the atom bombs being dropped in the Second World War, but these won the war.' E.g. against the statement: 'The point of war is to win and create peace, not to kill the enemy. Showing compassion towards the enemy means there will hopefully be less tension when the war ends, making reconciliation easier. Helping the enemy to survive also demonstrates Christian teachings such as Jesus' teaching to love your neighbour and Paul's teaching to live at peace with everyone.'*

9 Religion, crime and punishment

Please note that these are suggested answers to the Apply questions, designed to give you guidance, rather than being definitive answers.

9.1 **A** Prison/ community service/ fine. **B** *For the statement*: intentions are the reasons for actions/ loving and compassionate intentions usually bring about good actions/ 'But I tell you that anyone who looks at a woman lustfully has already committed adultery with her in his heart' (Matthew 5:28 [NIV])/ having good intentions helps Sikhs to build good karma. *Against the statement*: nobody is helped or harmed by intentions but they may be by actions/ 'faith by itself, if it is not accompanied by action, is dead' (James 2:17 [NIV])/ Christians and Sikhs are expected to act in a positive way, e.g. Sikhs are expected to perform sewa.

9.2 **A** *E.g. in response to the reason of poverty*: Christians believe stealing is wrong, and they should help to create a society where it is not necessary to steal because of poverty/ Sikhs believe stealing is wrong and try to prevent the need for it, e.g. by providing food for all at the langar. **B** *Arguments for the statement might include*:

addiction takes away choice/ a person may need to commit crimes to fund their addiction. *Arguments against might include*: some other reasons (e.g. poverty and mental illness) are also good reasons for committing crimes/ addicts should be helped to defeat their addiction so they do not commit crimes/ Christians and Sikhs believe crime is very rarely justified/ Sikh teachings forbid the taking of any intoxicants.

9.3 **A** Hate crimes usually involve violence and possibly killing/ murder is unlawful killing/ hate crimes result from prejudice, murder can have other reasons/ murder is generally considered to be worse/ some murders are classed as hate crimes. **B** *For*: hatred of a criminal is not constructive/ reasons why the criminal committed the crime should be considered/ love and compassion are religious teachings that should extend even to criminals/ Christians and Sikhs believe in the importance of rehabilitation. *Against*: criminal actions can cause great harm and upset/ some victims never fully recover from a criminal action/ 'let everyone be subject to the governing authorities, for there is no authority except that which God established' (Romans 13:1 [NIV])/ crimes break Christian and Sikh teachings and morality.

9.4 **A** *Retribution*: getting your own back/ the offender should receive the same (not greater) injuries and harm that their actions caused. *Deterrence*: putting people off from committing crimes/ the punishment should be severe enough to prevent repetition of the offence. *Reformation*: changing someone's behaviour for the better/ offenders are helped to change so they do not reoffend. **B** *For*: severe punishment can help prevent future crimes/ the criminal deserves severe punishment for what they have done/ 'eye for an eye' means punishment should equal harm caused, so more serious crimes deserve severe punishment. *Against*: less severe punishment may lead more easily to repentance and change/ positive methods (e.g. reformation) are more likely to have a lasting effect/ 'Do not take revenge, my dear friends' (Romans 12:19 [NIV])/ many Sikhs believe offenders should be treated with compassion, forgiveness and equality.

9.5 **A** 1: Christians believe suffering is a result of free will given by God/ Adam and Eve misused their free will to bring sin and suffering into the world/ suffering can be reduced by following the example and teachings of Jesus. 2: Sikhs believe that if they cause suffering to others, they will receive suffering later in this life or in the next/ this is a result of the law of karma. **B** *Arguments might include*: Sikhs believe that God allows suffering as a test of faith, courage, understanding and being content with God's will/ people who are suffering can bring out positive qualities in others/ 'people show compassion; then, they become immortal' (Guru Granth Sahib 340)/ Christians believe that suffering can lead to good things/ 'We also glory in our sufferings, because we know that suffering produces perseverance; perseverance, character; and character, hope' (Romans 5:3–4).

9.6 **A** Christians oppose all punishment that causes harm to offenders/ corporal punishment has no element of reform/ Sikhs oppose corporal punishment because it does not treat the criminal with decency and compassion/ a better aim is to reform them. **B** *Arguments for*: 'eye for eye' suggests offenders who commit serious crimes should receive severe punishment. *Arguments against*: 'love your neighbour' suggests criminals should be treated well/ all humans are deserving of respect as they are created by God/ the parable of the Sheep and the Goats teaches that showing kindness to prisoners is good.

9.7 **A** Christians and Sikhs believe they can condemn the offence but should forgive the person who has done wrong/ both Sikhism and Christianity teach that forgiveness is very important/ but also that in order to be just the offender may need to be punished. **B** *E.g. 'I agree that nobody should expect to be forgiven more than once because they should have learnt from their original mistake. If they were punished on the first occasion they should have used the chance to repent and promised not to offend again. On the other hand, Christians are taught they should forgive again. When asked how many times they should forgive, Jesus said, 'not seven times, but seventy-seven times.' Sikhs also believe forgiveness is important/ 'Where there is forgiveness, there is God himself' (Guru Granth Sahib 1372)/ this implies that someone might be forgiven more than once.'*

9.8 **A** Some Bible passages agree with retribution (e.g. Genesis 9:6)/ others with reform (e.g. Ezekiel 33:11)/ 'You shall not murder' (Exodus 20:13 [NIV])/ the death penalty does not reform the offender, which Christians and Sikhs believe is an important aim/ does not respect the sanctity of life/ goes against Sikh teachings that only God has the right to take life/ 'He alone has the power in His Hands' (Guru Granth Sahib 7). **B** The death penalty is not loving or compassionate/ may kill an innocent person by mistake/ life is sacred and only God has the right to take it/ evidence suggests that it does not deter/ a dead offender cannot be reformed/ the victim's family may not want it to happen/ Sikhs believe only God has the right to take life/ the death penalty is based on retribution and revenge, which cannot be justified as they are linked to anger and will lead to bad karma.

10 Religion, human rights and social justice

Please note that these are suggested answers to the Apply questions, designed to give you guidance, rather than being definitive answers.

10.1 **A** A fair trial/ education/ free elections/ family life/ life/ liberty/ security/ privacy/ marriage. **B** *For*: everyone is entitled to have rights/ they allow the more disadvantaged to be treated with justice and compassion/ promote equality/ allow people freedom to live their lives as they wish. *Against*: some people (e.g. murderers) do not deserve rights/ rights should be earned/ those who do not respect the rights of others should have no rights themselves/ it is sometimes best to restrict the rights of some people to ensure the welfare of others.

10.2 **A** *Similarity*: in both religions, men and women are encouraged to serve others/ in Sikhism and some Christian denominations (e.g. Baptists), women can lead worship. *Difference*: in Sikhism, women can lead worship services/ in some Christian churches, such as the Catholic and Orthodox churches, only men can be priests and lead worship. **B** *For*: leadership of the Christian Church has traditionally been male/ 'Women should remain silent in the churches' (1 Corinthians 14:34 [NIV])/ men and women should have different roles. *Against*: there is no reason why women cannot make equally good leaders to men/ Jesus treated women as equal to men/ women can now become priests in the Church of England/ women successfully lead worship in Sikh services.

10.3 **A** Christianity supports freedom of religion, and encourages tolerance and harmony between different religions/ 'If it is possible [...] live at peace with everyone' (Romans 12:8 [NIV])/ Sikhism teaches that the devotion of other faiths should be genuinely respected/ 'Do not say that the Vedas, the Bible and the Koran are false. Those who do not contemplate them are false' (Guru Granth Sahib 1350). **B** *Points might include*: it is a basic human right to be allowed to follow a religion/ following any religion can only be helpful to a person and society as a whole/ *any reference to the answers in 10.3 A*/ some sects and interpretations of major religions may be harmful and so should be avoided/ people should follow the religion of their country to show patriotism.

10.4 **A** Christians oppose racism because they believe all people have been made equal in the image of God/ 'There is neither Jew nor Gentile [...] for you are one in Christ Jesus' (Galatians 3:28 [NIV])/ Sikhs oppose racism because they believe everyone has been created by God and is of equal value. **B** *E.g. 'I believe all discrimination is wrong because it can cause great harm to people. It is also completely unjust because Christians believe all humans are created by God, in his image, and with equal rights. Behaving in any other way shows no love and respect to others and makes them feel that they are in some way inferior and wrong through no fault of their own. However, positive discrimination is an exception because it is not harmful. This means to treat people of some minority groups better than others, for example by giving disabled people special areas of seating in sports stadiums and theatres. This allows them equal opportunity to see sports or arts performances because it removes problems with access. Christians see this as fulfilling the prophecy of Amos: 'Let justice roll on like a river and righteousness like a never-failing stream' (Amos 5:24).'*

10.5 **A** Christians believe God blesses people with wealth in response to their faithfulness/ excess wealth should be shared with those who have less/ wealth can be dangerous (1 Timothy 6:10)/ can cause neglect of the spiritual life (Matthew 6:24)/ Sikhs believe wealth can be seen as a blessing if it used to help others/ Sikhs should earn an honest living/ wealth can't be taken on into a new reincarnation/ greed is one of the five evils. **B** *E.g. 'If giving to charity was compulsory, it is likely that charities would receive much more than they do at present, so could help more people in need throughout the world. This might help to fix many problems in society, which for Christians would demonstrate good stewardship and help in the pursuit of justice (Amos 5:24). Sikhs are already encouraged to give dasvandh (a tenth of their income) to support community projects. However, perhaps it should only be compulsory for people who earn a certain amount of money, as otherwise it could contribute to forcing more people into poverty.'*

10.6 **A** Unemployment/ low wages/ high cost of living/ debt from loans or credit cards/ gambling/ addiction/ financial mismanagement. **B** *Arguments for might include*: if people have got into poverty through their own fault, they should take responsibility for getting out of poverty/ Sikhism teaches that it is important for people to do honest work/ 'the one who is unwilling to work shall not eat' (2 Thessalonians 3:10 [NIV]). *Arguments against might include*: Christians and Sikhs believe it is important to show compassion to those in poverty and help them out of it if possible/ people living in poverty may not be able to get themselves out of it without the help of others.

10.7 **A** By not being paid fairly for the work they do/ by being forced to work in poor conditions/ by being charged excessive interest on loans/ by being exploited by people-traffickers. **B** *E.g. 'Developed countries that prefer to buy cheap goods do cause exploitation. In order to have cheap goods, the cost of making them has to be reduced to a minimum. This means exploiting workers by paying them next to nothing. If people in developed countries were prepared to pay a little more, the workers could be paid more. Exploitation goes against religious ideas of justice, compassion and love, and shows that Amos' vision that justice should flow like a river and righteousness like a stream has not yet been reached. However, another opinion is that it is the multinational companies that make the goods, and the shops that sell the goods, who are to blame. Designer goods are often made in poor countries by people who are exploited, yet they are expensive to buy because the producers and shops are keen to make ever bigger profits because they are so greedy. In 1 Timothy it says, 'the love of money is the root of all evil', so exploitation of poor countries is caused by the greed of rich people, not poor people who want to buy decent things at prices they can afford.'*

10.8 **A** Long-term aid educates people in skills such as literacy, numeracy and basic training to allow them to access work/ teaches them agricultural methods to grow their own crops/ provides assistance for setting up a small business to earn enough to provide for their needs. **B** *E.g. of an argument in favour: 'Aid sometimes does not get to the root of the problem. For example, aid might provide necessary supplies like food and clothing, but this does not address the underlying causes of poverty and so does not really change anything. Aid can also make a country dependent on whoever is giving out the aid, rather than encouraging the country to solve its problems by itself.' E.g. of an argument against: 'Long-term aid does help people to lift themselves out of poverty and become less dependent on aid. It does this by addressing the root causes of poverty, such as a lack of education. For example, educating farmers about more effective farming techniques means they can produce more food for their families, even after the aid has been withdrawn.'*

Exam practice answers

1 Christianity: Beliefs and teachings

Test the 1 mark question

1. B) Incarnation

2. C) Benevolent

Test the 2 mark question

Suggested answers, other relevant answers would be credited. 1 mark for each correct point.

3. Through good works/ through the grace of God/ through faith/ through Jesus' death/ through obeying the Ten Commandments/ through loving one's neighbour/ through prayer/ through worship/ through the Holy Spirit.

4. Christians believe everyone will be raised from the dead (resurrection)/ face judgement of God/ immediately or at the end of time/ Judgement Day/ Second Coming of Christ/ Jesus rose from the dead/ people will be judged on how they lived their lives/ sent to heaven, hell or purgatory/ resurrection of the body/ restoration to glorified bodies.

Test the 4 mark question

Suggested answers, other relevant answers would be credited. 1 mark for each simple contrasting or similar point, another mark for developing each point, so a maximum of 4 marks for two developed points.

6. Christians may show respect towards all of God's creation/ actively work for conservation/ show stewardship/ take practical steps like recycling/ be energy efficient.

Christians may treat others with respect/ all are created 'in imago dei' (in God's image)/ work for peace between people/ support charities that help people in need/ reflect God in all they do.

Christians may take care of themselves (both body and soul)/ adopt healthy lifestyles/ develop spiritual practices/ prayer/ worship/ meditation.

7. Christians believe that because God is loving, God wants the best for them/ they accept God's will as being for their benefit, even if it does not appear to be so/ they love others because God loves them.

God's greatest act of love was sending his Son Jesus/ to save people from sin/ to gain eternal life/ so they are grateful to God/ express their thanks through worship or praise.

God is love/ qualities of love described in Paul's letter to the Corinthians/ patient/ kind/ not easily angered/ Christians try to live according to these descriptions of love.

Test the 5 mark question

Suggested answers, other relevant answers would be credited. 1 mark for each simple contrasting or similar point, another mark for developing each point, so 4 marks for two developed points, 1 extra mark for a correct reference to a source of religious belief or teaching.

9. Christians believe God is omnipotent (all-powerful)/ has supreme authority/ can do all things/ 'Nothing is impossible with God' (Luke 1:37 [NIV])/ is loving (benevolent)/ wants good for God's creation/ wants people to love God freely in return/ 'God so loved the world that he gave his one and only Son, that whoever believes in him shall not perish but have eternal life' (John 3:16 [NIV])/ is just (fair/righteous)/ wants people to choose good over evil/ punishes wrongdoing/ is the perfect judge of human character.

Christians believe there is only one God/ 'The Lord is our God, the Lord alone' (Deuteronomy 6:4 [NIV])/ but within God there is a Trinity of persons/ Father, Son (Jesus), Holy Spirit/ 'Our Father in heaven' (Lord's Prayer)/ the Spirit's presence at Jesus' baptism.

God is the creator of all that is/ 'In the beginning, God created the heavens and the earth' (Genesis 1:1 [NIV])/ the Spirit was present at creation/ the Word of God (the Son) was involved in creation too.

10. Christians believe Jesus restored the relationship between God and humanity/ Jesus atoned for the sins of humankind/ God accepted his death as atonement for sin by raising Jesus from the dead/ 'Jesus Christ [...] is the atoning sacrifice for our sins, and not only for ours but also for the sins of the whole world' (1 John 2:1–2 [NIV]).

Through the atonement of Jesus, humans can receive forgiveness for sin/ be able to get close to God/ gain eternal life/ sin has been defeated/ 'For the wages of sin is death, but the gift of God is eternal life in Christ Jesus our Lord' (Romans 6:23 [NIV]).

Jesus' death atoned for the original sin of Adam and Eve/ Adam chose to disobey God, but Jesus chose to offer his life as a sacrifice/ 'For since death came through a man, the resurrection of the dead also comes through a man. For as in Adam all die, so in Christ all will be made alive' (1 Corinthians 15:21 [NIV]).

Test the 12 mark question

Suggested answers shown here, but see page 10 for guidance on levels of response.

12. Arguments in support

- Hell is not a place/ exploration of the earth and space have not discovered a place where spirits are punished forever/ although hell is shown in paintings as a place of fire and torture ruled by Satan (the devil) somewhere beneath the earth, no such place exists.
- The idea of hell is inconsistent with a benevolent God/ Christians believe God is loving/ a loving God would never send anyone to eternal damnation in hell/ like a loving Father, God will give people another chance if they repent.
- The idea of hell is just a way of comforting those who want to see justice/ some people get away with many bad things and seem not to receive punishment in this life/ the idea of hell ensures the idea of justice being done, but it does not really exist.

Arguments in support of other views

- Today hell is more often thought to be an eternal state of mind being cut off from the possibility of God/ the state of being without God, rather than a place/ a person who did not acknowledge God or follow his teachings would necessarily end up without God in the afterlife.
- Christians believe God is just/ it is only fair that someone who has gone against God's laws should be punished eventually/ it is a just punishment for an immoral life.
- Jesus spoke about hell as a possible consequence for sinners/ 'But I tell you that anyone who is angry with a brother or sister will be subject to judgment [...] And anyone who says, 'You fool!' will be in danger of the fire of hell.' (Matthew 5:22 [NIV])/ 'If your right eye causes you to stumble, gouge it out and throw it away. It is better for you to lose one part of your body than for your whole body to be thrown into hell.' (Matthew 5:29 [NIV])/ 'For if God did not spare angels when they sinned, but sent them to hell, putting them in chains of darkness to be held for judgement' (2 Peter 2:4 [NIV]).

13. Arguments in support

- Salvation means deliverance from sin and admission to heaven brought about by Jesus/ saving one's soul/ sin separates people from God who is holy/ the original sin of Adam and Eve brought suffering and death to humankind/ so God gave the law so that people would know how to stay close to him/ Jesus' teaching takes the law even further.
- One way of gaining salvation is through good works/ by having faith in God and obeying God's laws/ obeying the Ten Commandments (Exodus 20:1–19) is the best way of being saved because by doing so Christians are avoiding sin/ following other Christian teachings such as the Beatitudes (Matthew 5:1–12) helps gain salvation through good works/ being merciful/ a peacemaker.
- Christians believe God gave people free will to make moral choices/ following God's law shows the person is willing to use their free will wisely.

Arguments in support of other views

- The best way of gaining salvation is through grace/ grace is a free gift of God's love and support/ it is not earned by following laws/ faith in Jesus is all a person needs to be saved/ 'For it is by grace you have been saved, through faith – and this is not from yourselves, it is the gift of God – not by works, so that no one can boast.' (Ephesians 2:8–9 [NIV]).
- Merely following the law is a legalistic approach/ it can hide sinfulness inside a person/ Jesus criticised the Pharisees for following the law but having evil hearts/ Jesus said, 'The teachers of the law and the Pharisees sit in Moses' seat. So you must be careful to do everything they tell you. But do not do what they do, for they do not practise what they preach.' (Matthew 23:2–3 [NIV]).
- Most Christians believe both good works and grace (through faith in Jesus) are needed to be saved/ you can't prove you have faith unless you show it in your outward behaviour/ a danger in believing in salvation through grace alone is that people can feel specially chosen so look down on others/ not feel they have to obey God's law as they are already 'saved'.

2 Christianity: Practices

Test the 1 mark question

1. D) Liturgical worship

2. C) Christmas

Test the 2 mark question

Suggested answers, other relevant answers would be credited. 1 mark for each correct point.

3. By setting up charities/ Christian Aid/ CAFOD/ Tearfund/ by raising or donating money/ by working overseas in poor countries/ by praying for justice for the poor/ by campaigning for the poor.

4. Prayer helps Christians communicate with God/ develop and sustain their relationship with God/ thank God for blessings/ praise God/ ask God for help for oneself or others/ find courage to accept God's will in difficult times.

Test the 4 mark question

Suggested answers, other relevant answers would be credited. 1 mark for each simple contrasting or similar point, another mark for developing each point, so a maximum of 4 marks for two developed points.

6. *Ways must be contrasting*:

Infant baptism: Catholic, Orthodox, Anglican, Methodist and United Reformed Churches baptise babies/ 'I baptise you in the name of the Father, and of the Son, and of the Holy Spirit'/ blessed water poured over the baby's head/ sign of cross on baby's forehead/ anointing with oil/ white garment/ candle/ godparents' and parents' promises.

Believers' baptism: others such as Baptist and Pentecostal Christians baptise those who are old enough to make their own decision about baptism/ baptise people who have made a commitment to faith in Jesus/ full immersion in pool/ minister talks about meaning of baptism/ candidates are asked if they are willing to change their lives/ Bible passage/ brief testimony from candidate/ baptised 'in the name of the Father, and of the Son, and of the Holy Spirit'.

7. *Interpretations must be contrasting*:

Catholic, Orthodox and some Anglican Christians believe the bread and wine become the body and blood of Christ/ Jesus is fully present in the bread and wine/ a divine mystery/ those receiving become present in a mystical way at the death and resurrection of Christ/ receive God's grace/ Holy Communion is a sacrament.

Protestant Christians see Holy Communion as a reminder of Jesus' words and actions at the Last Supper/ bread and wine are symbols of Jesus' sacrifice/ they help them reflect on the meaning of Jesus' death and resurrection for their lives today/ it is an act of fellowship.

Test the 5 mark question

Suggested answers, other relevant answers would be credited. 1 mark for each simple contrasting or similar point, another mark for developing each point, so 4 marks for two developed points, 1 extra mark for a correct reference to a source of religious belief or teaching.

9. Evangelism is spreading the Christian gospel/ by public preaching/ by personal witness.

Evangelism is considered a duty of Christians because of the Great Commission/ 'Therefore go and make disciples of all nations, baptising them in the name of the Father and of the Son and of the Holy Spirit, and teaching them to obey everything I have commanded you' (Matthew 28:19–20 [NIV])/ people have a desire to share the good news with others because they have experienced it themselves.

Christians believe they are called to do more than just know Jesus in their own lives/ they are called to spread the good news to non-believers that Jesus is the Saviour of the world.

When the early disciples received the Spirit at Pentecost they were given the gifts necessary to carry out the Great Commission/ the Spirit gives some people wisdom/ knowledge/ faith/ gifts of healing/ miraculous powers/ prophecy/ the ability to speak in tongues and understand the message of those who speak in tongues.

10. Christians may work for reconciliation in their own lives by forgiving their enemies/ making up with people they have offended/ going to the sacrament of Reconciliation to be reconciled with God/ 'But I tell you, love your enemies and pray for those who persecute you' (Matthew 5:44 [NIV]).

Christians may work for reconciliation between political or religious groups through organisations/ e.g. through the Irish Churches Peace Project/ the Corrymeela Community/ which sought to bring Catholic and Protestant communities together in Northern Ireland/ through discussion and working on their differences together.

Christians could work for more global reconciliation through an organisation such as the Community of the Cross of Nails at Coventry Cathedral/ which works with partners in many countries/ to bring about peace and harmony in areas where conflict and violence are present.

Christians do this work because of Jesus' teaching and example/ as Paul says, 'For if, while we were God's enemies, we were reconciled to him through the death of his Son, how much more, having been reconciled, shall we be saved through his life!' (Romans 5:10 [NIV]).

Test the 12 mark question

Suggested answers shown here, but see page 10 for guidance on levels of response.

12. Arguments in support

- A pilgrimage is a journey made for religious reasons/ to a holy place/ a place where Jesus or saints lived and died/ it can teach people more about their religion's history/ can strengthen faith as it increases knowledge about holy people/ Christians make pilgrimages to the Holy Land as it is where Jesus lived, preached, died and resurrected from the dead/ Christians can experience for themselves what it was like to live there/ they follow in the footsteps of Jesus/ meet others who share their faith.
- Some Christians go on pilgrimage to places where miracles are said to have occurred/ e.g. Lourdes in France/ they pray to be healed from sin/ mental or physical illness/ to thank God for a special blessing/ to help others who are disabled or ill, putting into practice love of neighbour.
- Some Christians go on pilgrimage to a remote place/ e.g. Iona in Scotland/ they go to have quiet time to pray/ read scriptures/ connect with God through nature/ reflect on their lives/ particularly if facing a big decision/ refresh their spiritual lives in today's busy world.

Arguments in support of other views

- Pilgrimage does not always bring people closer to God/ some places are very commercialised/ it can disappoint people who had a certain mental image of a place to see that it is touristy/ it can be very crowded so not a place for reflection/ some people on the pilgrimage may just see it as a holiday, making it hard to concentrate on God.
- Pilgrimage can be expensive/ not everyone can afford going abroad/ not everyone has time to make a pilgrimage, e.g. getting time off work/ family commitments.
- Other ways of becoming closer to God are better than pilgrimage/ daily prayer in one's own home can bring the peace of mind and heart the person needs/ receiving Holy Communion brings people closer to God than any journey/ going to the sacrament of Reconciliation can be done locally.

13. Arguments in support

- The Church (meaning all Christians) has a mission to spread the good news/ that Jesus Christ is the Son of God/ came into the world to be its Saviour/ the Great Commission/ 'Therefore go and make disciples of all nations, baptising them in the name of the Father and of the Son and of the Holy Spirit, and teaching them to obey everything I have commanded you' (Matthew 28:19–20 [NIV]).
- Christians believe they are called to do more than just know Jesus in their own lives/ they are called to spread the good news to non-believers that Jesus is the Saviour of the world.
- When the early disciples received the Spirit at Pentecost they were given the gifts necessary to carry out the Great Commission/ the Spirit gives some people wisdom/ knowledge/ faith/ gifts of healing/ miraculous powers/ prophecy/ the ability to speak in tongues and understand the message of those who speak in tongues/ Christians today receive the Holy Spirit at their Confirmation/ they are called to be disciples of Jesus, like the first disciples/ so they must spread the faith fearlessly as the disciples did.

Arguments in support of other views

- The main job of a Christian is to believe in Jesus/ follow the commandments/ worship God/ love one's neighbour as oneself/ live a good life in the hope of eternal life in heaven.
- Many Christians do not have the personality to preach to others about their faith/ do not have the time if working/ have family responsibilities/ are not public speakers/ do not want to antagonise people who are unsympathetic non-believers/ cannot go abroad to work as missionaries.
- There are other ways of showing one's faith to others without actually 'telling them'/ being a good neighbour/ helping those in need/ working with charities/ worshipping God/ showing integrity/ having high moral principles that make non-believers notice that faith makes a difference to the Christian believer.

3 Sikhism: Beliefs and teachings

Test the 1 mark question

1. A) Haumai

2. B) Mool Mantra

Test the 2 mark question

Suggested answers, other relevant answers would be credited. 1 mark for each correct point.

3. Everyone seated on the floor showing equal status/ all are welcome to prepare, serve and clear up/ vegetarian food makes it inclusive/ food is served to everyone regardless of race, gender, religion, etc.

4. Anger/ lust/ greed/ worldly attachment/ pride.

Test the 4 mark question

Suggested answers, other relevant answers would be credited. 1 mark for each simple contrasting or similar point, another mark for developing each point, so a maximum of 4 marks for two developed points.

6. Amritdhari Sikhs are expected to offer daily prayers/ these include morning and evening prayers, as set out in the Rehat Maryada.

Amritdhari Sikhs are expected to practise the Sikh virtues/ these are truth, compassion, contentment, humility and love.

Amritdhari Sikhs should practise self-control/ they should not use tobacco, alcohol and illegal drugs.

7. A gurmukh aims to have their mind centred on God at all times/ this means they are becoming a perfect person as God intended.

A gurmukh is removing haumai (pride or egotism) from their lives/ removing haumai means they understand their reliance on God.

Performing sewa is an important part of being gurmukh/ this implies that to become gurmukh a person must live in a community/ 'One who performs selfless service, without thought of reward, shall attain his Lord and Master' (Guru Granth Sahib 286).

Test the 5 mark question

Suggested answers, other relevant answers would be credited. 1 mark for each simple contrasting or similar point, another mark for developing each point, so 4 marks for two developed points, 1 extra mark for a correct reference to a source of religious belief or teaching.

9. Sikhs believe in karma, which determines what happens to a person in the future/ Guru Granth Sahib 78 explains it as 'The body is the field of karma in this age; whatever you plant you shall harvest'/ this metaphor shows that a person's actions and attitudes (what they 'plant') will affect their future (their 'harvest').

The belief in karma means that rebirth is not a random event/ rebirth depends on what Sikhs have done previously/ once born as a human a person has the opportunity to make further progress to liberation.

Doing bad deeds brings consequences/ this is shown in the Sikh story of the proud man who met a blind man and did not help him/ the blind man explained that he was blind because he had refused to help a sick person.

10. Sikhs believe God is the creator/ God creates and sustains the universe/ the opening words of the Mool Mantra ('One Universal Creator God') show this importance of this belief.

Sikhs believe God in immanent/ he is present in the souls of humans/ this makes it possible for humans to have a personal relationship with God/ the Mool Mantra refers to this as 'Creative Being Personified'.

God makes himself known through his word/ the Mool Mantra says 'By Guru's Grace'/ Sikhs try to understand God's word through worship and prayer.

Test the 12 mark question

Suggested answers shown here, but see page 10 for guidance on levels of response.

12. Arguments in support

- Sewa (selfless service) is a way of life for Sikhs/ it is a way of worshipping and serving God/ it is an integral part of the langar at the gurdwara.
- Sewa will help lead Sikhs to God/ 'One who performs selfless service, without thought of reward, shall attain his Lord and Master' (Guru Granth Sahib 286)/ sewa helps a person become gurmukh and move away from pride, greed and self-centredness.
- Service demonstrates the key belief of equality of all/ serving others is a way to show that all people have value/ when serving others in the langar, there are no distinctions of race, gender, religion etc.

Arguments in support of other views

- Others would argue that belief in God is more important/ the Mool Mantra, which opens the Guru Granth Sahib, describes God and his qualities, showing how important he is/ without belief in God 'they are like dead bodies in the world' (Guru Granth Sahib 88)/ without belief in God Sikhism would not exist.
- Sewa should be performed while keeping God in mind/ sewa is an important way of serving and becoming closer to God/ 'One who performs selfless service, without thought of reward, shall attain his Lord and Master' (Guru Granth Sahib 286)/ this shows that sewa first requires belief in God, which is more important.

13. Arguments in support

- Mukti may be achieved while someone is alive (jivan mukti) so cannot be very difficult to achieve/ by being born human, a person is born into the stage of piety, which enables them to meet with God through commitment or devotion to him/ they can then focus on devoting time to God.
- Sikhs are encouraged to lead ordinary lives in their community and do not need to withdraw from the world or give up all their belongings to achieve mukti/ much of Sikh teaching is about sewa (practical acts of service), which may take effort but is still achievable/ 'One who performs selfless service, without thought of reward, shall attain his Lord and Master' (Guru Granth Sahib 286).

Arguments in support of other views

- Sikhs have to pass through several stages to reach mukti/ these stages require knowledge, time and effort/ one of the stages (grace) relies on help from God/ 'By the grace of the Holy, let your mind be imbued with the Lord's love' (Guru Granth Sahib 866).
- There are a number of barriers to mukti, including the five evils/ Sikhs have to give up anger, lust, greed, worldly attachment and pride, which can be difficult to do/ Sikhs also have to let go of their ego or self-centredness as this prevents them from getting close to God.

4 Sikhism: Practices

Test the 1 mark question

1. A) Amrit Sanskar
2. D) Nam japna

Test the 2 mark question

Suggested answers, other relevant answers would be credited. 1 mark for each correct point.

3. Vaisakhi/ Divali/ Guru Nanak's birthday/ Bandi Chhor Divas.

4. Sikh flag (Nishan Sahib)/ prayer hall (Darbar Sahib/ the langar/ the throne (takht)/ the canopy (chanani)/ the bed (manji).

Test the 4 mark question

Suggested answers, other relevant answers would be credited. 1 mark for each simple contrasting or similar point, another mark for developing each point, so a maximum of 4 marks for two developed points.

6. Sikhs pray by themselves in the morning after they bathe/ they recite the Japji, Jap and Swayyas prayers given to them by Guru Nanak and Guru Gobind Singh.

Any service of worship in the gurdwara begins and ends with the Ardas prayer/ Sikhs stand during this prayer.

Sikhs aim to remember God throughout the day/ one way they can do this is by quietly reciting the name of God/ they might use a mala to meditate on the name of God.

7. In India, celebrations take place on the date of the original event/ schools and workplaces are closed for some of the gurpurbs/ there are colourful processions, firework displays and fairs.

In Great Britain, celebrations take place at the weekend/ celebrations tend to be quieter than in India/ celebrations tend to be centred around the gurdwara.

Test the 5 mark question

Suggested answers, other relevant answers would be credited. 1 mark for each simple contrasting or similar point, another mark for developing each point, so 4 marks for two developed points, 1 extra mark for a correct reference to a source of religious belief or teaching.

9. Sikh worship includes the singing of hymns (kirtan)/ these include verses from the Guru Granth Sahib/ focusing on the meaning of the words encourages worshippers to concentrate on God's name.

All services start and end with a recitation of the Ardas prayer/ Sikhs are reminded to remember God and the ten Gurus as well as praying for individuals and the welfare of all people/ the Ardas prayer encompasses important Sikh beliefs, for example in the line 'The light of the Ten Gurus shines in the Guru Granth Sahib.'

10. Processions are held in many towns for Vaisakhi/ the Guru Granth Sahib is carried on a decorated float/ there is singing, dancing and music/ special sweets are made and given away.

Divali is celebrated with light/ homes are lit up and there are bonfires and firework displays/ it is a celebration of freedom and good over evil/ Sikhs remember the story of when Guru Hargobind was released from prison with 52 Hindu princes.

Test the 12 mark question

Suggested answers shown here, but see page 10 for guidance on levels of response.

12. Arguments in support

- Sikhs are expected to remember God at all times/ Guru Granth Sahib 305 says, 'One who meditates on my Lord… that GurSikh becomes pleasing to the Guru's Mind'/ as a Sikh becomes more focused on God and less on themselves, they become gurmukh/ the morning and evening routines of bathing and praying are set out in the Guru Granth Sahib, showing that remembering the name of God in daily life is vital.

Arguments in support of other views

- Although God is present everywhere, special reverence is shown at gurdwaras/ services offer an opportunity to be completely focused on God/ listening to the Guru Granth Sahib helps focus the worshipper/ talks or sermons can help Sikhs to understand God better/ kirtan offers an opportunity to concentrate on God and his name/ It is important for Sikhs to be part of a community and worshipping at the gurdwara is one way of doing this.

13. Arguments in support

- Many Sikhs believe that the spiritual reflection on a pilgrimage will deepen their faith and understanding/ visiting the Golden Temple helps pilgrims to learn about the faith and courage of Sikh Gurus and leaders/ a pilgrimage is time taken out of the normal routines of daily life and so offers greater opportunities to focus on God.

Arguments in support of other views

- 'There is no sacred shrine equal to the Guru' (Guru Granth Sahib 1328)/ Guru Nanak and the other Gurus believed that ritual and ceremony could sometimes get in the way of true faith and wisdom/ to become gurmukh it is important for Sikhs to make the effort to understand God and meditate on his name/ 'One who meditates on the Lord… that GurSikh becomes pleasing to the Guru's Mind' (Guru Granth Sahib 305)/ performing sewa is an important way to become more selfless and God-centred.

5 Relationships and families

Test the 1 mark question

1. D) Stability
2. B) A couple and their children

Test the 2 mark question

Suggested answers, other relevant answers would be credited. 1 mark for each correct point.

3. Christians believe all people are created equal by God/ 'love your neighbour' applies to everyone/ Christians follow Jesus' example in treating women with equal value/ 'There is neither Jew nor Gentile, neither slave nor free, nor is there male and female, for you are all one in Christ Jesus' (Galatians 3:28 [NIV])/ men and women can have different roles in the family but this does not mean they are not equal in God's sight/ Christian marriage is an equal partnership.

Sikhism teaches that men are women are equal before God/ Guru Nanak said that 'without woman, there would be no one at all' (Guru Granth Sahib 473)/ women in Sikhism should be treated with respect and consideration/ it is important to demonstrate equality in family life and worship in Sikhism/ e.g. both men and women are allowed to lead worship and serve food in the langar.

4. Christians who oppose sex before marriage think cohabitation is wrong/ Catholic and Orthodox Churches believe a sexual relationship should only take place within marriage/ many Anglican and Protestant Christians accept that although marriage is best, people may live together in a faithful, loving, committed way without being married.

Sikhs do not approve of cohabitation because they believe sex should only take place in marriage/ sex outside marriage lowers one's self-esteem and respect for others/ the Rehat Maryada says that anyone who has sexual relationships without marriage is not a true Sikh.

Test the 4 mark question

Suggested answers, other relevant answers would be credited. 1 mark for each simple contrasting or similar point, another mark for developing each point, so a maximum of 4 marks for two developed points.

6. *Beliefs must be contrasting:*

Christians believe marriage is for life/ vows made in the presence of God should not be broken/ Jesus taught that anyone who divorced and remarried was committing adultery (Mark 10:11–12)/ except in the case of adultery (Matthew 5:32)/ for Catholics marriage is a sacrament that is permanent/ cannot be dissolved by civil divorce/ Catholics can separate but cannot marry someone else while their partner is still alive/ for some

Christians divorce is accepted as the lesser of two evils/ some Christian Churches (e.g. the Methodist Church) accept civil divorce and allow remarriage in church.

Sikhs believe that marriage is for life/ the Rehat Maryada teaches that, in general, no Sikh should marry for a second time if their spouse is still alive/ Sikhs reluctantly accept civil divorce if a marriage cannot be saved/ grounds for divorce include adultery, desertion and change of religion.

7. *Beliefs must be contrasting*:

Many Christians believe heterosexual relationships are part of God's plan for humans/ God created male and female/ told them to 'be fruitful and increase in number' (Genesis 1:28 [NIV])/ sex expresses a deep, life-long union best expressed in marriage/ some Christians oppose same-sex relationships because they go against God's plan/ the Catholic Church teaches that homosexual sex is a sinful activity/ some Christians think loving, faithful same-sex relationships are just as holy as heterosexual ones.

Sikhism teaches that it is important to remain chaste before marriage/ for Sikhs, sex is a creative act and means of spiritual growth/ many Sikhs believe heterosexual relationships are intended by God/ '[same-sex marriage] is unnatural and ungodly' (Manjit Singh Kalkatta)/ some Sikhs accept same-sex relationships are a valid way to express love and commitment/ Sikhs promote equality between all people regardless of sexual orientation.

Test the 5 mark question

Suggested answers, other relevant answers would be credited. 1 mark for each simple contrasting or similar point, another mark for developing each point, so 4 marks for two developed points, 1 extra mark for a correct reference to a source of religious belief or teaching.

9. For Christians, procreation is an important purpose/ procreation is part of God's plan for humanity/ God created man and woman, blessed them and said, 'Be fruitful and increase in number; fill the earth and subdue it' (Genesis 1:28 [NIV])/ protection of children is an important purpose/ educating children about Christian values is an important purpose/ 'Children thrive, grow and develop within the love and safeguarding of the family' (The Church of England website).

For many Sikhs, procreation is an important purpose/ marriage helps two people experience God in their relationship/ 'It is a Sikh's duty to get his children educated in Sikhism' (the Rehat Maryada)/ in Sikh families, the mother has a strong role in educating her children in the faith.

10. The Christian Church teaches that both parents and children have responsibilities in a family/ the commandment to 'Honour one's father and mother' (Exodus 20:12 [NIV]) applies to children of all ages/ it includes the respect and care given to the elderly members of the family/ children should obey their parents/ 'Children, obey your parents in everything, for this pleases the Lord' (Colossians 3:20 [NIV]).

In Sikh families, children are expected to obey and respect their parents/ to learn the history of Sikhism and the stories of the Gurus/ to learn religious values and customs/ for example, wearing the five Ks.

Test the 12 mark question

Suggested answers shown here, but see page 10 for guidance on levels of response.

12. Arguments in support

- Most Christians think marriage is the proper place to enjoy a sexual relationship/ sex expresses a deep, loving, life-long union that first requires the commitment of marriage/ it is one of God's gifts at creation/ 'That is why a man leaves his father and mother and is united to his wife, and they become one flesh' (Genesis 2:24 [NIV]).
- Having sex is part of the trust between partners in a marriage/ sex should not be a casual, temporary pleasure/ 'The sexual act must take place exclusively within marriage. Outside of marriage it always constitutes a grave sin' (Catechism 2390).
- The Rehat Maryada says that anyone who has sex before or outside marriage is not a true Sikh/ Sikhism teaches that sex outside marriage lowers one's self-esteem and respect for others.
- Marriage brings security/ protects each partner's rights/ the rights of children/ provides a stable environment in which to raise a family.

Arguments in support of other views

- Society has changed/ many people do not see sex as requiring the commitment of marriage/ contraception has reduced the risk of pregnancy before marriage/ many people engage in casual sexual relationships.
- The cost of marriage prevents some people from marrying immediately/ some couples want to see if the relationship is going to work before marrying/ some people do not think a marriage certificate makes any difference to their relationship.
- Some Christians accept that for some people sex before marriage is a valid expression of their love for each other/ some Christians may accept cohabitation, particularly if the couple is committed to each other/ more liberal Christians may accept that people may live together in a faithful, loving and committed way without being married.

13. Arguments in support

- The Orthodox and Catholic Churches teach that using artificial contraception within marriage is wrong/ against natural law/ against the purpose of marriage to have children/ having children is God's greatest gift to a married couple/ 'Every sexual act should have the possibility of creating new life' (*Humanae Vitae*, 1968).
- God will not send more children than a couple can care for/ if Catholic couples wish to plan their families they should use a natural method, such as the rhythm method.
- Some Sikhs are against the use of artificial contraception as they believe sex is a God-given gift that should be used to have children/ contraception is seen as killing life.

Arguments in support of other views

- Other Christians accept the use of artificial contraception provided it is not used to prevent having children altogether/ by mutual consent of the couple.
- Its use may allow a couple to develop their relationship before having children/ prevent sexually transmitted infections/ help reduce the population explosion.
- The Church of England approved the use of artificial contraception at the Lambeth Conference in 1930/ 'The Conference agrees that other methods may be used, provided that this is done in the light of Christian principles.'
- Most Sikhs accept the use of artificial contraception within marriage if it is used for responsible family planning/ but it should not be used to prevent having children altogether.

6 Religion and life

Test the 1 mark question

1. C) A painless death

2. D) The theory of evolution

Test the 2 mark question

Suggested answers, other relevant answers would be credited. 1 mark for each correct point.

3. Christians believe the world is on loan to humans, who have been given the responsibility by God to look after it (Genesis 1:28)/ pollution is not loving towards others – Jesus teaches Christians to 'love your neighbour' (Luke 10:27 [NIV]).

Sikhs are keen to reduce pollution because they believe it damages God's creation/ there is a divine presence in every living being and pollution harms or kills some of those beings.

4. Christians believe animals were created by God for humans to use and care for/ humans are more important than animals but should still be treated kindly/ God gave animals to humanity to use for food, so it is fine to eat meat.

Sikhs believe animals have souls/ animals are sentient, feeling beings/ they should be treated with respect and compassion/ the Guru Granth Sahib forbids killing living beings/ for these reasons, most Sikhs are vegetarian.

Test the 4 mark question

Suggested answers, other relevant answers would be credited. 1 mark for each simple contrasting or similar point, another mark for developing each point, so a maximum of 4 marks for two developed points.

6. *Beliefs must be contrasting*:

Most Christians believe animal experimentation can be justified to help save human lives/ Christians believe humans have dominion/are more important than animals, so they can use animals for this purpose.

Most Sikhs oppose animal experimentation/ particularly for nonessential reasons (e.g. testing cosmetics)/ they believe animals have souls and should be treated with respect and compassion/taking part in animal experimentation can negatively affect a person's karma.

7. *Beliefs must be similar*:

Christians believe the Earth is a priceless gift from God, loaned to humans as a result of his love/ the earth's resources should be used responsibly so the world still has value for future generations.

Sikhs value the world because God created it and cares for it/ because of this they should look after the world, for example by trying to live sustainably.

Test the 5 mark question

Suggested answers, other relevant answers would be credited. 1 mark for each simple contrasting or similar point, another mark for developing each point, so 4 marks for two developed points, 1 extra mark for a correct reference to a source of religious belief or teaching.

9. Christians believe stewardship means humans have a responsibility to look after the earth on behalf of God/ God put Adam into the Garden of Eden 'to work it and take care of it' (Genesis 2:15 [NIV])/ it is an act of love to protect the earth for future generations.

Sikhs believe that the world was created by God/ there is a divine presence in every living being/ this means that humans should protect the environment and live in harmony with it/ 'The Lord infused His Light into the dust and created the world, the universe. The sky, the earth, the trees and the water – all are the Creation of the Lord' (Guru Granth Sahib 723).

10. Christians believe the universe was designed and made by God out of nothing/ Genesis 1 says that God made the universe and all life in it in six days/ 'In the beginning God created the heavens and the earth' (Genesis 1:1 [NIV])/ some Christians believe God used the Big Bang to create the universe.

Sikhs believe the universe was created by God/ before this, there was 'utter darkness' for a long time (Guru Granth Sahib 1035)/ then God spoke and his word created everything/ the Guru Granth Sahib supports the idea of an expanding universe, in line with the Big Bang theory.

Test the 12 mark question

Suggested answers shown here, but see page 10 for guidance on levels of response.

12. Arguments in support

- Many Christians believe abortion doesn't respect the sanctity of life/ Christians who believe life begins at the moment of conception think abortion is wrong, as it is taking away life given by God.
- Most Sikhs oppose abortion because they believe life begins at conception and ending it deliberately is a sin/ 'The Lord infused His Light into you, and then you came into the world' (Guru Granth Sahib 921).
- Disabled children can enjoy a good quality of life/ unwanted children can be adopted into families that will care for them/ those who choose abortion can suffer from depression and guilt afterwards.

Arguments in support of other views

- The mother has to carry the baby, give birth to it and bring it up, so she should have the right to choose whether to continue with the pregnancy/ some Christians might argue that having an abortion should be a matter of personal choice – not dictated by the law.
- Life doesn't start until birth (or from the point when the foetus can survive outside the womb), so abortion does not involve killing.
- It is cruel to allow a severely disabled child to be born/ if the child would have a very poor quality of life then abortion may be the lesser of two evils/ some Christians would agree with this view.

13. Arguments in support

- A minority of Christians believe humans were given dominion over the earth so can do what they want with it/ 'Rule over the fish in the sea and the birds in the sky and over every living creature that moves on the ground' (Genesis 1:28 [NIV]).
- If resources are destroyed or used up, scientists will develop alternatives.
- Humans need natural resources to sustain their way of life.

Arguments in support of other views

- Most Christians believe humans were put on the earth as stewards to look after it on behalf of God for future generations/ God put Adam into the Garden of Eden 'to work it and take care of it' (Genesis 2:15 [NIV])/ it is wrong to destroy something that belongs to someone else (i.e. God).
- Many of the earth's natural resources are non-renewable so there is only a limited supply of them/ using them up too quickly will probably make life much harder for future generations/ this shows a lack of love and respect for others.
- Sikhs believe the world was created by God and every living being in it has a divine presence/ this means Sikhs should live sustainably and respect and care for nature/ Sikhs should avoid the five evils, including greed, which arguably is at the root of many of the abuses of the environment.

7 The existence of God and revelation

Test the 1 mark question

1. C) Outside space and time

2. B) God directly revealed through a vision

Test the 2 mark question

Suggested answers, other relevant answers would be credited. 1 mark for each correct point.

3. If everything that exists has a cause, why doesn't God have a cause?/ if God is eternal then the universe could be eternal too/ the idea that everything has a cause doesn't mean the universe has to have a cause/ or that the cause is God.

4. Suffering is a result of free will/ without suffering, no one would be able to actively choose good over bad/ God allows suffering to test people's faith and courage/ God has reasons for allowing suffering that humans can't know.

Test the 4 mark question

Suggested answers, other relevant answers would be credited. 1 mark for each simple contrasting or similar point, another mark for developing each point, so a maximum of 4 marks for two developed points.

6. *Beliefs must be contrasting:*

Christians and Sikhs believe miracles are events performed by God which appear to break the laws of nature/ *an example of such an event*/ they confirm God's existence/ they show God is at work in the world.

They are not real/ they are lucky coincidences that have nothing to do with God/ may be made up for fame or money/ healing miracles may be mind over matter or misdiagnosis/ can be explained scientifically in a way we don't yet know.

7. *Beliefs must be similar:*

Comes through ordinary human experiences/ seeing God's creative work and presence in nature/ Christians and Sikhs believe God is revealed through his creation to be creative, clever and powerful/ comes through worship or scripture/ the Bible can help to reveal what God is like and how he wants people to live/ the Guru Granth Sahib teaches Sikhs how to become closer to God and become people of truth.

Test the 5 mark question

Suggested answers, other relevant answers would be credited. 1 mark for each simple contrasting or similar point, another mark for developing each point, so 4 marks for two developed points, 1 extra mark for a correct reference to a source of religious belief or teaching.

9. For Christians and Sikhs, a way of God revealing something about himself/ direct experience of God in an event, such as a vision or prophecy/ e.g. Moses receiving the Ten Commandments/ Mary finding out she is pregnant from the angel Gabriel/ Saul's vision/ Guru Nanak seeing a vision of God/ can have a great influence on people's lives/ started Sikhism.

10. Omnipotent/ omniscient/ benevolent/ immanent/ transcendent/ personal/ impersonal/ creator/ *any ideas in scripture related to creation, possibility of relationship with God through prayer, incarnation of Jesus, work of Holy Spirit.*

Test the 12 mark question

Suggested answers shown here, but see page 10 for guidance on levels of response.

12. Arguments in support

- Christians and Sikhs believe miracles are events with no natural or scientific explanation that only God could perform.
- If they occur as a response to prayer, they are a response to asking God for something/ prove that God is listening and responding to prayers.
- They are usually good and God is the source of all that is good.
- The fact that some people convert to Christianity after experiencing a miracle is proof of God's existence.
- 69 healing miracles have officially been recognised as taking place at Lourdes.
- Miracles exist and are caused by God, therefore God exists.

Arguments in support of other views

- Miracles are lucky coincidences and nothing to do with God.
- Whether something counts as a miracle is a matter of interpretation.
- They may have scientific explanations we haven't yet discovered.
- Healings could be mind over matter or misdiagnosis.
- Some miracles are made up for fame or money.
- If God is involved in miracles, this means he is selective and unfair (as only a few people experience them)/ but God cannot be selective and unfair/ therefore he cannot be involved in miracles.
- If miracles don't exist or have other explanations, they are nothing to do with God, so do not prove he exists.

13. Arguments in support

- A loving God would not allow people to suffer.
- God should be aware of evil and suffering because he is omniscient/ if so, he should use his powers to prevent it because he is omnipotent/ because God does not do this, he cannot exist.
- If God made all of creation to be perfect then there would not be earthquakes, droughts, etc./ suffering caused by the natural world is an example of poor design, which no God would be responsible for.

Arguments in support of other views

- It is unfair to blame God for suffering because he doesn't cause it.
- Suffering is a result of the disobedience of Adam and Eve/ the result of humans misusing their free will.
- If there was no evil, no one would be able to actively choose good over bad/ learn from their mistakes/ show faith and courage/ show compassion and kindness towards others who are suffering.
- Humans are in charge of looking after the earth and God chooses not to interfere.
- The existence of evil doesn't necessarily prove God does not exist, but could suggest he is not all-loving or all-powerful.
- Suffering is caused as a result of karma, which is caused by the actions of people, not God.

8 Religion, peace and conflict

Test the 1 mark question

1. C) Justice

2. D) Conventional weapons

Test the 2 mark question

Suggested answers, other relevant answers would be credited. 1 mark for each correct point.

3. Just cause/ correct authority/ good intention/ last resort/ reasonable chance of success/ proportional methods used/ focused on what God wants/ no personal reward/ selfless reasons for fighting.

4. For Christians violent protest goes against Jesus' teachings not to use violence/ goes against the commandment 'Do not kill'/ does not show 'love of neighbour'/ goes against the sanctity of life/ goes against 'So in everything, do to others what you would have them do to you, for this sums up the Law and the Prophets' (Matthew 7:12 [NIV]).

Sikhs are expected to protest against threats to their faith and oppression, but are expected to use peaceful means if at all possible.

Test the 4 mark question

Suggested answers, other relevant answers would be credited. 1 mark for each simple contrasting or similar point, another mark for developing each point, so a maximum of 4 marks for two developed points.

6. *Beliefs must be contrasting*:

Christians who support pacifism (e.g. The Religious Society of Friends/Quakers) believe that war can never be justified/ all killing is wrong/ it breaks the commandment 'You shall not murder' (Exodus 20:13 [NIV])/ Jesus taught 'Blessed are the peacemakers, for they shall be called children of God' (Matthew 5:9 [NIV])/ conflicts should be settled peacefully.

Christians who do not support pacifism believe that war is sometimes necessary as a last resort/ they would fight in a 'just war'/ to stop genocide taking place/ to defend one's country or way of life/ to help a weaker country defend itself from attack.

Most Sikhs believe war is sometimes necessary to combat oppression or defend their faith/ they agree with the Sikh just war theory/ Sikhs should be 'saint-soldiers' with the courage to fight in a war if necessary.

7. *Beliefs must be similar*:

Forgiveness is showing grace and mercy/ pardoning someone for what they have done wrong/ Christians believe forgiveness is important as in the Lord's Prayer it says 'Forgive us our sins as we forgive those who sin against us'/ this means God will not forgive if Christians do not forgive others/ Christians believe God sets the example by offering forgiveness to all who ask for it in faith.

Sikhs believe forgiveness is important for people to live peacefully/ 'Where there is forgiveness, there is God Himself' (Guru Granth Sahib 1372).

Test the 5 mark question

Suggested answers, other relevant answers would be credited. 1 mark for each simple contrasting or similar point, another mark for developing each point, so 4 marks for two developed points, 1 extra mark for a correct reference to a source of religious belief or teaching.

9. Some Christians and Sikhs believe in the just war theory/ it is right to fight in a war if the cause is just/ war can be the lesser of two evils/ it can be justified if its purpose is to stop atrocities/ people have a right to self-defence/ 'If there is a serious injury, you are to take life for life, eye for eye, tooth for tooth' (Exodus 21:23–24 [NIV])/ 'Love your neighbour as yourself' (Matthew 22:39 [NIV]) demands protection of weaker allies through war.

Sikhs believe they should be 'saint-soldiers'/ they should pray and work for peace but be willing to fight to defend their faith or resist oppression.

10. Reconciliation is a sacrament in the Catholic Church/ Christians believe it is important to ask God for forgiveness for sins/ reconciliation restores a Christian's relationship with God and other people/ it is when individuals or groups restore friendly relations after conflict or disagreement/ it is important to build good relationships after a war so conflict does not break out again/ justice and peace must be restored to prevent further conflict/ to create a world which reflects God's intention in creation/ Christians believe they must be reconciled to others before they can worship God properly/ 'Therefore, if you are offering your gift at the altar and there remember that your brother or sister has something against you, leave your gift there in front of the altar. First go and be reconciled to them; then come and offer your gift.' (Matthew 5:23–24 [NIV]).

Test the 12 mark question

Suggested answers shown here, but see page 10 for guidance on levels of response.

12. Arguments in support

- Some religious people believe in the concept of a holy war/ a holy war is fighting for a religious cause or God/ probably controlled by a religious leader/ these believers think that it is justifiable to defend their faith from attack.
- Religion has been a cause of such wars in the past/ e.g. the Crusades, wars between Christians and Muslims, were fought over rights to the Holy Land/ in the Old Testament there are many references to God helping the Jews settle in the Promised Land at the expense of those already living there.
- There are many examples of conflicts that involve different religious groups/ e.g. Catholics and Protestants in Northern Ireland during the 'Troubles'/ Israeli–Palestinian conflict/ conflict in India and Pakistan between Muslims and Hindus.
- Some atheists claim that without religion, many conflicts could be avoided/ religiously motivated terrorism would cease.

Arguments in support of other views

- Religion is not the main cause of wars: greed, self-defence and retaliation are all more common causes/ academic studies have found that religion plays a minor role in the majority of conflicts/ most wars have many causes/ e.g. opposition to a government/ economic reasons/ objection to ideological, political or social systems/ e.g. political differences played a greater role in the conflict in Northern Ireland than religion.
- Christians today believe they should defend their faith by reasoned argument, not violence/ many Christians think no war can be considered 'holy' when there is great loss of life/ "Put your sword back in its place,' Jesus said, 'for all who draw the sword die by the sword" (Matthew 26:52 [NIV])/ 'You have heard that it was said to the people long ago, 'You shall not murder […] But I tell you that anyone who is angry with a brother or sister will be subject to judgement" (Matthew 5:21–22 [NIV]).

13. Arguments in support

- Religious people should be the main peacemakers because of their beliefs/ e.g. Christians believe in 'love your neighbour'/ the sanctity of life/ equality/ justice/ peace/ forgiveness/ reconciliation/ Jesus taught 'Blessed are the peacemakers'/ Sikhs believe in equality and justice/ working to create peace follows Guru Nanak's teachings.
- Prayer and meditation can bring inner peace to individuals/ this helps avoid quarrels with others/ peacemaking begins with each person/ Sikhs believe genuine peace is not possible where there is an absence of absolute forgiveness.
- Many religious people are engaged in peacemaking in today's world/ e.g. the Anglican Pacifist Fellowship works to raise awareness of the issue of pacifism/ the 'Peace People' (Mairead Corrigan, Betty Williams and Ciaran McKeown) in Northern Ireland work to bring the Catholic and Protestant communities together to stop violence.

Arguments in support of other views

- Religious people should be peacemakers, but not the main ones/ the problems of global conflict require global solutions that are beyond any individual to solve/ the United Nations should be the main peacekeeping organisation/ only large organisations or governments with powerful resources can hope to affect peacemaking in the world.
- Religious people can be peacemakers in their own families and support justice and peace groups locally, but they cannot take the lead as peacemakers/ their main duty is to their family/ people have jobs that do not allow them to stop violence across the world/ the most they can do is contribute to organisations which help.
- Everyone should take equal responsibility for helping to contribute towards peace, whether they are religious or not/ some situations might benefit from peacemakers who are not religious.

9 Religion, crime and punishment

Test the 1 mark question

1. A) Corporal punishment

2. C) Happiness

Test the 2 mark question

Suggested answers, other relevant answers would be credited. 1 mark for each correct point.

3. Retribution/ deterrence/ reformation/ protection.

4. Poverty/ upbringing/ mental illness/ addiction/ greed/ hate/ opposition to an unjust law.

Test the 4 mark question

Suggested answers, other relevant answers would be credited. 1 mark for each simple contrasting or similar point, another mark for developing each point, so a maximum of 4 marks for two developed points.

6. *Beliefs must be contrasting*:

Approved of by most Christians and Sikhs/ as allows offenders to make up for what they have done wrong/ helps to reform and rehabilitate offenders/ may involve counselling, treatment or education/ may include an opportunity to apologise to the victim/ no harm is done to the offender.

Some people disapprove of community service as it is not a sufficient deterrent/ there is no element of retribution/ it is too soft a punishment.

7. *Beliefs must be similar*:

Most Christians oppose retribution because it does not show forgiveness/ it is not as positive as reformation/ 'Do not be overcome by evil, but overcome evil with good' (Romans 21:21 [NIV])/ Jesus taught his followers to 'turn the other cheek'.

Most Sikhs oppose retribution as it doesn't help to reform the criminal/ it is like revenge and comes from anger, which is one of the five evils/ 'Do not be angry with anyone else' (Guru Granth Sahib 259)/ it is not compassionate.

Test the 5 mark question

Suggested answers, other relevant answers would be credited. 1 mark for each simple contrasting or similar point, another mark for developing each point, so 4 marks for two developed points, 1 extra mark for a correct reference to a source of religious belief or teaching.

9. Christians are expected to forgive those who offend against them and if they do God will forgive them/ forgiveness is not a replacement for punishment/ it should be unlimited/ 'not seven times, but seventy-seven times' (Matthew 18:22 [NIV])/ Jesus forgave those who crucified him and Christians should follow his example/ 'Father forgive them, for they do not know what they are doing' (Luke 23:34 [NIV]).

Forgiveness is a fundamental principle in Sikhism/ it is closely linked to equality/ all humans share weaknesses that can lead to wrong actions/ this understanding leads to compassion for others/ although Sikhs believe forgiveness is not a replacement for punishment/ 'Where there is forgiveness, there is God himself' (Guru Granth Sahib 1372).

10. Hate crimes are condemned by Christianity and Sikhism/ hate crimes target individuals and groups perceived to be different/ Christians believe God created all humans equal in his image/ 'There is neither Jew nor Gentile, slave nor free man, male nor female, for you are all one in Christ Jesus' (Galatians 3:28 [NIV])/ hate crimes are not loving ('love your neighbour').

Hate crimes make the Sikh ideal of a society without prejudice or discrimination impossible/ the Mool Mantra describes God as being without hate and Sikhs should be like God in this respect.

Test the 12 mark question

Suggested answers shown here, but see page 10 for guidance on levels of response.

12. Arguments in support

- Use of the death penalty means there is a chance of killing an innocent person.

- There is little evidence it is an effective deterrent.
- It is never right to take another person's life/ this does not show forgiveness or compassion.
- Society can still be protected by imprisoning criminals instead of executing them.
- For Christians, sanctity of life means life is sacred and special to God, and only he has the right to take it away/ Ezekiel 33:11 teaches that wrongdoers should be reformed/ 'I take no pleasure in the death of the wicked, but rather that they turn away from their ways and live' (Ezekiel 33:11 [NIV]).
- Sikhism teaches that only God has the right to take life, so the death penalty is wrong.

Arguments in support of other views

- The death penalty should be allowed as retribution for people who commit the worst possible crimes.
- It protects society by removing the worst criminals so they cannot cause harm again.
- It may deter others from committing murder.
- It creates happiness for the greatest number of people (the principle of utility).
- Teachings from the Old Testament seem to support it/ 'Whoever sheds human blood, by humans shall their blood be shed' (Genesis 9:6 [NIV]).

13. Arguments in support

- Committing crime is wrong whatever the reason/ all crime causes someone to suffer.
- People should obey the law/ God put the system of government in place to rule every citizen so it is his law that is being broken (Romans 13:31).
- Christians and Sikhs believe it is wrong to commit crime because of poverty/ people should focus on creating a fairer society where the need to steal because of poverty is removed.
- Those who commit crime through illness or addiction should be provided with treatment so they have no reason to commit crimes.
- People who want to protest against an unjust law can do so legally, e.g. through a peaceful protest.

Arguments in support of other views

- Society is not fair so crimes because of need/poverty are justified in some circumstances/ e.g. it may be better to steal food than allow a child to starve.
- Some laws are unjust and the only way to change them is to break them/ peaceful protest is not always powerful enough to change the law.
- All humans have a tendency to do bad things, including crime, because of original sin.
- Those who commit crime because of addiction/mental illness cannot help it.

10 Religion, human rights and social justice

Test the 1 mark question

1. C) Negative thoughts, feelings or beliefs about a person based on a characteristic they have

2. A) Promoting tolerance

Test the 2 mark question

Suggested answers, other relevant answers would be credited. 1 mark for each correct point.

3. Unfair pay/ bad working conditions/ bad housing/ poor education/ high interest rates on loans or credit cards/ people trafficking/ modern slavery.

4. Give to the Church/ help people in need/ donate to charities/ use it to keep themselves safe/ give to the gurdwara/ provide pleasure and satisfaction for themselves, their family and friends.

Test the 4 mark question

Suggested answers, other relevant answers would be credited. 1 mark for each simple contrasting or similar point, another mark for developing each point, so a maximum of 4 marks for two developed points.

6. *Beliefs must be similar.*

Christianity teaches that prejudice is always wrong because it is unjust to single out individuals or groups for inferior treatment/ some Christians think same-sex relationships are unnatural and against the Bible/ cannot lead to the 'natural' creation of a child/ other Christians believe any relationship based on love should be cherished.

Sikhism teaches that God created and is in every person so Sikhs should not show prejudice against anyone/ most Sikhs believe same-sex relationships are not acceptable as they are not part of the lifestyle approved by the Gurus/ some Sikhs argue that the soul does not have a gender so same-sex relationships should be permitted/ most Sikhs believe seeking enlightenment is more important than a person's sexuality.

7. *Beliefs must be similar.*

The Bible stresses the importance of providing human rights to all people/ which includes creating a more just society/ 'Let justice roll on like a river' (Amos 5:24)/ Christians believe it is not loving to deny people their rights/ rights are written into law, and the law is inspired by God so must be obeyed/ Christians have a responsibility to help provide human rights/ 'faith without deeds is useless' (James 2:20 [NIV]).

Sikhism is founded on the principles of working towards the common good of all people/ 'All beings and creatures are His; He belongs to all' (Guru Granth Sahib 425)/ Sikhs are required to stand up for the weak and fight for the rights of the oppressed.

Test the 5 mark question

Suggested answers, other relevant answers would be credited. 1 mark for each simple contrasting or similar point, another mark for developing each point, so 4 marks for two developed points, 1 extra mark for a correct reference to a source of religious belief or teaching.

9. Poverty is sometimes caused by injustice and Christians must combat injustice/ poverty involves suffering and Christians are expected to help relieve suffering/ e.g. the parable of the Sheep and the Goats/ people have God-given talents that they should use to help overcome poverty/ tackling poverty is good stewardship/ Jesus' teaching to 'love your neighbour' encourages Christians to help those in poverty.

Sikhs are expected to show compassion to those in poverty/ give a tenth of their income to community projects/ perform sewa, which includes helping the poor/ 'In the midst of this world do sewa and you shall be given a place of honour in the Court of the Lord' (Guru Granth Sahib 26).

10. Christians should be careful that the pursuit of wealth does not lead to traits such as greed and selfishness/ 'the love of money is a root of all sorts of evil' (1 Timothy 6:10 [NIV])/ focusing on wealth brings the danger of ignoring God and neglecting the spiritual life/ 'You cannot serve both God and money' (Matthew 6:24 [NIV])/ Christians should use their wealth to help those in need/ the parable of the Sheep and the Goats.

Sikhs should earn an honest living while remembering God/ Sikhs should avoid greed, which is one of the five evils/ Guru Nanak said that the accumulation of wealth is not possible without sins/ Sikhs are taught that nothing should distract them from becoming God-centred (gurmukh), which includes the pursuit of wealth.

Test the 12 mark question

Suggested answers shown here, but see page 10 for guidance on levels of response.

12. Arguments in support

- Treating people equally is a very important teaching in Sikhism that goes back to Guru Nanak/ 'Recognise the Lord's light in all, and do not consider social class or status' (Guru Granth Sahib 349).
- Equality can be seen in practice in Sikhism in the way all are welcome to eat at the langar/ all Sikhs work together in the langar/ both men and women can lead worship.
- Christianity teaches that all people should be treated equally because they are all made in God's image/ 'There is neither Jew nor Gentile, neither salve nor free, nor is there male or female for you are all one in Christ Jesus' (Galatians 3.28 [NIV])/ Christians believe that Jesus died for all humankind.

Arguments in support of other views

- The Mool Mantra is the most important statement for Sikhs and it is all about God/ living a life centred on God leads to a belief in equality rather than the opposite way round.
- Christians believe in equality because they believe God created every person to be equal/ Paul explains that all people can be one in Christ Jesus – belief in Jesus comes first and leads onto equality of people.
- Both Sikhism and Christianity teach the importance of equality, but both faiths would say belief in God is more important.

13. Arguments in support

- Freedom of religion is a basic human right/ 'Everyone has the right to freedom of thought, conscience and religion' (The United Declaration of Human Rights)/ in the UK the law allows people to follow whichever faith they choose.
- It is wrong to try to force someone to follow a religion/ or to prevent them from following a religion/ it should be a matter of personal choice/ this makes choosing to follow a particular religion more significant/meaningful.
- Forcing people to follow a religion or preventing them from following a religion could lead to more conflict and fighting between different religions.
- Being a Christian is a choice that any person can make/ Christians believe religious freedom is important/ Jesus taught people to show tolerance and harmony.
- Sikhs don't claim to be the only path to God/ the Gurus taught that the faith someone is born into is the faith they should try to excel in/ Guru Tegh Bahadur was prepared to risk his life to protect Kashmiri Hindus.

Arguments in support of other views

- If a religion teaches hatred and intolerance, there should be limits on how it can be taught or practised/ people should not be allowed to join it for the wrong reasons.
- Some people might argue that to show patriotism, a person should follow the main religion in their country.
- Some people might argue that when people are allowed to join any religion, this can lead to conflict and tension between different religious groups, whereas if everyone followed the same religion then there would be more harmony between people.
- Some people might unintentionally harm/upset others through choosing a particular religion/ e.g. by choosing a religion that is different to their parents'/ so perhaps it should not be so easy to switch from one religion to another.
- Everybody also has the right not to follow any religion.